Working with Adolescents:
Building Effective Communication and Choice-Making Skills

Richard C. Nelson

Claire J. Dandeneau

Marsella Kay Schrader

Guidelines for Teachers, Counselors, and Others

Publisher-
Educational Media Corporation®
PO Box 21311
Minneapolis, MN 55421-0311
(612) 781-0088

Production Editor—
Don L. Sorenson, Ph.D.
Graphic Design—
Earl Sorenson
Artwork—
Dave Sattler

Table of Contents

Working with Adolescents: Building Effective Communication and Choice-Making Skills

Guidelines for Teachers, Counselors, and Others

Reader Introduction

People in leadership roles meet adolescents in a great variety of situations and environments, both one-to-one and in groups. Although the two most common settings are the school and the classroom, they are not the only places adult leaders meet young people; and the teachers, counselors, and others who work with adolescents in the schools also encounter those youngsters in many other situations.

Recreation directors, youth religious leaders, probation officers, wilderness camp counselors, scout leaders, house parents, and a wide range of volunteers and other adults work with young people in such varied formal and informal situations as organized meetings, residential settings, structured outdoor experiences, or in freeform wilderness ventures. Teachers, school counselors, and other educators may most often meet adolescents in offices or classrooms, but they also encounter them in their work with school activities and clubs, in in-school suspension rooms, on field trips, and at after-school programs such as school dances and sporting events.

The common experience of all of the various leaders to whom this book is addressed is that they meet adolescents one-to-one, in groups, or both. Our purposes are to meet two basic needs of leaders of youth: to point out effective ways of establishing leadership and maintaining control in work with adolescents, and to show how adolescents may be assisted to mature and grow in self-discipline and responsibility as they wend their way through the growing-up maze.

This book is designed to supplant or supplement adolescent psychology/development books and discipline/control books that are currently used in staff and in-service training and college classes. Adolescent psychology and development books are generally quite thorough in reporting on the status, needs, and problems of adolescents, but they offer little or no guidance concerning what youth leaders might do with that information. Classroom discipline and control books likewise tend to be thorough in

achieving their basic objective: suggesting to teachers how they might manage adolescents in classroom environments, but they offer little that builds an understanding of adolescents or suggests how to communicate with them effectively.

Those who work with young people day-to-day, in and out of schools, need something more than two disparate sets of information. They need a systematic, practical resource that integrates four essential elements:

1. current information about adolescents;

2. useful approaches for establishing discipline and control with adolescents;

3. skills for interacting effectively with adolescents one-to-one and in groups; and

4. suggestions for helping adolescents learn to make more effective choices as they cope with the mysteries they encounter on the road to maturity.

H. B. Gelatt, in a 1993 American Counseling Association Convention program, suggested that educators and others need to make a paradigm shift, directing at least some of their efforts to helping youth imagine and then create the world they will live in. Those who work with adolescents can help them imagine and create the world they want for themselves in two ways: first, by becoming more responsive to their needs, and, second, by helping them develop essential communication and choice-making skills for engaging the world effectively. Leaders must then stand aside, remaining available to assist young people as needed, while at the same time encouraging them and allowing them to find their own way.

Most adolescents are offered little direct assistance in evolving their everyday behaviors and communication patterns. Instead, their patterns evolve haphazardly as a result of trial and error, imitation, and incidental feedback. Most adolescents could benefit from direct training designed to help them shift from the vague or overpowering sense of "choicelessness" they feel to a realization that they are in charge of a great many aspects of their own lives—and that they can and do make choices all the time.

Substitute "you," change verb forms, and make other appropriate modifications in the paragraph above and it may apply to you as well. You, too, have learned your skills of action and interaction through imitation, trial and error, and incidental feedback. More likely than not some of your habit patterns are functional and valuable and serve you well in your life and in your work with young people, while others are not useful and ought to be modified or discarded. More likely than not you too could benefit from becoming more aware of your patterns of choices and from developing more effective choice-making skills. Greater awareness and enhanced skills should help you become more effective both in assisting youth and in relating to others.

In this book we seek to achieve three basic objectives:

1. To make realistic and immediate your understanding of the needs and characteristics of adolescents—where they are "coming from" and what their concerns and challenges are. To this end we summarize key findings concerning young people and we present a large number of critical incidents for your exploration and discussion.

2. To help you expand the repertoire of choices and communication skills you have available to you for helping adolescents, for interacting with them, for exercising leadership, for applying controls, and for encouraging their self-discipline and growth. To achieve that purpose we introduce you to a variety of communication skills and to the concepts of Choice Awareness (Nelson, 1977; Nelson, 1990; Nelson, 1992).

3. To assist you to help young people learn how they might act in more positive and responsible ways in their lives—through making better choices. To that end we offer numerous activities and suggestions you may use with young people to build awareness of how they make their choices and how to expand their choice repertoire.

The content, the journaling suggestions, and the activities in *Working with Adolescents: Building Effective Communication and Choice-Making Skills* are designed to help you make more effective choices in communicating with the adolescents you encounter, and to assist you in achieving what may well be your most important professional goal: working successfully with young people. A related benefit is that it may also help you make more effective choices in your interactions with others in your life.

Working with Adolescents *The Basic Elements*

Working with Adolescents: Building Effective Communication and Choice-Making Skills presents a unique program that has been employed and refined over several years at Purdue University. Those who work with adolescents have been helped in several ways through the program; they have improved their communication and choice-making skills, expanded their understanding of adolescents, learned how they might establish more effective controls and promote greater self-discipline in adolescents, and explored ways in which they might help adolescents learn to make more effective choices. The program uses a variety of procedures including readings, journaling suggestions, skill-building exercises, and small group and dyadic activities to achieve those objectives.

The essential elements of the program include: (1) *markers*, key concepts concerning adolescents; (2) *critical incidents*, events that those who work with youth may face, spelled out in ways that elicit immediate action; (3) *choices and communication skills*, techniques and skills that leaders may use to improve their interactions with young people; (4) suggestions for *sharing Choice Awareness with adolescents*, numerous activities and discussion options for expanding the understanding of young people concerning the skills and choices they have available to them, and (5) *supplementary materials*, a variety of other information that we have found useful in enhancing the learning of those who lead youth.

These essential elements are introduced below, then are delineated in greater detail throughout this resource so that you and others may follow the model. You are encouraged to use each of the elements flexibly, applying them to your own needs—whether you are reading on your own or being guided through the experiences in an extended workshop, a graduate or undergraduate class, or another training setting.

Adolescence Markers. The adolescence markers presented in Part 1 are briefly-stated key concepts that express some of the basic understandings we have concerning adolescents and that stage of development. They may be used individually or in clusters as bases for additional exploration or research. Learners may build brief handouts and design presentations that incorporate one or more of the markers; they may then share those key understandings concerning adolescence with others in unique, engaging ways. This approach enables those involved to tie their learnings and their observations together.

The journaling suggestions that are made encourage you to relate the adolescence markers to your own and your contemporaries' experiences during that period of life, as a way of enhancing your understanding of young people.

Critical Incidents. Over their careers, alert, sensitive teachers, counselors, and others who work with adolescents meet a great many situations that demand effective immediate and long range responses. We refer to these events here as critical incidents and present a large number of them in Part 1 of this source. Individuals who have practiced a variety of effective ways of responding to critical incidents like these are in a better position than they would otherwise be to meet the challenges presented by young people and others.

As you expand your knowledge concerning adolescents and the problems and possibilities they face, and as you develop more effective skills in communication and choice-making, you need to apply those learnings. The critical incidents presented here provide opportunities for you to practice making immediate responses and to contemplate future actions. You are encouraged to use these incidents in a group, with a partner, or individually, in creative, challenging, and interactive ways; to discuss them; and to revisit them again and again, employing familiar skills and choices in new ways, and using others you are introduced to that you may never have tried before.

Choices and Communication Skills. Part 2 of this source presents a large number of choice-making and communication skills that are valuable in dealing with young people in any setting, whether individually or in groups. It is our conviction that in the education of those who work with adolescents an important consideration has been neglected: that well-developed and effective interactive choices and communication skills are essentials in successful work with youth. As a consequence, choices and communication skills are explored here in some depth.

Creating a CREST Plan for Group Management and **Choices** *and Communication Skills for Adolescents.* Chapter 15, Part 2, presents a design for building a group management plan that is adjustable to various kinds of groups. Chapter 16 closes Part 2 by suggesting how various choice-making and communication skills might be shared with young people. For convenience sake it follows the sequence of the *Choices and Communication Skills* chapters that precede it. The objective of this chapter is to make it easy for you to help adolescents understand the choices they have been making, and to enable and encourage them to broaden their repertoire of effective choices.

Supplementary Materials. Part 3 of this source presents a number of additional materials we have used with our groups. Examples include: Suggestions for Team Presentations built on the adolescence markers, Communication Skills, and Sample Taping Activities; the latter has proven to be a successful device for providing skill practice. These materials are intended, first, to expand the range of experiences we have included in the program; and second, to stimulate your creativity so that you might more readily achieve the essential purpose of *helping adolescents to improve their communication and choice-making skills.*

Instructor, Presenter, or Leader Introduction

Congratulations! You have in hand an exciting, relevant resource that is designed to help you achieve three important objectives with teachers, counselors, and others who work with youth. The objectives are:

(1) to assist them in gaining a greater understanding of adolescents and the realities that affect their lives;

(2) to extend the range of communication skills and choices they have available in their work with young people, in both individual and group settings; and

(3) to help them work with adolescents to expand their repertoire of effective choices, on the road to greater self-discipline and more positive personal growth.

Please be sure to explore the Reader Introduction to *Working with Adolescents: Building Effective Communication and Choice-Making Skills* which sets forth the essential elements of the program: *adolescence markers, critical incidents, choices and communication skills, choices and communication skills for adolescents,* and *supplementary materials.* The following paragraphs expand the previous discussion for you as instructor, presenter, or leader.

Adolescence Markers. You are encouraged to use the adolescence markers—key concepts concerning adolescents—that are presented here in two ways: (1) as bases for reflection and group discussion, and (2) as foundations for further exploration and research by the participants in your course, workshop, or program.

Among the Supplementary Materials in this source you will find an extensive discussion of how your group members might design presentations keyed to the adolescence markers. At Purdue University we have used these materials as a basis for encouraging creative use of markers from the *Adolescence Markers* chapter as well as from the *Choices and Communication Skills* chapters (Part 2). We have invited our learners, in small groups or individually, to explore the markers and to design creative, activity-based presentations; we have then scheduled brief blocks of time so that they might present these key understandings to their colleagues. We encourage you to make similar use of markers whether you are teaching a course or conducting workshops or other intensive training programs.

We also encourage you as leader/presenter to make use of the journaling suggestions throughout this source. Writing journal entries should help learners fix the markers and concepts in their minds and relate them to their own experiences.

Critical Incidents. The critical incidents presented here offer examples of situations that teachers, counselors, and other youth leaders may face that require immediate action and followup. In the introduction to the section several suggestions are given for use of the incidents. Also, you may wish to ask your learners to develop their own critical incidents—to challenge their own thinking and that of their peers.

A fundamental assumption here is that people who work with youth, as well as the adults around them, need a variety of strategies for responding to the critical incidents they encounter. We encourage you to use the critical incidents presented here, and the taping activities (see Supplementary Materials for suggested procedures) as bases for interaction and discussion. We also encourage you to invite your learners to revisit selected incidents as new choices and skills are explored, so that they might apply their developing skills to a variety of challenging situations.

Choices and Communication Skills. As we noted in the Reader Introduction, it is our belief that one of the greatest voids in the education of youth leaders is a consideration of the interactive choices and communication skills that are essential if they are to function in effective ways in their individual contacts and in their group work with adolescents. To fill that void, in these several chapters we explore choices and communication skills and suggest ways in which they may be useful in responding to young people and in encouraging the development of self-discipline and personal growth.

We invite you to encourage use of the journaling suggestions and to promote the development of the concepts and skills by the members of your group. You may wish to invite individuals and/or small groups to select specific markers in the chapters and to develop brief presentations and design activities to share with others that will emphasize these key ideas.

Creating a CREST Plan for Group Management and *Choices and Communication Skills for Adolescents.* Following the several chapters devoted to *Choices and Communication Skills*, we offer a design your learners may use for developing a management plan tailored to their groups. Also, keyed to the *Choices and Communication Skills* chapters, we have included a chapter that suggests how various choice-making and communication skills might be shared with adolescents. We suggest how the leader may help them understand the choices they have been making and how they might broaden their repertoire of effective choices. The role plays, activities, and demonstrations are designed to offer your learners starting points for suggesting how they might help young people learn to make more effective choices. Given minimal encouragement, your learners should be able to design their own creative activities and experiences for extending the concepts in interesting and meaningful ways. Those activities and experiences in turn should enable the young people they work with to expand their range of useful choices.

Supplementary Materials. The final section of this source incorporates a number of materials we have used to enhance the activity level of the program and to extend the thinking processes of those involved. Among the inclusions are items alluded to in the paragraphs above as well as other materials you might wish to adapt for your use.

We encourage you to employ these materials in creative, interactive ways that challenge your learners and assist them in *helping adolescents to improve their communication and choice-making skills.*

Part 1
Adolescence Markers and Critical Incidents

An Introduction

Part 1 of *Working with Adolescents: Building Effective Communication and Choice-Making Skills* explores adolescence in two ways.

First, some of the most basic information concerning adolescence is presented in the form of markers, or key concepts. These markers, drawn from a number of sources, represent current information concerning youth and ranging over a wide range of topics. The adolescence references that follow the markers provide good starting points for further exploration and research (see pp. 134-135).

It should be noted that many issues for young people arise through the normal developmental processes of maturation and striving for identity. Growth, occasionally, has its negative side, but the positive, hopeful realities involved in the adolescent's striving for maturity should be kept in view. Most adolescents at any given moment can be found moving toward adulthood in healthy, positive, ways.

Second, an extensive collection of brief critical incidents has been included with four objectives in mind: to make the realities of adolescence more salient and meaningful, to provide grist for the discussion mill concerning the experiences of adolescents, to challenge the reader with situations that demand effective immediate and long range responses, and to provide lifelike opportunities for trying out new skills as they are developed.

Nothing can substitute for the real-life challenges that you face in your work with youth, but you are likely to make more effective responses if you have tried out a variety of behaviors in situations in which there is no risk of harm, and if you have learned to modify your first impulses over time and employ other skills and choices.

We invite you to make an immediate response to these critical incidents and to try out other possibilities; then, as you explore the various choices and skills presented in this source, we encourage you to return to these incidents from time to time and try some different ways of responding to them. Journaling about your experiences will mean that you do not have to rely on memory concerning the progress you are making in your use of skills and choices.

Once you have become comfortable and skillful in using a wide range of choices—and only then—you will be in a good position to decide what types of responses would be most effective and appropriate for you to make in similar situations.

1

Adolescence Markers

The markers cited in this section suggest many of the realities adolescents face within themselves or in their life space. It takes little imagination to see how the lives of young people would be affected by each of these realities.

At any given time, due in some measure to the situations adolescents encounter, and in some measure due to the responses they choose to make to these situations, the behaviors of adolescents may range widely along a continuum. We find it useful to categorize the two ends of the continuum as OK to OD, concepts which are developed more thoroughly in subsequent chapters. Suffice it to say at this point that OK choices range from *major*, meaningful, positive behaviors to everyday behaviors that take care of the ordinary tasks of life or contribute in relatively *minor* ways to our relationships. By contrast, OD choices (think: overdone) are those that range from everyday behaviors that block our effective completion of the tasks of life and contribute in *minor*, negative ways to our relationships to the *major*, destructive, negative behaviors that often hurt ourselves as well as others.

In most instances, the markers that follow emphasize the problems that face adolescents, but they may only reflect the tip of the iceberg—the OD actions that show above the surface and become the subject of headlines or newspaper and magazine articles about the "terrible state" of youth today. Truth to tell, frequently, invisible below the surface, not cited in statistics, is an even larger group of young people who may be less dramatically affected by whatever the problem is, but for whom the problem has some present or potential effect.

It may be argued that during the period of adolescence nearly every individual comes to be at risk from time to time, legally or otherwise. In support of that point has been our experience with a Secret Pooling activity. We have asked adults to write on slips of paper a way in which they were at risk during adolescence, or to indicate that they never had that experience. As the slips have been read aloud anonymously it has become clear that nearly all participants experienced something that put them at risk during adolescence—poor self image, underage drinking, sexual activity, cheating, theft, and so forth.

Three points need to be made that put the adolescence markers that follow in perspective: (1) many young people are highly self-actualized and fully functional; (2) by no means do all young people face problems at a given time; and (3) most of the adolescents who are faced by severe problems prove to be survivors, and some even thrive, tempered like fine steel by the fires they have faced.

The adolescence markers presented here suggest appropriate topics for discussion and research. Current educational and psychological journals, as well as selected items in the summary list of references, should provide useful starting points for expanded exploration. Where a concept may be associated with a single source, or where a direct quote is used, a citation has been made, otherwise the reader may assume that the finding is cited in more than one of the references.

Markers like those that follow each section have been used by pre-service and in-service teachers, counselors, and others at Purdue University in a highly useful way. They have taken one marker or a cluster of them and created a brief handout and designed a presentation through which they have initiated or expanded the knowledge of their fellow group members on the topic.

You are encouraged to make journal entries according to the suggestions in this chapter and to use your creative powers and make your own connections between these markers and the critical incidents and the skills and choices that are explored elsewhere in this source.

Theories of Adolescence

M-1. Adolescence has been conceptualized in a number of ways. There are biological, psychoanalytical, anthropological, social learning, and developmental views of adolescence. (Note that the sample handout in the Supplementary Materials gives some information on these theories and at the same time it provides a model of a handout which you may wish to follow.)

M-2. The Choice Awareness view of adolescence acknowledges the role of *choice*—how the individual *chooses* to respond to events—as central in whether storm and stress or smoothness, characterize the adolescent period of life. (See the sample handout in the Supplementary Materials, and the contents of the *Choices and Communication Skills* chapters, for further development of this idea.)

- **Journal Entry.** Following each of the subsequent sections of this extended chapter you are invited to reflect on the markers above and make a journal entry. In each instance we suggest that you spend a few moments on *meaning*—deciding what the marker means to you and how it connects to other theories and concepts; on *relating*—considering how the ideas related to you and to others you observed when you were an adolescent, and have observed since; on *relevance*—what significance the ideas have for you in understanding adolescents; and on *implications*—exploring how the ideas might impact on young people with whom you work. To avoid repetition we list only the heading and the four key words as follows:

- **Journal Entry**—*meaning, relating, relevance, implications.*

Physical Development

M-3.   Human babies experience the most extraordinary growth spurt through age two, then their growth tends to be more constant and gradual over the next sixteen to eighteen years, with the exception of a second spurt, the adolescent growth spurt, which occurs within early or middle adolescence. Feet, noses, and other parts of the body do not necessarily all grow at the same rate.

M-4.   On average, girls experience the adolescent growth spurt approximately two years before boys. Boys tend to have a more extended growth spurt, thus they end adolescence taller than girls by an average of eight per cent. Girls may feel stress if they enter adolescence taller and heavier than boys; boys may feel stress if their growth spurt is delayed, and they are shorter and lighter than girls their age.

M-5.   The onset of menstruation and the development of various secondary sex characteristics vary greatly among individuals. Menstruation onset may occur any time between ages 9 and 18, and female breast development may also occur over a wide age range. The same age group may include boys who have fully-developed sex organs, have deep voices, and shave regularly, while others may be just beginning, or have not yet begun, the process of puberty. Both boys and girls who experience early maturation have a number of advantages over those who mature late; examples include: higher ratings from peers and adults on physical attractiveness, athletic prowess, status, self-confidence, and independence. However, early maturation for girls tends to correlate with less satisfaction concerning both weight and appearance.

M-6.   Apparent change over the years in such factors as height, weight, and the onset of menses can be corroborated factually; between 1880 and 1950, for example, average increases of about 4 pounds and 1 inch per decade occurred for adolescents.

- **Journal Entry**—*meaning, relating, relevance, implications.*

Sexuality

M-7.   Such visible body changes as enlargement of the breast or the penis and gonads, and increased body hair, are accompanied by numerous invisible bodily changes in the adolescent.

M-8.   Hormonal secretions from a variety of organs, including the pituitary, the hypothalamus, the gonads, and the ovaries, are initiated or changed in adolescence. The number and variety of these bodily changes may cause adjustment problems for adolescents.

M-9.   Menstruation itself and understanding the menstrual cycle are two key challenges that adolescent girls must meet.

M-10. Untimely erections and nocturnal emissions are two key challenges that adolescent boys must meet.

M-11. The most commonly-reported source of information regarding sex is that of friends, with school, books/magazines, parents, siblings, doctors/nurses, and church following in that order. It may be that parents transmit important values and attitudes concerning sex, but relatively few parents contribute significantly to the knowledge of their sons and daughters in this area.

M-12. Sexual urges, leading to sexual experimentation, put many adolescents at risk for sexually-transmitted diseases. Chlamydial infections are the most common STDs. Gonorrhea is more common than chicken pox, measles, mumps, and rubella combined. Genital herpes and syphilis are not uncommon among adolescents. Approximately one-third of adult males and one-fifth of adult females report having had homosexual experiences during adolescence.

M-13. Adolescents who are sexually active, who engage in homosexual contacts, and who use intravenous drugs are a high-risk group for becoming HIV-positive or for contracting AIDS. Since the incubation period for AIDS may last up to ten years, an adolescent can carry the virus for years without knowing it, and not exhibit symptoms of the disease until long after adolescence is over.

M-14. Pregnancy, and unwed motherhood, adoption, and abortion choices face over one million adolescent girls each year. Approximately one-quarter of the pregnancies result in hasty marriages, another quarter result in babies born out of wedlock, forty per cent result in induced abortions and ten per cent result in miscarriages or stillbirths.

M-15. Over ninety per cent of babies carried to term are kept by their teenage mothers. Pregnancies result in approximately a half million teenage girls marrying or becoming single parents each year.

M-16. Boys' attitudes toward pregnancies they have helped to produce range widely. Although the percentages may still be small, more males than in past decades are evidencing genuine interest in the growing fetus, as increasing numbers of teenage males have taken parenting classes or have taken action to block abortions, for example.

- **Journal Entry**—*meaning, relating, relevance, implications.* (Note that you may wish to make more than one entry on this or any other topic.)

Cognitive Development

M-17. Intellectual changes accompany the physical changes of adolescence. Cognitive changes for this age, as identified by Piaget and called formal operations, are the increased abilities to think abstractly, to think about thought (introspection), to think logically, which includes inductive and deductive reasoning, and to think hypothetically.

M-18. The ability to think about one's thoughts can result in hypersensitivity in adolescents' awareness of themselves and their ideas, and is reflected in their increased egocentrism and increased self-consciousness.

M-19. Like other developmental characteristics, the development of thinking and rate of cognitive changes varies and is highly individual. Such development is influenced by the maturation of the nervous system and the level of intelligence. Some individuals never reach the formal operational stage.

- **Journal Entry**—*meaning, relating, relevance, implications.*

Moral and Value Development

M-20. Development of moral judgment is theorized to be a gradual cognitive process influenced by increasing and changing social relationships. Many of these changes occur in adolescence and thus adolescence is a crucial time in moral development.

M-21. Due to their increased cognitive development, adolescents tend to use an internalized set of standards when evaluating others; they take into account the intentions of others and they begin to question societal and parental values.

M-22. Adolescent values remain relatively constant over time.

M-23. Contrary ι. ιssumptions, adolescents possess much the same values as their parents. For example, with regard to education, 90% of adolescents and their parents have similar attitudes. There is also a high degree of consensus in the areas of religion, racial issues, roles of women, and even dress style. (Cobb, 1992)

M-24. Many family factors have been shown to correlate with moral learning. These are parental warmth, acceptance, mutual esteem, and trust; frequency and intensity of parent-teen interactions, parental discipline measures, and parental role modeling.

M-25. Surveys indicate that religion plays an important role in the lives of adolescents. Approximately one-half of high school seniors surveyed attend church weekly or one to two times per month.

- **Journal Entry**—*meaning, relating, relevance, implications.*

Adolescents and the Family Structure

M-26. Even though conflicts increase during adolescence, parent-adolescent relationships usually remain reasonably close and harmonious. When conflict does occur, adolescent girls report greater conflict than boys, and more adolescents report difficulty in getting along with their fathers than with their mothers. Also, conflicts tend to occur more often in authoritarian homes than in more democratic homes.

M-27. Adolescents in single-parent families, which are typically headed by females and have substantial financial concerns, are given more responsibilities, more autonomy, and a greater role in family decision-making.

M-28. Adolescents in single-parent families often believe they must take on part-time jobs to pay for personal items.

M-29. Approximately a fifth of the children under the age of 18 live with a step-parent, which more likely than not is a step-father, and re-marriage frequently occurs within three years after a divorce. Adolescent reactions to step-fathers is mixed, however the transition seems to be easiest for young boys, while girls may remain hostile and antagonistic. Reactions to step-mothers may be more pronounced because they play a more active role in relation to the household and the children and thus more often come into conflict with step-children.

M-30. Adolescent reactions to parental divorce are varied. Reactions involve self-centered concerns as to how the divorce will affect them, their academic future, vocational responsibilities, and financial responsibilities. Right after the divorce, youth responses may parallel the grieving process for the absent parent; thus, anger, resentment, anxiety, depression, and guilt may be observed.

- **Journal Entry**—*meaning, relating, relevance, implications.*

Adolescents and Peers

M-31. Friendships in adolescents are developed in many different ways and fulfill a variety of needs: for emotional support, for intimacy, and for advice. Girls seem to develop close friendships through talking and sharing their feelings. Boys may share their feelings through disclosure, but they are more likely to develop closeness through sharing experiences.

M-32. There are two types of adolescent peer groups, the clique and the crowd. A clique is a small group of close friends with whom the adolescent shares similar interests and spends time. The crowd is a larger, less personal group, often including twenty or so members. The function of the crowd is to furnish a setting in which young people can experiment with social skills. The clique's function is to provide feedback on social skills and to assist with social skill development.

M-33. Adolescents experience peer pressure: the pressure to conform and think and act like their friends. Boys tend to respond to peer pressure by evaluating the expected outcome. Girls tend to respond to peer pressure in order to gain friendships or peer approval. Dependency on the peer group lessens as young people become more secure in themselves.

M-34. Dating for adolescents, which begins between the ages of twelve to sixteen, with girls starting earlier than boys, serves many purposes. Dating is recreation. Dating provides companionship. The dating relationship allows young people to explore themselves in a social context, and to develop their potential.

- **Journal Entry**—*meaning, relating, relevance, implications.*

Adolescents in the School Setting

M-35. Adolescents, in a national survey in the mid-1980s, rated the overall quality of their education and graded their schools: 27% of schools received an A; 57% received a B. Teachers did not fare as well; 14% were given A's, and 55% were given B's. Approximately half of the adolescents thought that the way to improve education was to improve the quality of the teachers. Addressing the problem specifically, they suggested that teachers failed to make the subject matter interesting, did not challenge students to work hard enough, and lacked classroom discipline. (Solorzano, *et al.,* 1984).

M-36. Each year a substantial number of students dropout of high school. In the mid-1980s, of the young people aged sixteen to twenty-one, approximately one-eighth of White students, well over a sixth of African-American students, and over a fourth of Hispanic students were early school leavers.

M-37. Causes for early school withdrawal are numerous, often involving a whole series of events that lead to the final withdrawal. Warning signs include such factors as: poor school achievement, poor school performance in relation to potential, low grade level placement according to age, antagonism to school authorities, lack of interest in school, a sense of not belonging, a lack of acceptance by other students, low scholastic ability, frequent changes of schools, friends who are much younger or older, an unhappy family situation, larger or smaller than agemates, unable to afford the expenses of school or make purchases similar to those of schoolmates, a lack of participation in activities, an inability to compete with or feeling ashamed of brothers and/or sisters, a serious physical or emotional handicap, frequent disciplinary difficulties, and involvement in delinquency. (Rice 1990)

M-38. Youth who drop out of school are approximately twice as likely to be unemployed as those who graduate; they also are more likely to obtain lower paying jobs and have lower lifetime earnings than non-dropouts.

- **Journal Entry**—*meaning, relating, relevance, implications.*

Adolescents, Work, and Careers

M-39. Part-time employment for young people, ages sixteen to seventeen, has increased dramatically in recent years. Current estimates are that forty per cent of these youth are employed part-time while still in high school. A large part of this increase is the considerable number of adolescent girls who now seek and secure jobs. The advantages of youth taking part-time jobs include: they develop their social skills, they learn time management, and they develop good work habits and traits. The main disadvantage is that the work may interfere with their school work, especially homework.

M-40. There are many theories as to how individuals, particularly adolescents, make vocational choices and their subsequent career decision-making processes. There are social-cognitive theories, developmental theories, self-concept theories, and personality and work environment theories. No matter which theory is accepted it is certain that adolescents feel pressure to make vocational choices. They are frequently asked such questions as: What do you want to be when you grow up? What are you going to do after you graduate? Their responses and their choices are influenced by parents, peers, and school personnel.

M-41. Important factors involved in vocational choice are the individual's intelligence, aptitude, special abilities, interests, job opportunities, socioeconomic status, sex, and race.

   • **Journal Entry**—*meaning, relating, relevance, implications.*

Adolescent Risks

M-42. Alcohol is usually the first drug tried by adolescents and the most widely used drug, followed by tobacco, then marijuana. Drug use increases substantially for youth between sixth and ninth grades.

M-43. Rates of alcohol and drug use for rural youth are similar to those of urban youth.

M-44. Almost all high school seniors have tried alcohol and approximately two-thirds are users on a somewhat regular basis. (Cobb, 1992)

M-45. Motivations for adolescents to use drugs, particularly the first time, include: curiosity and experimentation; fun and pleasure; social pressure; relief of tension, anxieties, and pressures; escape from problems; a way of coping with problems; or a desire for creativity or self-awareness. (Rice, 1990)

M-46. It is estimated that anabolic steroids, synthetic male hormones, are used by a half million adolescent athletes of the over seven million adolescents who participate in competitive sports in high school, and the additional thirteen million who take part in sports outside of school. Athletes rationalize their use of steroids by stating their need to be competitive. Steroid use can result in excessive hostility, increased sexual aggression, and such physical complications as adverse chemical changes in the brain, and damage to the liver, heart, and reproductive system.

   • **Journal Entry**—*meaning, relating, relevance, implications.*

Self-Concept Development

M-47. The self-concept in childhood is largely based on a physical view of self. In adolescence that view changes gradually and becomes more psychological. There is a change from only seeing one's outward appearance to also seeing the deeper psychological attributes of self, including one's thoughts and emotions.

M-48. Self-concept relates to sex-role orientation. A masculine orientation in females tends to be predictive of self-esteem, and among males both a masculine and a feminine orientation surface as important in self-esteem. (Rogers, 1985; Manaster, 1989)

M-49. In general, boys have a more positive body image than girls, especially if the boy is among those who mature early. As male adolescents mature, the single most important aspect related to their sense of self is facial hair. Female adolescents are most satisfied with their body images if they see themselves as slightly underweight. Beyond that, the single most important factor related to the female's sense of self is breast development. The sense of self in adolescence thus focuses on the appearance of visible characteristics that represent adult status.

   • **Journal Entry**—*meaning, relating, relevance, implications.*

Adolescent Problems: General Health

M-50. Rapid physical growth is often associated with adolescence; with this rapid growth there is also a change in nutritional needs. Many adolescents, particularly females, have inadequate diets. Adolescents tend to skip meals, snack often, eat small quantities of desirable foods, particularly fruit and vegetables, and have inadequate knowledge of nutrition. (Rice, 1990)

M-51. Health concerns for adolescents focus on such matters as dental problems, getting along with friends, nutrition, sex, vitamins, getting along with adults, acne, sports injuries, sleep, and headaches. (Sobal, 1987)

- **Journal Entry**—*meaning, relating, relevance, implications.*

Adolescent Problems: Eating Disorders

M-52. Anorexia is a life-threatening emotional disorder in which individuals severely restrict their food intake and are obsessed by food and weight. Females between the ages of twelve to eighteen account for ninety-five per cent of all cases, but the problem is becoming more common among males. Some high school students, estimated at under five per cent of the population, are thought to have bulimia, a disorder that involves binge eating. That pattern is often followed, usually within a year of the onset of bulimia, by purging. It should be noted that anorexia is more common among young adolescents than bulimia, whereas bulimia is more likely to occur in older adolescents. Both conditions require medical intervention to prevent permanent damage.

M-53. A considerable proportion of adolescents are overweight, and approximately ten to fifteen percent are truly obese. There are considerable health risks associated with being overweight. For the adolescent, overweight is likely to have an adverse impact on social relationships as well as on self-image and self-esteem.

- **Journal Entry**—*meaning, relating, relevance, implications.*

Adolescent Problems: Delinquency

M-54. Most delinquent behavior is neither observed nor reported. Nearly all children and youth commit at least one delinquent act at some time or other, and of those who become involved with the police approximately one-third never go to court. Instead they may be given a warning, released to their parents, held in temporary custody, or referred to other social agencies.

M-55. Causal factors associated with serious delinquent behaviors are deficient academic skill—those involved are usually two or three grades behind their peers; low self-esteem and poor self-images; from families characterized by violence, abuse and/or neglect, excessively harsh punishment, parental rejection; poor social skills; and impulsiveness and lack of internal constraints for behavior. (Cobb, 1992)

M-56. Males who commit criminal offenses tend to receive harsher treatment than their female counterparts. However, for status offenses, or offenses related to age, females tend to receive harsher treatment (Cobb, 1992). People of color tend to receive harsher punishments than Whites.

- **Journal Entry**—*meaning, relating, relevance, implications.*

Adolescent Problems: Suicide and Depression

M-57. Suicide rates for the age group between fifteen and twenty-four years of age have nearly tripled over the past thirty years; suicide is now the second most common cause of deaths for that age group, second only to accidents. The rates for suicide attempts have also been increasing even more dramatically. Approximately one million attempts per year occur for persons fifteen to eighteen years of age, and the ratio of attempts at suicide to completions of suicide has jumped to over three hundred to one.

M-58. Various factors associated with increased risk of suicide have been identified. The characteristics include mental illness, substance abuse, negative personality traits such as aggression and impulsivity, psychosocial stresses resulting from school or family problems, having access to lethal means (guns, drugs, etc.), and having made a prior suicide attempt.

M-59. Suicide warning signs include sudden changes in behavior, changes in sleeping or eating patterns, loss of interest in usual activities, withdrawal from others, experiencing a humiliating event, feelings of guilt or hopelessness, inability to concentrate, talk of suicide, and giving away important possessions.

M-60. Suicidal adolescents exhibit various symptoms such as depressed moods and loss of interest in productive activity. These reactions are likely to result in academic problems, family problems, and masked depression, each of which may be expressed in a wide variety of ways. Acting-out behavior and such inappropriate conduct as aggression, stealing, and social withdrawal may be observed as the adolescent attempts to avoid feelings of loneliness and depression.

- **Journal Entry**—*meaning, relating, relevance, implications.*

Adolescent Problems: Runaways/Throwaways

M-61. Runaways most often do so because of family conflict, alienation, or poor social associations. Throwaways have been encouraged or asked to leave home; they frequently report that their relationships with their parents are strained: their parents called them names and frequently punished them or beat them.

M-62. Recent evidence has suggested a link between abuse and neglected youth and running away. Adolescent abuse occurs with some frequency. Almost fifty percent of serious injuries resulting from abuse involve youth between the ages of twelve and seventeen. Running away seems to be symptomatic of other problems.

M-63. Running away is seldom planned. Many youth leave home suddenly without money or clothes and end up staying with friends or relatives. Many do not stay away for long, returning within the same day or week; many often run away again.

- **Journal Entry**—*meaning, relating, relevance, implications.*

Adolescent Problems: Growing Up in a Materialistic World

M-64. A great many adolescents work part-time and many earn more than fifty dollars per week; as a result they have become a huge consumer market, and businesses and advertisers cater directly to them.

M-65. Trends over the past dozen years indicate that there has been an increase in the emphasis on materialism. For youth, there has been a decline in the intrinsic value of work and it is partially being replaced with extrinsic values such as achieving status and security through earning money.

- **Journal Entry**—*meaning, relating, relevance, implications.*

Adolescent Problems: Gangs

M-66. Gangs are typically formed from neighborhood associations and often focus on protection of turf. More and more often gangs are linked with some form of organized crime and the goal of the members is that of making money. Crimes committed by gangs run the gamut from harrassment, intimidation, and extortion to selling drugs, rape, and murder.

- **Journal Entry**—*meaning, relating, relevance, implications.*

Race, Cultural Diversity, Ethnicity, and Adolescents

M-67. Most minority adolescents are very much aware of their ethnicity, though some may not see themselves as members of a particular ethnic or racial group.

M-68. Multicultural diversity is a reality. Adolescents from different cultures may react differently to the same stimuli. For example, Chinese, Hispanic, and African-American adolescents tend to be more group-oriented and focus more on the feelings and expectations of others than their White contemporaries. Cultural differences also exist in the area of mannerisms; interactions in some cultures are very informal and easy-going, while in others interactions are ritualized and restrictive. For example, African-American adolescents may be quick and open in expressing their emotions, whereas Asian-American adolescents may act in a more reserved manner.

M-69. In terms of behavior problems in children and adolescents, there appear to be very few racial or cultural differences. (Achenbach and Edelbrock, 1981)

- **Journal Entry**—*meaning, relating, relevance, implications.*

Adolescents with Special Needs: Learning Disabled

M-70. Adolescents with learning disabilities often have difficulties in school, particularly with such matters as turning in homework, paying attention, and following classroom discussions. Learning disabled young people tend to be at increased risk for psychological and emotional problems due to the fact that compared to others they have poorer social skills, are less aware of the effects of their behavior on others, and are less likely to key into others' non-verbal cues and moods.

M-71. Despite the overwhelming negative consequences of their disabilities, learning disabled adolescents tend to have normal relationships with their families, and as they go through adolescence their self-concepts tend to show improvement. Most of them find avenues other than school success upon which to base their improving self-concepts.

- **Journal Entry**—*meaning, relating, relevance, implications.*

Adolescent Problems: Gifted

M-72. The most common criterion for identifying young people as gifted is a score of 130 or higher on an intelligence test. Although intelligence is the focus of the definition, other factors associated with gifted youth include: more maturity, better-developed social skills, more self-confidence, a higher level of responsibility, and more self-control when compared to their peers.

M-73. Several specific characteristic of gifted youth have been identified:

1. They ask many questions.
2. They have information on numerous topics.
3. They become impatient when they cannot complete a task perfectly.
4. They are often loners.
5. They may become bored and complain that they have nothing to do.

6. They may complete part of an assignment but leave it unfinished as they move to another activity.
7. They like to solve problems.
8. They have their own ideas about how things should be done.
9. They tend to adopt a questioning attitude. (Clark, 1988)

- **Journal Entry**—*meaning, relating, relevance, implications.*

Adolescents as Contributors

M-74. Adolescents represent a vast, often-untapped reservoir of energy that may be mobilized for their advantage and the advantage of the society at large. One way in which adolescent energy is currently being utilized is in peer helping programs which may involve peer tutoring, peer counseling, and the like.

M-75. The energies of youth have been tapped both within and outside the school setting through all manner of volunteer activities. Young people have contributed through a variety of social, ecological, and political projects. They have cleaned highways and streams, met with and read to children and the infirm, raised funds to meet individual and community emergencies, acted on behalf of political candidates or supported political issues, and engaged in all manner of other useful activities.

M-76. Adolescents have done much themselves to counter the frequent complaint, "There's nothing to do." Citing but one example, young people have helped to organize a great variety of Friday Night Live activities—a vast array of engaging Friday evening events that provide them drug-free opportunities to socialize and entertain themselves. These gatherings for social purposes have resulted in many social service spinoff activities of the kinds enumerated above (M-75). (An address that can be used for further information is: California Friday Night Live, State Department of Alcohol & Drug Programs, 1700 K Street, Sacramento, CA 95814)

- **Journal Entry**—*meaning, relating, relevance, implications.*

2
Critical Incidents

Critical incidents—incidents that demand immediate action and followup—inevitably occur in your work with adolescents and others. From time to time the young people in your charge, their parents, your supervisors and colleagues, act or speak in surprising or troubling ways, based on the realities they face and the patterns of choices they have learned to make, and you must respond. To a large extent, the effectiveness of your choices and responses to critical incidents detemines your success or failure in your work with adolescents and others.

Here we offer numerous critical incidents that are designed to expand your understanding of some of the stresses of adolescence in graphic, dramatic ways. Through your responses to these incidents, you may test your satisfaction with the present state of your choices and skills and implement new skills and choices. We invite you to make immediate responses and decide on possible future actions you might take in response to these incidents. Then, as you read the Choices and Communication Skills chapters, we encourage you to re-play the incidents using the skills and choices you are learning about. Doubtless, you will notice greater sensitivity and suitability in your responses.

If you are reading this book on your own, we encourage you to find a way to use these incidents interactively in a group or with a partner. If that is not possible, we suggest you read the context of these incidents aloud, initiate the interaction in the way it is presented here, then continue the two-way dialogue as best you can, enacting it and re-enacting it following your first impulse, then in other ways you believe might be more effective. If you are reading this book in conjunction with a class, a workshop, or other program, your group leader may invite you to enact these incidents as role plays, initiating them as they are presented, then continuing the dialogue with a partner.

In any event, we encourage you to use these incidents interactively, to find opportunities to discuss them, and to re-enact them using new skills and choices.

•J. This coding appears after each incident as a journaling reminder. You may wish to write journal entries in which you discuss your responses to incidents, answer key questions (see page 12), and/or reflect on your use of new skills and choices.

Some of the critical incidents occur in non-school settings, while others are school- or classroom-based. If an incident does not fit your situation, we encourage you to adapt it so that it does. Adolescents offer challenges; they also seek out adults they believe may be understanding, and they share their problems with them. If you are a teacher you may have occasion to be with adolescents off the school grounds, on a trip, or in an in-school suspension room, so some of the events that occur outside the classroom may relate to you. If you are a counselor or administrator you may find yourself conducting a special activity or taking over a group for a period of time until other arrangements can be made, or you may recast the incident so that someone else is reporting the incident to you and asking you what your response would have been in the situation. If you work in a non-school setting, it is likely that from time to time you have occasion to provide leadership to a group of young people; thus, whatever happens in a classroom might occur while adolescents are in your charge. We encourage you to give yourself to these experiences, adapting them as needed.

We would like to thank the teachers, counselors, and others who have participated in this program for their suggestions of the incidents presented here. Nearly all of the incidents were written by participants, based on their own observations and experiences with adolescents and the adults in the lives of those young people. We have altered circumstances, changed names, and rewritten the incidents so that they have the broadest applicability, but we tip our hats gratefully to those who have helped us build this challenging, interactive resource.

Note that not all the incidents are ideally initiated—but the dialogues begin with what the writers have said to young people, have heard others say, or thought they might actually say in the situation.

Using a Critical Incident

The example that follows suggests how a critical incident may be structured: Note that this incident has applicability both in- and outside the school environment.

CI-sample: Adam—A Good College Prospect

Adam is a very bright boy who comes from a lower-middle class environment. He is involved in several activities and is very popular. You have let him know that when it comes time you will be happy to help him with an application to college and that you may have some ideas concerning scholarships.

Lately, Adam has been scowling a lot, his effort has not been up to his usual level, and most of his work has been sketchy or incomplete. You create an opportunity to meet with him, and open up the dialogue.

You: Adam, I'm concerned about you. Your work seems to be falling off lately and I've noticed a different attitude on your part. If something is bothering you, I'd like to help if I can.

Adam: Oh, it's nothing. *(Pause)*. I know you think I ought to go to college some day, but it's just not in the cards.

You: Hmm. Talk about that some more, would you please?

Adam: Well, my parents didn't go to college and they are doing fine running the family grocery store. I'm already in the business with dad and I can make money lots earlier if I don't go to college. I just can't see wasting four years there. Anyway, if I don't go, I can use the money I've got to buy a new car pretty soon. •J.

[As noted in the introduction, the symbol above (•J) suggests that you build a journal entry at this time. For any incident you may wish to respond to one or more of the questions in the adjoining column.]

As you can see, the first portion of the critical incident establishes the context, and the second portion provides an immediate dialogue opportunity.

Here, and in most other examples, the context is very brief. You may believe you would have more information, but think of what is presented here as the sketchy kind of information you might have about an adolescent very early in your contact.

Note: *Dialogue typically ends with a challenge to YOU that requires an immediate response of some kind. In using these critical incidents, you are encouraged not to just think about or "talk around" what you would do. Rather, construct an immediate sample verbal response or demonstrate the action you would take.*

Assume that each incident includes the following suggestions and questions:

1. *Continue the dialogue several steps—with a partner if possible. You may wish to begin with your "first impulse" response, then try what you believe might be a more effective response.*

2. *What is the essential problem? What is going on with the other person?*

3. *What key concepts of adolescence are playing out in the incident?*

4. *What are your long-range goals for the relationship?*

5. *Have "you" responded suitably in the printed dialogue?*

6. *What might have been a more effective initiation or first response?*

7. *What followup actions, if any, would you want to consider?*

8. *What are several alternative things you might do or say in the moment?*

9. *What would be the advantages of each of these approaches?*

10. *What would be the disadvantages of each of these approaches?*

11. *What question(s) might you want to raise for discussion?*

As you read in the *Choices and Communication Skills* section that follows, return to these incidents from time to time and ask—

12. *In what ways can you apply your readings about skills and choices to the particular situation?*

The above suggestions and questions are the same for all incidents, so space is not used to repeat them for subsequent incidents.

Critical Incidents

CI-1: Julie—That Don't Make Me No Never Mind

(This incident is a natural for a school setting, but is applicable in other group settings as well. Use your creative powers to apply it to a non-school setting.)

Julie is not very bright, is undermotivated, and can be sullen and impolite. You've heard her brag that she intends to drop out of school the minute she turns sixteen. You find yourself wishing she would make that landmark soon, since that would take her out of your group—but she will be with you for many months to come.

The one thing Julie has going for her is her long, dark, glossy hair—which she endlessly combs in your presence and everywhere, it seems. You have asked her to stay involved and not to use her comb while she is in your charge.

You look at the back of the room and see Julie combing her hair. A few moments later, after you have given the group a task to do, you work your way back to her. She is still preening her locks.

You: Two things, Julie. I've asked you not to comb your hair in here, and I've just given out work you should be doing.

Julie: *(Scowls and goes on combing her hair)* You know what? That don't make me no never mind. •J.

CI-2: Carl—I Thought I Needed to Change

Carl has always been well-behaved and quiet. He gets along well enough with other boys, though he tends to remain in the background.

Recently, though, Carl has been making his presence known more. He has become more assertive, almost to the point of being a bully. In addition, his work has begun to deteriorate. You arrange to talk to him, and he appears in your doorway.

Carl: Howdy! You wanted to talk to me?

You: Come on in, Carl. *(He comes in and sits down.)* I've noticed that your work has been slipping lately and I've been concerned about the changes I've seen recently in your behavior. I thought the two might be connected. I'd like to know if there is anything going on that I might be able to help you with.

Carl: Well, something has been bothering me, but I'm not sure you can help me with it.

        (You wave your hand and he continues.)

        Well, all of my friends now have dates on the weekends, and they're always seeing girls, but not me. I thought I needed to change, and if I was more, you know, forceful, that the girls would be more interested in me, too—but it hasn't worked so far. •J.

CI-3: Cora—I Hate the Class!

(This incident clearly belongs in a school setting, but responses like these occur in other situations as well. Use your creative powers to apply it to a non-school setting.)

Cora is a high achiever and a good class participant. She seems to be enjoying school and learning the material well, though she is often the last student to complete her work. On the day of the first test she arrives in your room five minutes late with a terrified look on her face. You hand her a test and quietly repeat the instructions you gave the class. She writes very quickly and finishes in plenty of time. As she turns in her test, she bursts into tears and starts to run out of the room. You call her name quietly, and she turns back to you.

You: Cora, what's the matter?

Cora: *(Loud enough so all can hear)* Oh, I just know I failed that terrible test! It was unfair and too hard! I hate the class and I hate you! Why did you give such a rotten test? •J.

CI-4: Sam—It's Great to be Home

Sam has been a problem for the authorities and school since third grade. He is presently in the 9th grade. He has been involved with the local probation office since fourth grade when he began skipping school and was reported to the courts for truancy. Sam has little supervision at home and when he does get in trouble at school; it is suspected that his father "whips him." He was recently adjudicated as delinquent for auto theft. He and two other boys stole and wrecked a car. The judge committed him to a state school. Sam spent six months in the school and is now returning to the community. Reports from the state school indicate that Sam worked well in their structured environment.

Sam has always seemed to like you and it does not surprise you when he stops by to visit with you.

Sam: Boy it feels great to be home! I sure did learn my lesson. I'm never going back to *that* place again.

You: It's great to have you back. It really sounds like you've got your act together.

Sam: Yeah, but no one wants to believe me. I think everyone still thinks I'm just a punk, except you. You always treated me different. You're cool!

You: Thanks, Sam. *(You nod your head and wait for him to go on.)*

Sam: Look, there are these guys. . ., you know, the ones I got in trouble with before. Well, they're up to no good. I'm afraid that they're gonna set me up and I'll get blamed for something I didn't even do. •J.

CI-5: Jamie—The Junior Adult

Jamie is a tenth grader who recently moved into your area. You have learned that Jamie moved due to his parents' recent divorce. Jamie is the oldest of four children. He has a 13-year-old brother and two younger sisters, ages 11 and 8. It is apparent that Jamie is responsible for much of the care of his brother and sisters while his mother is working. Additionally, Jamie has taken a job at a local fast food restaurant and he works some weekday nights and weekends. Jamie's past school performance has been average and his adjustment to his new school and community has been uneventful; however, he has begun to slack off in his school work. Because he has had a favorable contact with you, one of his teachers encouraged you to talk with him.

You: Jamie, thanks for stopping by. I asked you to come in because one of your teachers is concerned about your school work lately.

Jamie: Uh huh.

You: Well, I thought you might like to talk.

Jamie: Nah, I don't need to talk to anyone. Thanks, anyway. Besides, I hardly know you and you don't have any idea what I've been going through. I'd best be going, I have to get home. •J.

CI-6: Barb—Will You Help Me?

(The context here is school, but the dialogue is as likely to occur in any other situation in which adolescents meet responsive adults. If appropriate, apply this incident to your non-school setting.)

Barb seems to be genuinely interested in school and has said she wants to become a teacher. She is a hard worker and a good student. She often stays after school to talk to you and to ask questions.

She hasn't been acting like herself the last couple of days. She stops by and you notice that she appears to be very nervous.

You: Hi, Barb. You wanted to see me?

Barb: Well, I really need some help and I'm hoping you'll want to help me.

You: I'll be glad to help you if I can.

Barb: I found out on the weekend for sure that I'm pregnant. I just can't have this baby because it will mess up all my plans for the future. I want to get an abortion. I don't want my boyfriend or parents to find out. Will you help me and keep it between us? PLEASE!!!

Play this incident through as is, then a second time as if you are a single male who works with Barb in a group. Does it make a difference? Consider the possibility that Barb's parents might see you as a better potential father to their grandchild than the boy who is actually involved. What actions might that lead them to take? •J.

CI-7: Jack—This Place Stinks

Jack is a tenth grader. Jack's family has lived in the community for many years. Jack's father is a machinist in a local factory; he has a sixth grade education. His mother is unemployed and she, too, only completed sixth grade. Jack has four siblings, two older brothers and two younger sisters. The two older brothers do not live at home any longer. The family lives in a trailer on the outskirts of town. Jack is very uninvolved in school. He hardly ever does his homework. He never attends any of the school athletic activities and admits that he is "bored" with school. Jack has told school officials that as soon as he can legally do so he will drop out of school.

Jack is in a group you work with and his attitude seems infectious. He has gotten the majority of the group members to talk about the benefits of quitting school.

Jack: Yeah, I'm gonna quit in five weeks—35 days—I can't wait. Who needs school anyway.

        (Others chime in, saying they can't wait until they can quit school. Billy looks at you in a strange way, and you nod to him, inviting him to speak.)

Billy: I think Jack's stupid for quitting school. He'll just end up flipping burgers. Don't you think he's stupid? •J.

CI-8: Kevin—Young Father

Kevin is a senior in high school and a fine athlete. For two years he has been a participant in the community recreation program you work with. He is well liked. You have heard that his academic performance is a little above average. However, this year his grades have begun to fall and his performance, both in your program and in school, has deteriorated. A teacher has told you that Kevin has fallen asleep in class a few times recently and you note that he is often late for your practice sessions. He reports that he is working a part-time job after school to have money he needs for "personal reasons."

After talking with you several times, Kevin shares those personal reasons. He is working to help provide support for the baby he has fathered. He is presently thinking about dropping out of school so that he can work full time.

Kevin: I'm really sorry. I should have told you sooner. I was just really embarrassed. Things are real hard right now.

You: Kevin, I'm glad you shared what's going on. I was beginning to get really worried.

Kevin: See, Peg, that's my girl, she wants to get married, but I'm not sure what to do. I'm having enough trouble just making enough money to buy the things the little guy needs. I don't think I can handle getting married. I guess this means no college and no athletic scholarship, huh? •J.

CI-9: Toni's Father— Teen-Parent Trouble

You are aware that Toni is being raised by her father. Until recently she had been doing well in your group. When she seemed to lose motivation you talked with her about that, but nothing changed. You have invited her father in to talk with you.

Mr. Reece has listened patiently and has agreed to make an effort to get through to Toni and give her some encouragement. You are about to close the discussion when you make a simple observation, and that opens a new topic.

You: You seem discouraged.

Mr. R.:   I am discouraged. My daughter has been having some friends in after school when I have to be at work. Some are older boys. I'm not sure what's going on, but I'm afraid of the worst. I forbid her to have them over, but she only laughs and goes right on doing it. She can't live with her mother, and I can't seem to control her. I just don't know what to do. Can you help me? •J.

CI-10: Toni— The Other Side of the Coin

After talking with Mr. Reece you had hoped to visit with Toni. An opportunity comes up and you take advantage of it.

You: I'm sure you know I talked with your father the other day.

Toni: *(Sighs deeply)* You know, Dad's got me all wrong. He's right about one thing. I do have kids over, but we only talk and listen to tapes. I get bored out of my mind if I stay there for hours by myself. •J.

CI-11: Max's Mother— Another Teen-Parent Problem

Max's mother, Mrs. Warringer, asks to talk with you because she thinks Max may trust you more than anyone else. She tells you at length about her concerns: Max is clearly sexually active and he brags over the phone to other boys about how often he's "scoring" with the girls. He's keeping a log of his conquests and she has heard him claim that he's already got a list of over thirty "victims."

Mrs. Warringer tells you that she has strong religious beliefs and has tried to get through to Max, but with his father out of the picture she complains that he doesn't listen to her. She believes that Max may already have

gotten one girl pregnant, but, fortunately for him, the girl miscarried. What is worse—if anything can be worse—rumors abound that two or three girls in the school may be HIV-positive.

Mrs. W.: I'm just at my wit's end. Would you be willing to talk to him. He thinks I'm just old-fashioned and fuddy-duddy, but he tells me you're "cool." •J.

CI-12: Uproar— An Omitted Instruction

Because of an emergency you were called away for several minutes. You took a moment to assign a task before you left, but when you come back you find the group you were working with in an uproar. You realize right away that the problem is partly your fault because in your haste you omitted a key instruction.

How would you begin the dialogue right now? •J.

CI-13: John— A Bright, Mixed-Up Boy

(If you haven't been evaluating the initial approach used, be sure to do so here. But first, try this as is. We won't always start in the most effective ways.)

John has been in your school eight days, but his past history has made him a legend. He is a runaway and a throwaway—his mother did not want him at home and he did not want to be there. It is well-known that he spent three months on the streets of New York, where rumor has it that he survived through thievery and prostitution.

John's aunt, who is well-respected in the community, went to the city and brought him to her home. A few days later, she met with you and the other members of the school and community who were scheduled to work with John in various situations. She agreed the odds were not favorable for John to succeed, and even said, "Frankly, I know it's very difficult to reach any youngster who has lived on the streets for over a month." But she appealed to all of you to "help salvage this bright, mixed-up boy."

John has kept to himself and had very little difficulty so far. He does fairly well in your group. What bothers you most are his sullen attitude and his look of disdain.

You notice that John looks distracted and make an observation to him which you immediately regret.

You: John, you've been working thirty minutes and I see you're only half done.

John: Well, if that's not enough, I suggest you just shove it! *(He pauses, then adds in a bitter tone)* Better still, let me help! •J.

CI-14: Lou—
A Hard Kind of Kid to Like

Lou is your number one challenge. He can hardly read, is argumentative and rude, extorts money from younger boys ("Gimme a buck, or I'll beat the s... out of you"), wipes his nose on his sleeve, wears the same clothes day in and day out, and is a certain school dropout when he turns sixteen. Despite Lou's negative traits, you are determined to get through to him by building a good relationship with him and focusing on the flip side of some of his most negative traits.

In your mind you think of some of the things you *could* say to reinforce Lou. For example: "You read that sentence well." "You really have a mind of your own, Lou, and I think that's good." "You decide what you want and you go after it."

But, despite your hopes for a positive interaction, Lou arrives in your group just after a younger boy has come to you, crying, and complaining that Lou had beaten him up because he wouldn't pay him off.

You: Well, Lou, what happened this time?

Lou: Nothing much. •J.

CI-15: Sandy—An Accident

You are getting ready for your group when Sandy, a bright youngster you enjoy, comes in looking tense and fearful, slumps in a chair, and asks to talk to you.

You: Sure. I'm always ready to hear from you. What's the deal?

Sandy: Well, it's like this. I got to drive our car alone for the first time today. I was trying to light a cigarette and I dropped the match. When I tried to find it, I went off the road and I scraped the whole right fender. The car's only a year old. My parents will kill me! What do I do? •J.

CI-16: Willie—
Can a Guy Really Do That?

Willie is a cleancut, sensitive, caring young man who drops in to talk with you often.

You: Hey, Willie, nice to see you. *(Pause)* You look down in the dumps today.

Willie: I just got the report on some career tests I took a while back and I thought I'd like to talk with you. Seems like I'd fit pretty well in nursing. *(Laughs)* Can a guy really do that? •J.

CI-17: Sally—No Problem Anymore

Sally is very quiet. She is very well-developed for her age. She seems to be liked by her peers, yet she evidently has a poor opinion of herself. Anecdotal reports in her folder indicate that she has "always" had a boyfriend. The school nurse detected physical symptoms that she believed might be related to pregnancy. In a conference with you, the school counselor, the school nurse, Sally's parents, and Sally, the nurse communicated with her parents that she thought Sally might be pregnant.

During the subsequent two month period, Sally was often absent. You let Sally know that you are available, and she comes by to talk with you.

Sally: Remember, that thing that we talked about awhile ago. *(She pauses)* You remember, we had the conference. . .

You: *(Nodding)* Yes, of course I remember.

Sally: Well, I don't have that "problem" anymore.

You: You don't have that problem anymore.

Sally: Nope, my parents made me take care of it. I got an abortion. •J.

CI-18: Jed—
I Don't Have No Problem

Jed, a ninth grader, has a poor school attendance record. His mother works the evening shift at one of the local factories and thus Jed has very little supervision. Jed's older brother was reported to be a "trouble maker" and "into drugs."

When he does go to school, Jed is rebellious and unruly. He associates with a peer group that seems to reinforce this behavior. There is some suspicion that Jed and his peer group are drug users. The administration has asked for help from Jed's mother. Her response is that she is aware that Jed is drinking and smoking marijuana some, but that he really is not a problem at home. She implies that Jed's problem stems from the school and "the group" he hangs out with. She agrees to make an effort to keep Jed in school but she reports that he doesn't always mind her and she cannot supervise him closely. Jed's father, who lives in the locale, has nothing to do with Jed. He has not been active in Jed's life for many years.

Because of the concern about drugs, Jed has been referred to a support group that you lead. He is resistant, but agrees to attend. Jed has been in the group for several weeks and has said little. During this week's group meeting, you decide to confront him.

You: Jed, I'm concerned. You come to group every week, but somehow I have the impression that you're really not interested.

Jed: Good guess.

You: I was hoping that you could help all of us understand what you hope to get out of the group.

Jed: Look, I don't need all that B.S. I'm here just to get those jerks, you know, the school people, off my back. I do some drugs, but I don't have no drug problem, so just leave me alone. •J.

CI-19: Cara—
I Just Wanted to Say Goodbye

Cara, a seventeen-year-old senior, is a near-perfect high school student. She is ranked in the top of her class, is a class officer, a member of the student council and the debating club, and she takes part in numerous other community organizations. Silently and secretly she is dealing with tremendous pressures. Her father appears to be a selfish, rejecting alcoholic whose inconsistent behavior keeps the family anxious and insecure about their financial and emotional futures. Cara, despite outward appearances and obvious strengths, appears to be a lonely, unsupported, and overextended individual who derives little pleasure from her activities and accomplishments.

It is late afternoon and Cara has been working along with you for nearly an hour on the decorations for an upcoming dance. You hear her sigh more than once. It occurs again, and you say:

You: My, but that sounds weary and sad.

Cara: Things are hopeless.

You: What do you mean, things are hopeless?

Cara: At home, I just can't stand it anymore. It's awful. I have to get out of there. I've had it. I'm at the end of my rope. Please don't tell anyone, but I just can't go on. (Before you can say anything, she adds)

         I just wanted to say goodbye and to thank you for being so nice to me. •J.

CI-20: Jeff—I Can't Stand It

Jeff is painfully quiet and shy. When you have gotten him to speak out, it has been a disaster. He becomes confused and trips on his words, and others tend to jump in to finish his thoughts. You have the impression that he is becoming even more introverted as your time with him goes on.

He has come by to pick up a form he needs and you decide to seize the opportunity to talk with him.

You: Hi, Jeff. I'm glad you're here, I've been wanting to see you.

Jeff: Huh? Well, OK.

You: I've become concerned about your participation lately. It seems to me that you are almost afraid to speak during our discussions now.

Jeff: Well, I don't like it when the other kids make fun of me for no reason.

You: I'd like to help. Can you see anything I might do?

Jeff: Could you get me excused from that physical ed stuff? That's the worst. You see, every time I can't do an activity like the other kids, they make fun of me. Now they pick on me all the time. I can't stand it. •J.

CI-21: Butch—
An Angry Young Man

(This incident is school-focused, but the same behavior may occur elsewhere.)

A group you work with has been really cooperative and pleasant. At least it was until Butch was switched in to it, due to "a personality conflict" with a leader in another group/class. Butch is a very angry young man who responds with hostility to your every move and to the outreach of his peers. It is the end of your time block and everyone has handed in the work except Butch. You approach him good-humoredly.

You: Time's up. I need you to hand in your work.

Butch: (For a moment Butch just glares at you, then he tosses his work on the floor and starts out the door.) You want it? There it is! •J .

CI-22: James—Am I Going to Have to Call Your Mother?

James has been a difficult young man to deal with from the first. His work is rarely complete, if it is done at all. He is under a court order to be in school and to pass all of his classes. At the present time, he is not passing in one class and if he does not shape up soon there will be no way for him to achieve a passing grade by the end of the term. You have been asked to keep track of him and act as his ombudsperson.

You: (Kiddingly) James, am I going to have to call your mother to get you to do your schoolwork?

Paul: (Gets your attention and says) James don't have no mother. She died last summer. •J.

CI-23: M. J.—A Reassignment

M. J. has recently been shifted into your group. She has never accepted the reassignment, which was made to separate her from two of her friends, and she has very evidently set out to make things difficult for you so that she might be returned to the group she came from. Today she has apparently decided to step up her campaign, has answered several questions sarcastically, and has functioned at the edge of rudeness since she entered the room. You decide you have had enough, you give the group a task to work on, and you ask M. J. to step out in the hall with you. She stands up, noisily grabs up her things, and as she follows you out the door she speaks up so that everyone in the room can hear:

M. J.: I'd be glad to go out in the hall and right on into my old group with my friends. This is the worst group I've ever been in, and you're a jerk. •J.

CI-24: Chris—Strong Interest

Chris is a young person of the opposite sex who is in a group you work with. *(Take the stance that you are single, regardless of your actual status.)* Chris arrives early and is always the last to leave. Chris often stops by to talk and to help set up and clean up the room. Chris is of average intelligence and doesn't seem to be highly motivated, but likes you.

Earlier today a colleague mentioned that Chris had been asking many personal questions about you. It is clear that Chris has a strong interest in you. You decide to express your concern to your supervisor and make an appointment to do so. You are hurrying out the door for the appointment when Chris stops by to ask if you will assist in chaperoning a school dance.

You: My name should already be on the list. I agreed to do that long ago.

Chris: Then, can we go together?

You: *(Starting out the door to go to your appointment.)* Look, Chris, I can't talk right now. Can you come by in the morning?

You turn back and see Chris smiling at you. A thought occurs to you. "Am I expected to say yes?"

As you meet the next morning how do you open the dialogue? •J.

CI-25: Your Supervisor—A Followup

When you arrive in the office to talk with your supervisor about Chris, you learn that he is in conference and has left a message saying he will call you to his office from the lounge as soon as he is available.

You spread out some work before you and busy yourself for a half hour. Instead of coming for you himself as usual, your supervisor sends a secretary for you. Later you learn that he had made several telephone calls and had hurried conferences—all relating to you and Chris.

You walk in the office smiling, but your supervisor looks very serious.

Super.: *(Gruffly)* Close the door, please.

You: Sure. *(You do so.)* Is something wrong?

Super.: Yes, something is very wrong and I'm sure you know what it is.

You: *(Your mind is a blank.)* I'm sorry. I don't understand.

Super.: *(Looks straight at you for a time.)* I'd heard that you often had someone in your room early and late, and that Chris Lane had a crush on you. And now Chris is reporting that you *might* go to the dance together. •J.

CI-26: Frances— I Don't Like Being Different

Frances was identified and subsequently labelled as learning disabled when she was in the second grade. Her school history indicates much academic difficulty. In elementary school, Frances was an isolate. She rarely socialized with any peer group and she was often "picked on" by her peers. As a result of having been involved with the school district's special education program, Frances has made remarkable progress. The parental support that the school and the teachers have received has been both welcomed and appreciated. Her parents have formed a partnership with the school in an effort to assist Frances. Presently she is in the tenth grade. She still has problems with her learning disability, but she has learned to accept it and adapt to it. She is now much more accepted by her peers.

She has stopped by and asked to speak with you.

Frances: I've got a problem and I need to talk with someone. Would you mind if we talked for a little while?

You: No, of course I wouldn't mind. Come on in and sit down.

Frances: Thanks. I don't know where to start, but you know that I've had problems with my LD, right? Well, everyone helped out a lot and I'm doing a lot better with my school work and all. It's just that now they won't leave me alone. I want to make my own decisions and all. 'Cept the teachers and my parents think they know what's best for me.

You: So what you're saying is that now that things are going well with school, you aren't really given much responsibility to make your own decisions.

Frances: Yeah, that's it. (She pauses and starts to cry quietly.) I just wish I wasn't so different and that I didn't have this LD thing. Maybe then people would treat me like a "normal" human being. •J.

CI-27: Mandie—I'm Just a Big, Clumsy, Lanky Geek!

Mandie seems very self-conscious about her appearance. She continually puts herself down. Ever since grade school, Mandie has been taller and bigger than most of the boys, and her peers have often made fun of her. Lately, she seems to be even harder on herself than in the past. During a break, you overhear her talking.

Mandie: No guys will ever want to date me! I'm just a big, clumsy, lanky geek! Why would some guy want to date me? (With that Mandie notices that you are standing within hearing distance and she looks directly at you, expecting a response.) •J.

CI-28: Jennie— I'm Having a Hard Time

Jennie, a strong academic junior, has recently been in contact with the local military recruiting office. She has indicated a desire to serve in the US Navy. Her interest in the Navy was sparked by her involvement with the high school ROTC program. Her parents are supportive of her interest in the Navy and have encouraged her. As part of the military screening processes, it is discovered that Jennie is HIV-positive and is thus denied consideration and subsequent naval/military admission. Following the diagnosis, Jennie admits to her parents that she has been sexually active with an older male, a naval reserve whom she met through the ROTC program.

Jennie has asked to see you. She says she needs someone to talk to and you are her favorite adult. You have heard some talk, but you know nothing of all this directly.

You: Jennie, come on in. Have a seat.

Jennie: I'm glad you had time to meet with me. I'm really having a hard time right now and I could use someone to talk to.

You: I'd be happy to listen. What do you have on your mind?

Jennie: I'm really scared. Everyone's talking about AIDS and stuff. I don't know how to deal with the fact that I have it. What should I do? •J.

CI-29: Tom—Dad Made It OK

Tom has good potential, and you know he is a good worker when he is motivated. His work, however, has been average. He enjoys sports and has some ability as a wrestler.

He is the youngest of eight children and the only one still at home. No one in his family has ever had post-high-school education of any kind, and you have the impression that schooling is not seen as important to them.

Tom's father, a self-educated man whom Tom admired, died recently. His mother moved two hundred miles away to her parents' home, and Tom lives with his older sister in their house in town. She works long hours so is seldom at home.

Tom seems depressed and unmotivated and has skipped school several times. You want to help him, so you ask him to stop by to talk with you.

You: Tom, I haven't had a chance to tell you how sorry I was to hear about your father's death. How are you doing?

Tom: OK, I guess. I miss him though—and my mom. She's moved in with her mom. Gram has been sick. It gets pretty lonely sometimes.

You: Yes. I've heard you say you're home alone a lot. I know that can be pretty lonely in itself.

Tom: Yes, but sometimes it's kind of nice to get to do what I want.

You: I know it's difficult to get your life back to normal after a loss like you've had, but I'm concerned about you missing so many school days.

Tom: Yeah. (Pause.) But I just don't care that much. My father never even went to high school. He made it OK. •J.

CI-30: Jill—Suddenly in Tears

Because of a specific interest of yours you are working with a health class (as a teacher or a volunteer). Jill has been actively involved in the group, but today she has been very quiet. A student has started talking about birth defects, and then begins to share information from a report he wrote about Downs Syndrome. As he describes the physical characteristics of children who have the defect, and how their treatment has changed over the years, Jill begins to cry and bolts out of the room. You ask the boy to continue the discussion, and look for Jill. You find her at the drinking fountain.

You: Jill, what's the matter?

Jill: Nothing. (You wait a few moments.) How do I get out of this class?

You: How come all of a sudden you want to get out of there?

Jill: I didn't know we were going to talk about that stuff. (She sobs.) My older brother has Downs Syndrome! •J.

CI-31: Lisa—Uncooperative

(Be sure to evaluate the comments presented here. But first, play it as written.)

From your first contact, Lisa has been causing trouble. She seems to harbor resentment toward any person in authority. During your group today she spent much of the time visiting with two girls in the back of the room. You arranged to meet with her. She arrives for the appointment and you wave her to a chair nearby.

You: Lisa, as I'm sure you are aware, I asked you to see me because you were talking so much today, and have often done so from your first day in here. When you carry on a conversation in the back of the room I feel disrespected.

Lisa: *(Turns and looks out the window.)*

You: It's not easy trying to reach everyone, and your talking makes things difficult for me, and, I think, for others as well.

Lisa: *(Looks back at you but says nothing.)* •J.

CI-32: Gina—Speech Defect

It is early in your contact with a new group and you don't know the members well. You are sharing a story, and you decide to have the group members who want to do so read aloud as you pass the book around. It is now Gina's turn to read. You are unaware that she has a speech defect; she pronounces many of her "S's" as "SH." The paragraph you gave her contains the word *sit*.

Reading aloud, she says, ". . . she was told to go s(h)it in the corner."

The group roars with laughter and, unprepared for the problem, you burst into laughter also. Gina looks at you with a pained expression. •J.

CI-33: Joe—Stepfather

Joe has been an above-average worker, but sometimes he shows little control and is disruptive. He has mentioned to you that his mother divorced and remarried when he was quite young. After an outburst on his part you ask to talk with him.

You: Joe, what is the problem with you? You're bright enough, yet you bother others while they're trying to get their work done.

Joe: I don't know. *(Shrugs his shoulders.)*

You: Is there anything I can do to help you?

Joe: Oh, it's just something at home—nothing to do with you. *(Long pause. You wait patiently.)* It seems that I can't get along with my stepfather. Nothing I do is OK with him. •J.

CI-34: Cliques—Rivalry

(Play this both ways—with girls, then boys. See if you notice differences.)

A rivalry is developing between two groups. The groups are like clubs, maybe the beginnings of gangs. Members dress alike, talk alike, and behave similarly. They play tricks on one another and occasionally fight with one another, usually when no grownups are around. Digs and negative actions are becoming increasingly cruel. You decide to confront the issue at the beginning of your time together today. How do you open the issue? What do you say? •J.

CI-35: Jake—Sissy Accusation

Jake, a hard-worker and a starter on the JV football team, has a good singing voice. You've heard that he has joined the chorus on the request of the director and that since then other members of the football team have been calling him a sissy and teasing him. In the last few days he has been creating minor problems everywhere he has been. As you are heading to your car you see Jake carrying his football gear and ambling toward the place where he is usually picked up after practice. You call to him.

You: Jake! Got a minute?

Jake: Oh, sure, Mom won't be here for a while.

You: *(Waving him to a bench nearby.)* I've been concerned about you, it seems like you've been creating a few problems lately. Nothing big, but it's unlike you.

Jake: Oh, I'm just being cool, like the rest of the kids on the team.

You: I thought you were getting along fine with the team.

Jake: I was. . . . Until I joined the glee club. •J.

CI-36: Randy—Hygiene

Randy is so advanced intellectually that he sometimes has problems relating to his peers. He is tall and overweight, but he shows signs of being a star wrestler.

Another wrestler, Wendell, asks to talk with you. "Coach won't talk to Randy, but somebody's got to do something. Anyway, I'm not gonna wrestle him any more, that's for sure." You invite Wendell to explain and after a pause he says, "Well, he stinks. He never takes a shower."

Hearing a sound, you turn. Randy is standing in the doorway and you are sure he has heard enough to know what the discussion was about. Wendell sinks in his chair.

Randy: *(Looking upset)* Oooh. •J.

CI-37: Joy—Takes Charge

Joy is quite bright. She is also attractive, popular, and a fine volleyball player. You have given small groups a task to do and have asked Joy to act as leader of one group. To your chagrin, you notice that Joy is too authoritarian as leader, so after a few days you shift the leaders in all the groups. However, Joy continues to give directions and monopolize the discussion. From the looks you see on the faces of others in the group with her, you are convinced that the other group members are disturbed by Joy's dominance. You arrange a private talk with Joy.

You: Joy, I've noticed that you seem to like small group work.

Joy: It's OK, but I have to do all the work.

You: Hmm. That's interesting. I'm sure the others have a lot to add also.

Joy: I doubt it. They never say very much. In fact, they just go along with what I say. •J.

CI-38: Jonah— Minority Group Member

Jonah is a minority member (could be African-American, Hispanic, or White) of a group you work with. You record a low evaluation on a key piece of work of his which you saw as too hastily done and too heavily dotted with errors. As you return his effort you hand him a note that invites him to re-do the work. You are walking away when Jonah stands up and demands to know why you didn't pass him.

You: I'll be glad to discuss that with you later today.

Jonah: Hey, I want to talk about it now!

You: I'm sorry, I can't. There are several things we need to do just now.

Jonah: Well, I know why you didn't pass me—because I'm Black (or White, or Hispanic)! •J.

CI-39: Sheri—Foster Child

Sheri is a heavy set girl of low-average intelligence. She recently came into your group as a result of her placement in a foster home in which she is showered with love and given a good deal of freedom. Perhaps to make up for her own deficiencies Sheri approaches other girls and even some adults with a bossy tone and attitude. Recently she has started bumping into others and then pretending she hasn't been paying attention to where she is walking. Twice she has done that to you as well.

The room you are assigned to is a lab in which much expensive equipment is located. (Envision a science lab, computer lab, or home economics facility—you may just

happen to use the room because it is vacant at the particular time in which you are meeting her group.)

You are moving in Sheri's direction when you see her bump into Carla from the side—hard, and nearly cause a table with expensive equipment to tip over.

You: Sheri!

Carla: (Before you can say more, Carla calls out.) There. That's what we've been telling you about. Sheri's just mad because we didn't follow her suggestion and she keeps ramming into us when we aren't looking.

Sheri: (Glares at you.) I suppose you're going to take her side. Nobody's ever on my side. •J.

CI-40: Manuel—New President

(Be sure to evaluate the comments presented here. But first, play it as written.)

Manuel is a very popular and highly capable individual. He was recently elected president of his group or grade level. Since then he has frequently acted disruptively and done less than his best work. You believe that he is following the lead of some other disruptive adolescents and wanting to be "one of the boys."

You have a good relationship with him, so you arrange to talk with him individually.

You: Manuel, I'm concerned about your attitude. I understand that you have often acted disruptive lately.

Manuel: I'm not the only one, so why are you talking to me about it?

You: The reason I decided to talk to you is that you seem to be following the lead of others who are not as gifted as you. You should try to set an example for the others to follow. How would it look if the newly-elected president was sent to the office for disciplinary reasons?

Manuel: Well, I've just been trying to have some fun. •J.

CI-41: Ward—Mainstreamed

(Be sure to evaluate the comments presented here. But first, play it as written.)

Mainstreaming has hit your group. Ward's legs are deformed due to a birth defect, but he can walk using braces and crutches. He has been the butt of many cruel jokes, and recently such incidents have occurred quietly in the back of your room. You realize that your initial approach, ignoring the matter, has not solved the problem, so you decide you will act, and have been waiting for the opportunity.

You have arrived in the room late after picking up needed supplies, and as you approach the door you hear Ward's voice.

"Leave me alone!" he says. Then you hear a voice imitate him, repeating his words in a whining way. At that point you enter the room.

You: I want to know who just repeated what I heard Ward say.

          (Long pause.) I'm waiting.

          (You notice that several others are looking at Sam, a rather quiet boy. You think it may have been his voice.)

          Sam, was that your voice I heard?

Sam: *(Gulps. His eyes fill with tears.)* Yes, it was.

Ward: But he's not the worst one. Lots of 'em pick on me worse than him. •J.

CI-42: Bill— I Think I'm Going to be Sick

Bill is popular, he is class vice-president, a star athlete, and a leader. He has usually done above average work, though his lately his work has often been messy or late.

It troubled you recently when one of his teachers said she thought she saw Bill drinking off the schoolgrounds. A recent out-of-school event raised that question in your mind as well, but you passed up the opportunity to talk with him.

Your group is well underway, and as you are making an important point, Bill and another boy arrive late. The two giggle and slur some of their words as they explain their lateness.

A few minutes later as you walk by Bill you catch a whiff of alcohol and see a bulge that could be a bottle inside his jacket pocket. You arrange to talk with him once you have given the group a task to complete. Bill agrees, then groans, burps, says, "I think I'm going to be sick," and hurries out of the room

While Bill is gone, you start the group on the activity, then watch for his return. As you see him coming, you step out in the hall and close the door with the two of you outside the room. What do you say—*right now?* •J.

CI-43: Melody—Unusually Bright

Melody, or Mel, as she is often called, is an unusually bright seventh-grade girl who is way ahead of nearly everyone in the school in all academic matters. She seems more mature than most other young people her age, but she doesn't seem to have many friends. Her parents have requested that she be advanced two grade levels. The school administrator has asked you to talk with her parents about the possible change. *(You may take the position that you have Mel in a group you work with now, or that you will have, if she makes the change.)* You have known Mel and her parents, Mr. and Mrs. Seaman, for some time, and you are now meeting them in the office. You have greeted the Seamans and talked in general terms, then Mr. Seaman begins the dialogue.

Mr. S: Well, you know us and you know Mel. I'm sure you're aware of how bored she is, because the work is so easy for her, and how well she fits in with older kids. Please tell us you'll support the change. •J.

CI-44: Jerry—Uncooperative

Jerry has been causing trouble ever since you've known him, but today he outdid himself by interrupting, bothering others, and tossing paper wads around. After you talked to him out in the hall, then changed his seat in the room, he even threw a paper wad at you. Your supervisor takes the view that you ought to handle your own problems whenever possible, so you ask Jerry to come to talk with you.

You: Jerry, I've noticed that you've had a lot of difficulties lately, but today was absolutely the worst. What seems to be the problem?

Jerry: Me? I don't have any problem.

You: Well, you keep bothering others and you were even throwing paper wads after I moved you.

Jerry: *(Long pause.)* Well, it's not just your group. It's everything. I get so bored here, I can't stand it. •J.

CI-45: Greg—A Questionable Tool

Greg is a member of a group you work with. He is usually quiet, but he seldom does much of anything. You give the group time to begin on a task and notice Greg cleaning his fingernails with a rather large, dangerous-looking knife. Although he is not intentionally bothering anyone, you realize that many of the other boys are watching him.

What do you say/do now? •J.

CI-46: Vinnie—Missing Exam

(This situation is school-specific, but the idea is not. Situations like this occur in other settings as well. Use your creative powers to apply it to a non-school setting.)

You have just finished grading the exams from your third period class. As you go through them you notice that you have no score for Vinnie. You flip through the tests to locate his, but it is not in the stack and there are no tests without names on them. You check your attendance book and confirm that he was present when you gave the test. You conclude that for some reason he did not take the exam or did not hand it in to be graded. You have to give a makeup exam to an absent student, so you go ahead and make an extra copy for Vinnie. You see him in the corridor before school and call him over to talk with you.

You: I didn't find your exam among the other papers when I graded them yesterday. I'm prepared to have you take a makeup exam in the library along with another student if that makes sense.

Vinnie: Why do I need to take a makeup exam? I took the same test the other students took the other day. What happened to mine? •J.

CI-47: Robby—I Didn't Mean To

Robby seems to personify learned helplessness and powerlessness. You've heard him say "I couldn't help it," or "They made me do it," and the like, dozens of times.

It is late afternoon and you are about to close your door behind you, when a girl whom you know Robby likes runs past you. You can see that her blouse is torn. Robby is right behind her. He stops when he sees you and says:

Robby: The other kids dared me to kiss her. I didn't mean to tear her shirt. •J.

CI-48: Gene— A Caustic Sense of Humor

Gene has a caustic sense of humor, and so do you. Occasionally the two of you engage in a competition of cutting repartee when Gene turns you on. Other young people have left and the two of you have been bantering as you get ready to leave. You make an effort to shift the conversation to serious ground, saying:

You: You know, Gene, if you really worked at it, you could have an excellent future ahead of you.

Gene: That's funny, I was just thinking that if you really worked at it, you could have a bright future ahead of you, too. •J.

CI-49: Kyle— Why Should I Try Anymore?

(You may play this as if Kyle is someone with whom you have contact at present, or as if you meet him by accident and are aware of the change he has undergone lately. Content in parentheses is used if your contact with Kyle occurred previously.)

Kyle had been a top student in grades and participation. He seemed to take school very seriously and always put a great deal of effort into his work. *(You have become aware that.)* In the last week, Kyle has become irritable, has not completed assignments, and failed a test. He has been hostile and unapproachable.

You encounter him by happenstance, mention a ball game you had both attended, laugh over a wierd play that occurred in the game, and decide that is enough of an opening for you to bring up your concern about him.

You: Kyle, I'm glad to have a chance to talk with you. *(I understand that.)* You haven't been your old self lately in school. Is there a problem?

Kyle: Yeah, I guess I've been a jerk lately and I flunked a test, but I just don't care anymore.

You: What do you mean?

Kyle: I don't care about school. I hate it.

You: Why the change in attitude?

Kyle: I thought I had a full ride scholarship to the University, but it fell through. Now I can't go on to college. My folks make too much money for me to get financial aid, but they can't help me pay for school. I don't have near enough money saved to pay for it, and they won't co-sign a loan for me. Why should I even try anymore? It won't get me into college. •J.

CI-50: Jan—Suddenly Reluctant

(School is the venue, but the accusation involved may occur anywhere.)

Jan has been an enthusiastic, helpful individual. She has spent a good deal of time helping other students when she has her work completed. Today, though, she looks worried, and seems reluctant to help other students. You find the change puzzling and arrange to talk with her.

You: Jan, something seems to be bothering you today. Can I help?

Jan: *(In a clipped voice)* No, I'm fine.

You: When I asked you for some help you seemed to ignore me. Why?

Jan: I'm not ignoring you.

You: Then what. . .

Jan: (Interrupts) Well. (Pauses) Some of the girls keep saying that I'm a brown nose and just trying to get on your good side for my grade. •J.

CI-51: Dale—Off in Another World

(Dale may be a male or a female. Try it both ways; see what difference it makes.)

You see Dale as a hard-worker, of average ability. Lately, though, Dale has been off in another world and has done sketchy or incomplete work. If work is turned in at all, it is of low quality. You ask Dale to meet with you.

You: I've been worrying about you lately, Dale. You've changed since the beginning of the year—you seem pretty unhappy.

Dale: Well, to tell you the truth, things haven't been going well lately.

You: Is there something I might be able to help you with?

Dale: No. I don't think so. (Pauses and looks downcast. You wait.) It's just that I didn't make the basketball team this year and I was looking forward to playing. Last year I was on the team and I was pretty good, but with the new plant opening in town, some new kids ** moved here and, like I said, I didn't make the team.

(After trying this the way it is written above, at the asterisks ** in the next-to-last line insert—some black kids, some white kids, or some rich kids—and try it again.) •J.

CI-52: Sara—I Don't Know What's Wrong With Me

(Be sure to evaluate the comments presented here, but first, play it out as written.)

Sara is a quiet junior high school aged girl who lives in a low-cost housing area in town. She is in a group you work with after school. You have noticed that she has looked tired and unkempt for the past few days. You are pleased when she asks to talk with you.

You: Sure, I can take some time. I'm glad you asked. I've been worried about you lately.

Sara: I don't know what's wrong with me.

You: I'm sorry, I don't quite understand. Why do you feel something's wrong with you?

Sara: Well, I keep gaining weight lately and I've been trying to diet and exercise. But mostly I'm just too tired. For the past few days I've been sick when I come to school.

You: (You think for many seconds.) Sara, could you possibly be pregnant?

Sara: I don't know. How do you get pregnant?

(Try this incident again as if you are a member of the opposite sex from your own. Discuss the difference that makes. Note: this incident occurred recently.) •J.

CI-53: John—Why Should I Care?

(Be sure to evaluate the comments presented here. But first, play it as written.)

John comes to your group dressed in dirty clothes that look sloppy on him. Furthermore, the products of his efforts are among the messiest you have ever seen; he seems to take no pride in his work. When he brings his latest effort to you, you decide to talk with him.

You: Are you turning this in as complete, or do you want suggestions?

John: What's wrong with it?

You: I didn't say anything was wrong with it, but do you think your work looks as nice as everyone else's?

John: What do I care how it looks? No one cares what I do, anyway. •J.

CI-54: Jenny— I Just Don't Know What to Do

Jenny and Tricia have recently become buddies. Jenny is friendly and outgoing, and many of the girls in her group have disapproved of her friendship with Tricia. Tricia's family is on welfare, she is poorly dressed, and she does not fit in with Jenny's other friends. For the last two days you have noticed that Jenny has seemed withdrawn. She has not been talking to other girls, and has taken a seat on the opposite side of the room from Tricia. Jenny asks if she may talk with you during lunch. After you greet her you open the conversation.

You: I can tell that something's bothering you. I'd like to help if I can.

Jenny: Thank you. I need to talk to someone I can trust.

You: Thanks. (You wave your hand for Jenny to continue.)

Jenny: Well, it's like this. Yesterday I was in the rest room after lunch. I was over in the corner by the paper towels and the trash barrel, there's sort of an alcove there, and someone came in. (Pause) Well, I looked in the mirror and I could see someone close the stall door. (Pause) She had set her purse on the shelf and no one else was there.

        Then I saw Tricia walk in. She glanced around and took out the wallet, slipped out a bill—I think a twenty, and put it in her pocket, then ran out.

I was already late, so I left, too.

I don't know what to do. Tricia's my friend. I feel sorry for her. She wears terrible stuff and the girls say she looks like a slob. She was probably taking the money to buy something nice.

I just can't squeal on her, but I figured I had to do something—so I decided to talk to you. •J.

CI-55: Tad—Something is Wrong

Tad and his girlfriend, Cindy, are both sixteen, and have been dating for some time. You meet Tad, and instead of his usual upbeat manner, he looks really upset.

You: You look like your world has come apart. Is something bothering you?

Tad: I don't know. (Long pause.)

You: Well, you do look awfully uptight, and one of your teachers mentioned that your grades have fallen off a lot. Maybe it'd help if we talked.

Tad: Well, you know, Cindy and I have been going together for almost a year. I thought she really loved me. (Another long pause.) She says she wants to break up. She tells me she wants some room. I'm all mixed up. •J.

CI-56: Rich—A Great Competitor

Rich is a participant in a club you direct because of your interest. (You decide on the club's nature: speech, tennis, science, agriculture, etc.) The club has been selected to send four representatives to take part in an upcoming area-wide competition. Rich, from whom you had an application, is your first choice to participate. You announce your four choices and you notice that Rich looks pained. He waits until the others have left the meeting and asks to talk with you.

You: Always glad to talk with you, Rich. What's on your mind?

Rich: It's about the contest. I know my mom signed my form, but I don't think I can go.

You: Could you share the reason with me?

Rich: My dad quit his job in the plant and started his own business, and I help a lot. I stuff envelopes and pack things for his mailings. He says he can't spare me on weekends. (Pause.) In fact, I'll probably have to quit the club so I can spend more time helping. •J.

CI-57: Dave—Just a Little Tired

Dave is evidently quite bright, but he generally does just enough to get by. He is the oldest of five children who live near town with their parents. Recently he missed handing in two assignments you had given him and he has appeared listless and tired. Today he even fell asleep. You walked toward his area of the room and began speaking more loudly. He stirred and stayed awake. You arrange to speak with him.

You: I notice that you seem very tired lately. Are you getting enough rest.

Dave: Oh, I was just a little tired this morning from working last night. Sorry I fell asleep today.

You: So, you're working some.

Dave: Yeah. I cook from eight to two at the truckstop three nights a week. •J.

CI-58: Lili—Ethnic Identity

Lili, who is from the middle east, arrived a year ago with a positive, out-going attitude, but lately she has seemed withdrawn. She is the only foreign student in your group. She now sits in a corner alone, does not talk with others, and has shown less interest in the group and the activities you have organized. You observe her one day in an apparent argument with another girl. You move in and hear her say:

Lili: You Americans are all alike. You are so rude to me. I'll be glad to go back to my country and tell all my people just how bad all you Americans really are.

        (The two girls turn and look at you.) •J.

CI-59: Andy—Attention Getter

(Be sure to evaluate the comments presented here. But first, play this as written.)

Andy, a skilled attention-getter, has decided the time with you is the best opportunity he has to show off. You are busily engaged with a small group that vitally needs your attention when Andy starts making noises, imitating a cat, a pig, and various other animals. The people sitting near him laugh and egg him on.

You: Excuse me, everybody! Since Andy is demonstrating his talents today, let's all listen to him perform, then maybe we can get back to business.

Andy: Hee haw. Hee haw. (Deep in the throat. A fine donkey imitation.) •J.

CI-60: Will—Family Tragedy

Will had been an average, hard-working young man, but lately his attitude has been negative and his work has been poor. One or two other boys have noticed the change and have made fun of him. Will has stopped by to drop off some materials he had borrowed. You chat with him for a few moments and decide the time is as good as it is likely to be to express your concern.

You: Will, I've noticed that you seem quite unhappy lately.

Will: Yeah, I guess I am.

You: Tell me, what's happened to the happy Will I used to know?

Will: I'll tell you. Mom has had Multiple Sclerosis for fifteen years, and she just went into the hospital last week. She's been there several times before, so the kids don't know how serious it is. *(Pause.)* But the doctors have told us they don't think she'll live another week. •J.

CI-61: Mary—A Special Need

It is the beginning of the first period of the first day of your first year of teaching, and the secretary introduces you to Mr. Workman and his daughter, Mary. The secretary then rushes off, saying that the office is loaded with other people.

You are pulled in several directions. Students are wandering around the room, the bell has rung for class to begin, you have many business details you must take care of, you want to create a good impression on students with your first lesson plan, and the father and daughter are standing before you.

You glance at the record, then look up. Mr. Workman looks irritated.

You: Yes, thank you Mr. Workman. I'll find a seat for Mary right away, as soon as I get everybody seated. *(You turn to Mary, who is looking around the room.)* Mary, if you'll just wait over by my desk I'll find you a place. *(She then turns to you and looks puzzled.)*

Mr. W: She can't hear you unless you get her attention first. She's almost completely deaf. That's what I need to talk to you about. I want to know what you plan to do to accommodate my daughter. •J.

CI-62: Dan—School is Just Not Very Important to Me

(Be sure to evaluate the comments presented here. But first, play it as written. Also, note that although this incident is school-based, the attitude involved can pervade any other situation.)

Dan has been a low-B student. Initially you were impressed with his effort, since his ability level is clearly modest. He is a quiet boy who seemed to have many acquaintances, but no close friends.

Lately you have seen Dan with some students various teachers have referred to as "hoods." You encounter him with the group in town one day and the signs lead you to believe they were all smoking marijuana. Over the next few days you notice a deterioration in Dan's work and attitude. His work, which he had always done at least reasonably well, has been sketchy or unfinished.

You arrange a meeting with Dan at the end of his lunch period.

You: Dan, I've been wanting to talk with you. To be honest with you, you never have been a super-strong student, but you did mostly "low-B" work and always completed your assignments. Recently, though, your attitude seems to have changed and you have failed to turn in some of your work. Is there some problem I might help you with?

Dan: Well, to tell the truth, school is just not very important to me anymore. *(He grins sheepishly.)* But you don't need to worry about my grades—my parents aren't worried, and I'm not, either. •J.

CI-63: Rita—It's My Other Brother

(If you haven't been evaluating the initial approach used, be sure to do so here—especially the promise that is given. But first, try this as is.)

Rita has always been very reliable—a happy, healthy, active young person. Her work is of good quality and always in on time. For the last few days, though, Rita has come in puffy-eyed and tired-looking. She has given excuses for tasks not being done and has complained that she doesn't feel well. You are baffled by her sudden change in behavior, so you ask to talk with her. She agrees. Later, you greet her, then say:

You: I'm really worried about you, Rita. There is obviously something going on in your life that's causing you to be unhappy.

Rita.   Yes, there is, and I'm sorry about my work, but I'm just too ashamed to talk about it. Besides, my parents would kill me if I told anyone what it's all about.

You: Rita, it's something you really need to talk about, isn't it? I promise to keep it between you and me if you want my help.

Rita: Well. *(Long pause.)* It's my older brother. He lost his job a couple of months ago, and he's moved back home. He's started drinking and taking drugs all the time. He stumbles into the house late at night and breaks things and threatens my parents and me. He says crazy stuff and I'm afraid to go to sleep at night. When I do, I have nightmares. I'm afraid he's going to kill us all some night. My parents don't know what to do. They won't even talk about it.

            I'd like to move out of the house, but I don't have any money or any place to go, and I don't want to leave them alone with him. I think I'd rather be dead than live like this. •J.

CI-64: Judy—Guilty

(Be sure to evaluate the comments presented here. But first, play it as written.)

Judy has been a bright and cheerful girl. Today, though, she seems distant and depressed. Toward the end of your time together you give the group a task to do, but Judy just lays her head down. You approach her and say, quietly—

You: Judy, are you feeling all right today? You seem to be troubled about something.

Judy: Yeah. I'm just kinda upset. My parents are getting a divorce, and I'm afraid it's partly my fault. My dad and I had a big argument just a couple of weeks ago.

You: I'm sure it's not your fault. You just have to let your parents deal with this.

Judy: Tell that to my dad. He *told* me he's about as mad at me as he is at Mom. •J.

CI-65: Myron— That's Just the Way I Am

Myron trusts you as a friend. He is bright and willing to help others when they need assistance. He seems to have a promising future ahead of him. You have noticed that he has a wide range of moods. Some days he seems alert and active, and other days he is quiet and tired-looking. His changes of mood have led you to wonder about him, but since they have not affected his work, you haven't explored the issue with him.

You are hurrying to your room when you observe Myron at the water fountain taking a pill. Over the next half hour you notice that he has become jittery and hyperactive, and you wonder if he might have taken an amphetamine. You ask him to step out in the hall with you after you start the other members of the group on an assignment.

You: Myron, I've been worried about you lately. Some days you seem really tired and other days you're very active.

Myron: Oh, don't worry about that. That's just the way I am.

You: I wonder if it isn't more than that.

Myron: Well, I have been under a lot of pressure lately. •J.

CI-66: Mona— I'm Really Confused, I Guess

Mona has participated well in your group, her attendance has been very regular, and her work has been consistently above average. Recently, though, her effort has declined, and she has appeared to be daydreaming a great deal. You decide to look into the problem, so you arrange to talk with her.

You: Mona, I've been concerned about you. Lately you seem to be in another world. Until the last few days, you've always been attentive, and a great contributor.

Mona: Yeah. Right.

You: I just wondered, is something upsetting you? Can I be of any help?

Mona: Oh, it's nothing, really. I guess everybody goes through it sooner or later. I don't know why I'm even worried about it.

You: I'm sorry, Mona. I don't understand. Everyone goes through what?

Mona: Well, I've been seeing a lot of Wesley lately, and well, I guess I'm sorta falling in love with him, and I'm not sure where our relationship will go or how he really feels. I'm kinda scared 'cause I don't want to get hurt, but right now I feel like I just can't control my feelings. I'm really confused, I guess. •J.

CI-67: Justine— Straight Out of a Magazine

(Be sure to evaluate the initial approach used. But first, try this as is. Note also that although the problem is set in a school, the concern often arises in other settings.)

Justine is a bright and popular girl who is involved in many extracurricular activities. Her parents are wealthy and influential in the community.

Justine has always done very well in school, but you learn by accident that she copied a considerable portion of a report she handed you from a feature in a current news magazine. You approach her cautiously because you know that she has a tendency to blame others for her mistakes and you have observed that she has "a smart mouth." You let the other group members go and ask her to stay and talk.

You: Justine, what's the matter? You haven't been yourself lately. I feel as if you haven't been putting enough time into your work.

Justine: Nothing is wrong. Besides, I have to go to cheerleading practice.

You: Well, something is wrong. I just happened across the place you got most of your last report. You copied it straight out of a magazine.

Justine: *(For a moment she looks nervous, she wrings her hands and looks all around, then she suddenly smiles and says)* Oh, dear. I bet I forgot to add the page that had that reference on it. Well, I'll get it and bring it to you tomorrow. But right now I have to go to practice. •J.

CI-68: Bella—And the Clique

Either as a part of your workload or in your capacity as a volunteer you are working with a recreational or physical education program for girls. You may envision this as a school program or as some kind of court-mandated or other special activity. In any event, both attendance and active participation of the girls involved are required.

In your group are four girls who are inseparable and who tend to do everything together, regardless of whether it is right or wrong. You begin warmup exercises and Maxine, one of the girls, decides she doesn't want to participate. She takes a seat against the wall and Bella and the other three girls follow her. You walk over to them.

You: C'mon now, you girls know you have to participate or I have to report it as an absence from the program for today.

(For a moment the only response from the girls is a "who-cares" look, then Bella speaks.)

Bella: Maxine doesn't feel so good today, so we just want to sit with her. •J

CI-69: Don—After Effects

Don and Linda are two young people you like very much. They have been very close. Their long-term plans have been to go to the university together and study the same subject area. They are both bright, energetic, and mature for their years. Your first indication of a problem came when Linda told you that Don had a painful lump under his arm and was off to see the doctor. The second came when Linda arrived in tears, saying, "Don has a malignant tumor. The best hope is that he will only lose his arm. If the cancer has spread too far it's unlikely that he will live out the year."

Action was rapid. You received a notice that Don's arm had been amputated, but that the cancer had been halted and he was expected to recover fully.

Don has recently returned to your group. He appears anxious and withdrawn and he seems to be uncomfortable, especially around Linda.

A task you assign makes it necessary for Don to stop by to see you. He works along with you silently for many minutes, then suddenly he begins to cry.

You: How can I help, Don?

Don: You can give me back my arm. •J.

CI-70: Bart—I Just Can't Do It

Bart is a mainstreamed special needs learner who tests high on individual intelligence measures, and who functions reasonably well one-to-one. He came into your group late because of a leg operation, he walks with a severe limp, he cannot use the right hand at all, he has a severe speech impediment, he has not settled into the group's routine after a month, he rarely completes his work, he makes many mistakes, he distracts others with his grunts and other subvocalizations, and he seems unable to sit still for more than a minute or two at a time.

Today has been especially bad. Bart has frequently mumbled to himself, shaken his head, waved his hands in the air, and otherwise distracted others working nearby. He did well enough when you stood by him for a while, but soon after you moved away problems again began to occur.

At a sudden howl you ask Bart to step ouside the room with you as the group continues to work. You sigh and begin.

You: Bart, You've simply got to try harder to control yourself in there.

Bart: *(Sighs, makes several jerky motions, then says)* But I do try. I try really hard to control myself. I just can't seem to do it. •J.

Part 2
Choices and Communication Skills

An Overview

Part 2 of *Working with Adolescence: Building Effective Communication and Choice-Making Skills* introduces you to Choice Awareness, a systematic model for choice-making, and to communication skills that are designed to help you in your work with adolescents and in your other interactions with people. These chapters will not lead you into avenues you have never explored before or introduce you to a whole new and impressive vocabulary. The terms and most of the ideas are familiar to you; the newness comes from both the direct consideration and the systematic organization of the ideas that are included.

The Choice Awareness model has been applied in a wide variety of settings, for example, with young children (Nelson, 1980), with retired people (Nelson, 1989a), to promote more effective teen-parent communication (Nelson & Link, 1982), in marriage enrichment (Nelson & Friest, 1980), in counseling (Nelson, 1990), and as a self-help process (Nelson, 1992).

The skills and choices chapters that follow use simple, direct, useful language to accomplish three objectives: (1) to help you look at the patterns of communication skills and choices you use in your interactions with those around you, and how you developed those patterns; (2) to suggest possible changes you might implement if you decide that you are not satisfied with the communication skills and choices you presently use; and (3) to offer you ideas for enabling young people to examine their choices and to consider how they might function in their world more effectively.

Why a new skills and choices model?

If you are like most teachers, counselors and others who work with young people, you tend to overlook two of the most important tools you have available to you in maximizing your effectiveness: your communication skills and your interactive choices. Instead, you focus primarily on policies, procedures, and the tasks or the content connected with your profession.

Overlooking communication skills and interactive choices in working with adolescents and others is rather like overlooking the floor game in basketball. Concentrating on procedures, plans, and knowledge of your role is like concentrating only on shooting baskets from various locations on the floor. True professionals develop all aspects of "their game."

The athletic analogy is a useful one. Athletes know they must focus on more than one aspect of the sport, and they understand that they continue to need new input and practice in the use of familiar skills. Unlike the members of the band in *The Music Man*, if anyone suggested that they read about a particular move, then use The Think System, and never practice the skill before using it in a game, they would reject that as ridiculous. They would be far more likely to try the move time and time again and use it in a game only when they are comfortable with it. We suggest the same thing with regard to communication and choice-making skills: use a skill time and again in practice before employing it "in the game" with others.

Most successful people who work with adolescents have gradually evolved reasonably-effective communication patterns for use with young people and with colleagues, parents, and others. Those around them learn that they can rely on them to respond reasonably whether they are met one-to-one or in groups within or outside the school setting. By contrast, most teachers, counselors, and others who have difficulties do so because they make poor interactive choices and they communicate ineffectively with young people and others.

Most leaders with youth, regardless of where they fall on the success continuum, could benefit by direct consideration of how they interact with others and how they might do so more effectively. And that applies to you. If you spend some time honing your communication skills and improving your patterns of choices you will be able to respond more effectively to those adolescents and others who present the greatest challenges in your life.

We invite you to read Part 2 of this book interactively and apply the ideas directly to *you*. Let yourself become involved and you will find that many of the ideas have relevance for you—both personally and professionally. You may well discover a number of ways in which you want to speak, act, think, and feel differently than you do at present in your relationships with adolescents and others. Of course, you are the judge of whether you need to or want to make changes. That is always *your* choice.

We suggest that as you read these chapters you make journal entries frequently and in some depth, using a new page to begin each entry and dating your entries. We invite you to reread the chapters now and again and make additional entries, inserting pages as needed; in that way you can explore different dimensions of the information and notice how your thoughts, attitudes, and skills change over time. We encourage you to follow as many of the end-of-chapter suggestions and engage in as many of the activities as time permits, that you return later and complete those you have omitted, and that you re-try later those you have already completed, with a fresh point of view.

In Chapter 15 of *Working with Adolescence: Building Effective Communication and Choice-Making Skills* we offer a Choice Awareness-based model for creating a plan for managing groups effectively. Chapter 16 is entitled *Choices and Communication Skills for Adolescents*. The activities presented are keyed to the *Choices and Communication Skills* chapters, and those who decide to help young people expand their choices and skills will want to review the related chapters in order to make the best use of the activities.

Part 2 of *Working with Adolescence: Building Effective Communication and Choice-Making Skills* is designed to help you think through how you might implement particular skills or choices in a variety of circumstances both within and beyond your work with adolescents. We encourage you to rehearse and role play these skills and choices "in practice," before you incorporate them "in the game" with young people, with colleagues, or with others.

Let this portion of *Working with Adolescence: Building Effective Communication and Choice-Making Skills* help you improve your communication skills and choice patterns. Let it help you join the ranks of the most successful and responsive individuals who work with adolescents. It is your choice.

Journal Entries

We have several specific suggestions for making journal entries in the *Choices and Communication Skills* chapters. First, we invite you to begin your entry by reflecting on the ideas presented in the chapter, then use the following key words to cue you in writing your entry:

Recall—an event you are reminded of by one or more of the ideas in the chapter.

Interpret—the event in the light of what you have read here, or interpret an idea you have read about in terms of you and your life.

+/-Feelings—consider the positive and/or negative feelings generated in you by one or more of the ideas presented, or an event you recall.

Freeing—explore in what way(s) the ideas presented are freeing for you—in what way(s) they help you realize that you can and do make choices.

Responsibility-taking—explore in what way(s) the ideas presented help you take more personal responsibility.

Relationship—explore the implications of the ideas for a particular relationship.

With adolescents—tie the ideas specifically to your experiences in, or to your concerns about, your work with adolescents.

Other—choose your own ways of responding to the ideas presented in the chapter.

You may also use your journal entry to discuss *To What Extent Are You Like These People, Ideas You Can Use. . .*, the *Critical Incident*, or to report on your experiences with *Choices and Communication Skills for Adolescents*.

Note that at the end of each chapter we make specific journal entry suggestions, and we reference this page for your convenience in writing your entries.

3

The Ways in Which
We Make Our Choices

** Choice is defined here as any behavior over which the person has some reasonable degree of control. Words and actions, and many thoughts and feelings, can be seen as choices.[1]

** It is important to bring the reality of constant choice-making to awareness, and practice the skills of effective choice-making.

** Every day affords a great many opportunities to choose, and each choice can be made in a great variety of ways. People make many choices on the basis of habits, labels, attitudes, and expectations—but they choose.

** Relationships often fall into stereotypical patterns of choices that evolve over time, but choice patterns do not have to remain fixed.

** Acting on long range relationship goals may improve many relationships since long range goals tend to be both global and positive.

Working Effectively with Adolescents Requires Effective Choices

Debbie D. works with adolescents in a halfway house in a rough, inner-city setting and loves her work. Paul P. is a teacher in a highly sought-after school situation, but by his own admission he is a failure and plans to leave teaching. Why is it that some people enjoy their work with young people in circumstances that offer a great deal of challenge, while others in less-demanding settings are frustrated and discouraged?

Work with adolescents requires continuous interpersonal interaction. Those who succeed in their work with young people communicate well and make effective interactive choices.

Four essentials affect success in working with young people. Those who succeed:

1. *understand the adolescents* with whom they work,

2. *master the tasks* for which they are responsible—*and the content*, in the case of teachers,

3. *use effective management techniques and procedures,*

4. *develop communication skills* that can help them interact effectively with young people in the positive and negative moments that inevitably occur.

All of these essentials involve choices. Debbie D. makes effective choices in her work in all four of these areas. Paul P. handles content well but lacks understanding of students and of good management procedures.

Think about the truly excellent teachers, counselors, and other people you have known. It is likely that they were unique in your eyes because of the effectiveness of the choices you saw them make in relating to you and to others.

*** You can achieve greater success and find greater joy in your interactions with others through making more effective choices.* More effective choices can lead you to more moments in which you feel a greater sense of meaning in life. And as you find more success, joy, and meaning in *your* life, you provide the adolescents and others around you with a positive model for *their* lives.

---

[1]Markers (symbol = **) are presented at the beginnings of these chapters and integrated in the text as well.

Choices and Choicelessness

** *Choice is defined here as any behavior over which the individual has some reasonable degree of control. What we say is a choice. What we do is a choice. Much of what we think and feel is a choice.*

Nobody pulls a string in your back and makes you do what you do, and nobody makes you say the words you say. Policies, rules, curricula, and the like aside, exactly what you say and do in your interactions with young people and others, and how you say and do those things, are choices you make.

The converse of effective choice-making, *choicelessness*, seems pervasive in our society. Other labels for choicelessness include powerlessness and irresponsibility. You hear evidence of choicelessness when young people make these kinds of statements:

"They made me do it."

"I couldn't help it."

"It's not my fault."

"I didn't mean it."

"I had to get back at 'em."

Adults, too, deny their power to choose; they just use more sophisticated language to voice their feelings:

"That's my personality."

"That's just the way I am."

"I was in a bad mood."

"There was nothing else I could have done."

"They should have learned that years ago."

"My boss (The administration) won't let me."

Our society allows us great freedom in our choices, but we often deny both the freedom we have and the responsibility that accompanies it. We excuse many things we do on the grounds that we "have no other choice." Many punitive actions taken in schools and in other settings, e.g., suspension of privileges, work release activities, suspensions, expulsions, and paddlings—are rationalized: "There was nothing else we could do." ** *We always have choices available to us.* At the very least we can choose to take action based on positive, caring attitudes toward the person involved in an infraction.

The literature on various discipline approaches supports a strong relationship between choice and discipline. Dreikurs, *et al.* (1982) put forward the point that discipline requires both freedom of choice and the understanding of consequences. Glasser (1969), too, suggested that behavior is a matter of choice, and, therefore, the focus of discipline, regardless of the environment involved, should be that of helping young people make responsible choices.

In exercising choices in general and with adolescents, most of the limits you experience you set for yourself. Where it is appropriate, you can learn to go beyond previous limits and choose more effectively—using the Choice Awareness system to counter feelings of choicelessness. The process and the outcome can be positive for you and for the adolescents whom you serve.

Effective Communication is a Key to Success

In your work with adolescents you need to give attention to the basic verbal and non-verbal communication you present to them, since the ways in which you talk and act are central to the outcomes you see. The basic skills you have available to you are your words and behaviors: how you use your voice, your body language (Jones, 1987), how you reinforce, and how you cope with the words and actions of young people.

Charles (1992) extrapolated from the discipline model presented by Dreikurs, et al., (1982), and made an interesting suggestion which he applied to teaching, but which has implications for a variety of other adult relationships with adolescents: that those who wish to use a democratic discipline model need to spend considerable amounts of time talking with young people about how their actions affect themselves and others. "[T]his puts teachers [and others, we would add] into a counseling role, which can produce very good results for [those] who have counseling skills. Unfortunately, most have never had such training" (Charles, 1992, p. 76). In this source we do not suggest that you attempt to function as a counselor unless that is your designated role; we are convinced, however, with both Charles and Dreikurs, that good communication skills "can produce very good results," and much of Part 2 of this source is designed to help you develop those skills.

You can develop effective communication patterns with young people, and to do that you need a repertoire of effective skills and procedures—which we see as choices. Effective communication requires effective choices, and effective choices do not come automatically on a single reading. They must be learned and practiced and improved over time. Pianist Lorin Hollander once lauded the virtues of practice in a PBS radio interview, saying, *Practice until it becomes easy. Practice until it becomes habit. Practice until it becomes beautiful.* The skills of communication, too, need to be practiced until they become *easy*, until they become *habit*, and if not until they become beautiful, at least until they become *comfortable and effective*.

Each Opportunity to Choose Allows for Many Choices

** *It is possible for you to make each of your choices in a great variety of ways.*

You pass a boy in your charge and compliment him on an accomplishment of which you have become aware. A girl tells you that she is sleepy, lost, and behind in her work (or homework) because her parents have been fighting late into the night for weeks. As you listen and respond to these two adolescents you make many choices. You do this continually throughout the course of your day, with young people and others, until you have made hundreds upon hundreds of choices. If you are like most people, you make many of your choices as if you are programmed to do so, but you are not.

** *One basis on which you make your choices is your habits.* Many of the things you do and say are basically habitual actions, and your habits can be useful or detrimental. If you are habitually generous with reinforcement, great! Keep it up! But not all of your habits are likely to be positive.

Studies have shown, for example, that when teachers call on students they habitually allow more "wait time" with those they expect will respond well than with weaker students. In one way this is understandable— since much of the time if teachers wait for strong students they will respond successfully. But, obviously, weaker students need *more* time to formulate their responses, not *less* than those who are strong. If they are given less time, they become discouraged and are likely to give up.

The good news is that habits are learned, and new habits can be learned, too.

** *A second basis on which you make your choices involves labels.* Labels become habits—patterns of choices of long duration. Do you see yourself as a *doer* or a *procrastinator*? A *responder* or an *initiator*? A *day person* or *a night person*? The labels you wear act as self-fulfilling prophecies, and are part of the patterns of habits that affect your interactions with others. Even positive labels, *the kind person,* or *the helpful one,* may create pressure on you at times and cause you stress; you can become overwhelmed by the neediness of young people, for example.

Many adults who work with adolescents see themselves as responders; they wait until young people have misbehaved and then they react. They could be initiators and make the first move—with positive statements, for example. "I'm really pleased; you're off to a good start today." "Thanks for cooperating."

Initiating an interaction may run counter to an important label of yours. Perhaps you think: I am a responder with other adults, but I am an initiator with young people. If that really works for you, fine. If it does not, you can change the way you think about yourself, or you can change your pattern of choices.

** *A third basis on which you make your choices involves your attitudes.* Many years ago, Viktor Frankl (1959) suggested in *Man's Search for Meaning* that people can always choose their *attitudes* even when all other freedoms have been taken away—and he discovered that truth in a concentration camp. In most instances when you make a choice, you have a vast array of possibilities available to you—but even when you do not, you can *always* choose the attitude with which you do what you believe you must.

Even when the responsibility you have is clear—for example, you must meet a severe violation of the rules with a strong disciplinary action—you still choose your *attitude*. You can be righteously indignant or fall back upon the old this-hurts-me-more-than-it-hurts-you line. On the other hand, you can calmly tell the boy or girl of the frustration you feel, discuss straightforwardly the action you believe you must take, and help him or her learn as a result of the infraction.

** *A fourth basis on which you make your choices involves the expectations you have of yourself.* When Teresa shouts out *another* smart remark, you may respond: "I've told you to keep quiet, now I want you out of here (to report to the director/the office) immediately!" When Dan breaks a rule, e.g., on gum-chewing, you may growl, "Get that gum out of your mouth!"

Behavior X calls for response Y. Right?

STIMULUS → RESPONSE.

Stimulus leads to response.

Is that the way life is?

Most young people think it is that way. Ask them what they do when someone hits them from behind. Some may say they punch the person. Others may say they yell, "What do you think you're doing?" Next, ask them what they do if they turn and see that the "hitter" is a friend, an enemy, a younger child, the school principal, Mom, Dad, a police officer, or *you*. The response changes. They make different choices.

The stimuli you encounter do not lead you to inevitable responses. ** *What you do or say is not just a response to a stimulus—it is your choice.* At the very least, when you take in a stimulus, you make an internal choice from among an array of possibilities— then you implement your response. The formula becomes:

STIMULUS → CHOICE → RESPONSE.

The stimulus leads you to your choice, and that leads you to your response. But it is even more complex than that.

You make choices about the stimuli to which you will respond—for example, you may ignore a behavior at one time and act upon it at another. And you even make choices *during* your response. If you see that your scolding is being ignored, or the person seems to feel hurt, you may switch your strategy in mid-sentence.

** *A fifth basis on which you make your choices involves your expectations of others.* Young people respond at least to some degree because of what they believe is expected of them. In Rosenthal and Jacobson's (1968) classic study, *Pygmalion in the Classroom*, teachers were told that randomly-selected students were likely to be late-bloomers. When teachers expected future growth of students they encouraged them more, and the outcomes were more positive. Higher expectations led to improved performance; improved performance led to higher expectations; and the spiral continued upward. If you expect more from young people than they have given in the past—if you make that choice—at least some of them are likely to improve their patterns of performance.

In a related point, it may be said that the expectations of you by the adolescents you encounter also become bases for the choices you make. Adults who work with young people are seen by them as fulfilling a number of psychological roles, among them: representative of society, judge, source of knowledge, helper, referee, detective, model, surrogate parent, target for hostility, object of affection, and so forth. Further, young people also assume various roles in the group: leader, clown, fall guy, instigator, scapegoat, and so forth (Redl and Wattenberg, 1959). Clearly, a variety of expectations influences your choices and the choices of the young people with whom you work, but no one has to be *controlled* by expectations.

Relationships and Choices

In addition to habits, labels, and expectations, a great many of the choices you make are based on the relationships you have with other people. If you are like most people, you let your relationships control many of your choices. Think about it. You probably interact quite differently with each individual member of your family, with various co-workers, and with casual acquaintances.

Think about the interactions you have with young people. Are they carbon copies of the relationships you have with friends and relatives? Do you use the same patterns of choices with those who are quick or slow, cooperative or troublesome?

In all probability, some of your relationships have evolved over time into narrow patterns of behaviors. You may "save" some of your most positive choices for your friends, and "spend" more of your negative choices on one or two family members or on a few young people. You may be a dynamic and skilled leader when it comes to your own tasks, but you may tend to wait for your supervisor or your father to take the lead within your relationship.

If you are like most people who work with adolescents you feel a great need to be predictable, so once you evolve a pattern of choices you tend to keep it that way. As a result, you may spend more time and energy in *maintaining* your relationships with young people as they are than you spend in *improving* them.

If you see yourself as a responder it is unlikely that you will make changes in the choice pattern you have with more difficult adolescents you encounter until *they* change. And guess what? The more difficult adolescents you know have also built habit patterns. Many of them see themselves as responders—so they believe they cannot change the interaction pattern until *you* or others do. If you are aware of your choices you are in a better position to make changes that can break the stalemate.

As Glasser (1990) suggested, for those young people who come from atrocious backgrounds, there may be few places where they might meet caring adults, and they deeply need someone who is genuinely interested in them. Choosing to build positive relationships with young people is among the most significant things you can do.

Goals and Choices

What do you want from your relationships with the person to whom you feel closest in this world, with your friends, with the adolescents you encounter, and in particular with any young person with whom you have been in conflict? If you take a moment to think about it, you are likely to find that from your closest relationship you want warmth and love; with your friends you want closeness, sharing, and trust; with young people you want respect and cooperation; and in your relationship with an adolescent with whom you have had conflict you would like to have a pleasant, easy pattern of interaction.

Your goals with others around you probably remain unspoken and unexamined. As a result, all too frequently, you may make choices that run counter to your goals. The view is taken here that looking closely at your goals with family members, with friends, and with the adolescents you encounter, can help you make life better for yourself and those around you.

The long range goals you have for your relationships are likely to be global, simple, and positive; and the extent to which you reach your goals depends largely on how you act upon them—through your choices. You cannot control the choices of an adolescent or any other person, but you can control your own choices. And you can do it more effectively if you keep your goals in mind.

In moments of stress, pause briefly, consider your goal for the relationship, *then* make a choice. If you find that you often make choices that run counter to your goals, either admit that your goals are not what you believed they were, or change your pattern of choices so that you move toward your goals instead of away from them.

It may never have occurred to you that you have goals for your relationships. In fact, your reaction to this point may be that you do not want to have goals—"*Que sera sera*—whatever will be will be," may be your thought. If that is a sticking point, what concerns you can probably be summed up in the word *manipulation*. You may think, "If I have goals, and if others do, too, might we not be manipulating one another to achieve our ends?" The key to avoiding manipulation is focusing on long range, relationship goals, rather than on short term goals, such as getting back at the person for something that happened recently, or a moment ago.

The alternative to making effective choices based on positive goals is acting out of habit. If you avoid relying on habit, if you choose your attitudes constructively—on the basis of both thought and feeling, and if you consider your goals, you are free to make more effective choices, both for yourself and in your relationships with young people and others in your life.

Note that at the close of the chapters in this section you will find a cluster of items that are intended to help you reflect on the ideas introduced. We suggest you explore these items and use them to build your journal entries.

To What Extent are You Like These People?

Julie Y.

Julie is a classic example of denial. Anyone who followed her around on any given day would inevitably hear her say such things as: "You leave me no choice." "You can't fight city hall." "Their parents should have taught them that." "I can't do it—it's not written into the program." She makes choices all the time, but she seems unaware that she is doing so.

How much are you like Julie Y.? What are your favorite copouts on a bad day? What other choices do you have?

Ruth Z.

Soon after Ruth was introduced to the idea that she had goals in her relationships she began to modify some of her interactions. She made the biggest change with Zack, whom she was supervising in a community service program for probationers. After some time she wrote in her journal, "I wanted a better relationship with Zack, and when I went after it, patiently, persistently, and with a caring attitude, I succeeded."

How much are you like Ruth Z.? How might you improve one or more of your relationships if you sorted out your goals and really acted on them?

Todd R.

Todd, a high school teacher, felt burned-out and he decided to take stock of himself and his attitudes. When he realized that it had become unpleasant for him to get up in the morning to face his classes, he decided to try to regain the joy he had once felt about teaching. He planned his program to include at least one enjoyable experience each week in each of his classes. Soon his attitude began to change, as did the attitudes of his students. "I'd started to see teaching as a job instead of a profession," he told a friend. "I thought I was putting too much of myself into it, but it was draining me because I hadn't been putting enough *positive* energy into it."

How much are you like Todd R.? To what extent do you need to infuse a more positive attitude into your work? How might you make a change along those lines, if needed? To what extent are you satisfied with yourself as an initiator or responder? What change(s), if any, do you need to make?

Ideas You Can Use with Individuals or Groups

** *Focus on your choices daily.* Take a few moments to consider the thoughts you have and what you say and do that denies that you have choices in instances where that is not really true—in your work with adolescents, in communicating with family members, in your everyday patterns of behavior. You are more likely to make changes in your patterns of choices if you spend time thinking about them daily.

For a journal entry, divide the page with a vertical line and list "Copouts" you use on the left and some "Alternative Choices" you could make on the right, as follows:

Copouts I Sometimes Use	Alternative Choices
1. I say, "It's not my responsibility."	1a. I could speak to the person whose responsibility it is.
	1b. I could take responsibility for my part of the problem.
	1c. I could find someone to work on the problem with me.

** ***Stress your positive habits.*** Select one or two of your more positive habits to emphasize in your interactions with young people. For example, if you see yourself as habitually optimistic and creative, emphasize those qualities, and appreciate them within yourself—every day. Suggestion: Letter a card that says, "I am optimistic and creative," and post it on your mirror.

** ***Decide on a goal and reach for it.*** Make a list of from two to four relationships you would like to improve. Specify one long range and one short range goal for each. Consider: will the short range goal help you move toward your long range goal? If not, revise either the short range or the long range goal. Select one of the relationships and go to work on achieving a positive short range goal. Keep notes on your progress.

Critical Incident

(*This incident is teaching-focused, but the problem can occur elsewhere. If you do not teach, adapt the situation to the environment in which you work.*)

Fourth period class. Assume for the moment that you are a new teacher and you have been given a fourth period assignment that is unrelated to your teaching credential— a filler for a free period, an overcrowded class of adolescents who are difficult to challenge. You have become aware that you sometimes feel negative about the group. Today you have just started class when a member of the clerical staff brings you a new student. "I'm sorry. There's no place else we can put her. It's the only time this class fits her schedule." What might you say at that moment—knowing that the new girl and some class members are listening?

A few moments later you have class members working at their seats. One of the students you like best, a boy you

have in another of your classes, comes up to you with a question. You answer him and he moves away, then he turns back to you and says, "You don't like this class very much, do you?" The room is hushed and the students who are seated close by look up. What might you say right at that moment? What kind of long range strategy might you use to change the atmosphere?

Respond to one or more of the Critical Incidents in Chapter 2. Decide what kind of choice seems to be called for in response to the adolescent or the group.

Sharing Choices and Communication Skills with Adolescents

As we noted in the introduction to Part 2, each chapter of *Working with Adolescence: Building Effective Communication and Choice-Making Skills* includes suggestions for sharing choices and communication skills with young people. Section A of Chapter 16 presents three suggestions under the following titles: *We make many choices. Each opportunity to choose allows for a wide variety of choices. Choices can be based on goals.*

Journal Entry

Date your entry and label it Ch. 3,—*Choices, Relationships, and Goals.* You may begin your entry by reflecting on the concepts in the chapter, *you, your choices, your relationships, your goals, and your progress in achieving your goals through your choices*—in your work with young people and beyond. You may also use the end-of-chapter activities or the key words on page 31 to further cue you in writing your entry.

4
OK/OD CREST Choices

** Life is a continuous series of choices. Each choice may be made in OK or OD (overdone) ways. OK choices can be major or minor—contributing in highly significant or less significant ways to the relationship. Likewise OD choices can be major or minor—detracting in highly significant or less significant ways from the relationship.

** It is useful to conceptualize that you and the adolescents with whom you work, and others who are close to you, have joint accounts to which each of you make deposits and from which each of you make withdrawals. You can contribute to your accounts, and move toward your goals at the same time, by making OK choices that counterbalance your OD choices.

** Choice Awareness suggests that you have the power to raise or lower the value of your accounts through five CREST choices. Through Caring choices you respond to your own and others' needs. Through Ruling choices you exercise leadership. Through Enjoying choices and Sorrowing choices you express positive and negative feelings. And through Thinking/Working choices you use your cognitive abilities and take action on the tasks before you.

A Continuum of Choices

You have been working hard with a group for many minutes. You were making really good progress, but now everyone seems worn out. What are some things you might say in that situation?

"Let's take the last ten minutes today for a fun activity. You've all been working really hard, but now you seem tired."

"Everybody stand up and stretch for a minute and move around; let's see if that helps."

"Come on, kids, just a little more to do."

"Those are the dumbest answers I've ever heard out of this group!"

Paula is often troublesome and seems not to care about anything. She surprises you by bursting into tears when you comment about her not having a brief assignment ready. What choices might you make in response to her?

"I'm sorry you're so upset right now, Paula, and I'd like to understand what is bothering you. Let me get the group started, then let's go outside the room and talk."

"Take it easy, Paula, and I'll come back and speak with you privately in a minute."

"*Now*, what's wrong?"

"If you'd worked instead of playing around yesterday you'd have had that done."

When you respond to young people you do so with what we call OK or OD choices. OK choices are those that are at least acceptable to yourself and the other person; OD choices are those that are not. The term OD stands for overdone as in cooking, an overdose as in drug or alcohol use, or overdrawn as in banking. OK and OD choices can be plotted along a continuum which demonstrates that they may be major or minor in their effects.

The OK—OD Continuum of Choices

| MAJOR OK CHOICES | MINOR OK CHOICES | MINOR OD CHOICES | MAJOR OD CHOICES |

Major and Minor OK Choices

** *Major OK choices are the things you say or do that are really special for the person involved.* You can make major OK choices in any relationship that is important to you. Adolescents and others around you crave major OK choices! One student felt complimented a whole year later because a high school teacher mentioned how attractively she always dressed. Even managers in business and industry are finding ways to make major OK choices for their workers—for example, a division of a major US industry rented the Meadowlands Stadium in New Jersey, and individual employees ran out of the tunnel to the applause of co-workers and supervisors as their names and their awards were announced. In whatever context in which you work with adolescents you can find effective ways to reinforce them creatively!

** *Minor OK choices include a great many everyday OK statements and actions.* You make minor OK choices when you say thank you or please, listen to another person, hand someone supplies he or she needs, make a favorable comment, or guide an adult or adolescent toward the solution to a problem. Minor OK choices are helpful in building relationships because they have cumulative effects. Compared to major OK choices, minor OK choices are not as significant, but they are essential elements in human interaction. The minor OK choices you make build your relationships with adolescents and others.

Major and Minor OD Choices

** *Minor OD choices are actions or statements that have a slight negative effect on the relationship.* If you scowl at someone or call someone's name to encourage him or her to return to work, your actions may well be seen as minor OD choices. Such everyday actions as telling young people it is time to finish up or clean up may also be seen by some as OD—though most will accept the need to do so.

** *Major OD choices are actions or statements that have a strong negative impact on the relationship.* Severe scolding, sarcasm, paddling, brow-beating, and shoving a person against a wall, are major OD choices that are not easily forgotten. Some of those choices may seem to be necessary, but they inevitably have an adverse effect on the person and on the relationship. In most such instances, little consideration is given to the other person's feelings or to the potential for learning in the event.

There is a risk in minor OD choices. The value of a relationship can be reduced through everyday, minimal, negative statements. But major OD choices are likely to destroy the value of the relationship far more quickly and completely. People who are effective in working with adolescents rarely feel the need to make major OD choices and they do not erode their relationships with numerous, minor OD choices.

If you are in a position of authority, it is inevitable that from time to time you will make choices some young people see as OD. The issue is one of balance. In relationships that are important to you, with adolescents and with others, let your OK choices outweigh your OD choices.

Building Your Accounts

When we introduced the term OD we spoke of overdrawn accounts. Let us take the banking analogy one step further. ** *One useful way in which we can think of our relationships with people who are of importance to us is to envision that we have joint accounts with each.* You add to the balance in each of your accounts with your OK choices, and you subtract from the balance with your OD choices. You can move toward your goals with young people by making choices that add to your accounts.

Let us make that explicit. Think of choices as having different numerical values on a scale from +10 to -10. If, in response to an activity you planned, your friend, Pat, or an adolescent in your charge, Sandy, says, "Wow, this is fun," your joint account has grown in value (+3, let us say). If you reply, "I'm glad. I wanted this to be fun," you have made another deposit (+2). If Pat or Sandy says, "This is stupid," and you reply, "Aw, quit your griping," you have both made withdrawals from the account (-3, -2).

When things are not going well in a relationship neither of you may add to the balance, and at times both of you may make withdrawals from an account that is already "in the red." As the adult in the relationship with an adolescent, you need to be the responsible, mature person who makes a continuous effort to build the balance in the account. This is not to say that the negative balance is totally your responsibility—both people in a relationship contribute to the account balance; nor do we want to suggest that no adolescent should ever be punished. Although the action of punishment itself is seldom an OK choice from the recipient's point of view, it may ultimately contribute to the relationship balance, if the action is seen as fair and reasonable.

One great thing about working with young people is that most of them are quite willing to forgive and forget. A strong, negative balance in an account with an adolescent may move closer to zero than it would with an adult on the basis of just a few good moves on your part: a friendly greeting, a pat on the back, a handshake, a smile, a comment that shows genuine interest, or saying, "I've decided to do what I can to make our relationship better. I know I haven't had a good word to say to you in weeks." Such actions may not change the balance with every young person, but they will reach many, and they are well worth the effort.

If you are like many teachers, counselors, and others who work with adolescents, in the hundreds of daily opportunities you have, most of the time you stay within the dull, safe, +1 or +2 to -1 or -2 range in making your choices. You do not have to.

** *You can build the balance in your accounts with adolescents by emphasizing OK choices and by interspersing major OK choices frequently in your interactions.*

To be of any value, any theory, Choice Awareness included, needs to offer realistic suggestions. We do not suggest that you should never make an OD choice, or even that you should avoid all major OD choices, for the rest of your natural life—with adolescents or with others. The overall balance is the important thing.

Any good relationship can tolerate a few negatives from time to time. There is no point in feeling guilty forever over a comment offered without sufficient thought. However, there is a vital point in counterbalancing OD choices with those that are OK—over time. Last moment's irritable comment to a young person may be countered by this moment's demonstration of genuine interest. Yesterday's glum attitude toward a group may be countered by a

statement today like, "Last night I thought about it and I decided I let something that had nothing to do with you affect the way I acted yesterday. I'm going to make sure we have a better day today." Young people expect you to be human, and most of them are willing to forgive your failings—if you show that you are interested in keeping a positive balance in your accounts with them.

Introducing the Five CREST Choices

** *Five CREST choices, Caring, Ruling, Enjoying, Sorrowing, and Thinking/Working, form the heart of the Choice Awareness system; these choices, individually or in combination, account for the vast majority of our behaviors.* In this chapter these choices are briefly introduced. The concepts involved are simple and familiar, but their implications are enormous. If you are to implement them effectively in your life and in your work with adolescents, you need to give them your best energy and attention.

People who work with adolescents need to develop ever-greater skill in making their choices; perhaps a musical analogy will do to reinforce that point. Most people, regardless of their work situation, make their everyday, interactive choices in ways that are analogous to the sound produced by a novice who "picks out a tune" on a piano; the result may be recognizable, but it is likely to be uneven, unmusical. It takes careful attention and extensive practice to "play" one's choices sensitively, creatively, and "musically." We encourage you to learn and to master the ideas and skills presented in the chapters that explore CREST choices so that you can go beyond the level of "picking out a tune," and "play" your choices skillfully and "musically."

Caring Choices

** *Caring choices are based on need, and need is ever-present.* When you ask an upset girl or boy how you might help, when you put an arm around a friend who is troubled, when you assist an overburdened colleague with a chore, when you reflect the feeling of another ("I can tell you're really upset right now"), or when you protect or defend someone, you are making caring choices. You are also making self-caring choices when you meet your own needs in similar ways.

Your caring choices may be offered verbally or nonverbally, may be made for yourself or another, and may be seen as OK or OD in terms of the relationship. Because you were raised in a cultural context, you are likely to make your caring choices in ways that are sex-, age-, or role-stereotyped, and you may habitually let those variables be more important than the immediate situation, your own needs, or the needs of the other person. Doubtless some of your relationships with others could be improved if you let yourself go beyond habits and stereotypical behaviors and made caring choices on the basis of your own needs and the needs of others.

Ruling Choices

** *Ruling choices show leadership, and opportunities for leadership are frequently present.* You make ruling choices when you ask someone to hand you something or to have lunch with you, when you make a request or give someone a direction ("How about giving Gene a hand with the editing after you finish what you're doing?"), or when you insist or forbid ("Don't you ever do that again!")—in short, when you demonstrate leadership in any way.

You may send your ruling choices verbally or non-verbally (e. g., with soft or harsh words, or through pointing, scowling, or finger-wagging), you may make them for yourself or for another, and you may make them in ways that are OK or OD in terms of the relationship. As with caring choices, because of your upbringing, you may have learned to make sex-, age-, or role-stereotyped ruling choices. For example, you may take the lead somewhat freely with young people, but feel powerless to do so with those who are older or in a supervisory relationship to you. It is likely that one or more of your relationships with adolescents or others would be improved if you changed your habitual patterns of lead-taking—either by making it easy for the other person to take the lead more often, or by more frequently filling the power vacuum that is likely to exist in some of your relationships.

Enjoying Choices

** *Through your enjoying choices you express your positive feelings.* When you listen deeply or pay someone a compliment, when you smile or say thank you, when you reinforce a young person through a note or a positive comment, when you function in creative ways, and even when you tease or enjoy yourself at the expense of another (as exemplified in the old psychiatrist's quip, "You don't have an inferiority complex, you are inferior"), you are making enjoying choices.

You may make your enjoying choices verbally or non-verbally, for yourself or another, and in ways that are OK or OD in terms of the relationship. You built your pattern of enjoying choices through imitation; thus you may make these choices, too, in ways that are sex-, age-, or role-stereotyped. For example, you may enjoy yourself readily with friends, but make few enjoying choices with adolescents.

You may have accepted the societal message that says that enjoying choices belong to children, or you may overlook the opportunity to make in-the-moment enjoying choices because you conceptualize such choices as events. It is likely that you could improve some of your key relationships with adolescents or others through increasing the quality and quantity of your enjoying choices.

Sorrowing Choices

** *Through your sorrowing choices you act on or express your negative feelings.* When you tell someone what is troubling you ("The worst thing happened at work today. . ."); when you are sad, hurt, or angry; when you pout, shout, cry, or call names; or if you ever go so far as to lie, become mean or vicious, cheat, or steal; you are making sorrowing choices.

As with caring, ruling, or enjoying choices, you may make your sorrowing choices verbally or non-verbally, but you can only make them for yourself. Society teaches people to hide their sadnesses, hurts, and frustrations; as a consequence it may be difficult for you to find ways to make sorrowing choices that are truly OK with the other person. From time to time you may need to settle for making choices that are OK just in comparative terms—that is to say, telling another person what is troubling you is likely to be more OK than either sulking or lashing out. It is likely that you could improve some of your key relationships with young people or with others through briefly stating what is troubling you, rather than making your sorrowing choices in sex-, age-, or role-stereotyped ways.

Thinking/Working Choices

** *The term thinking/working includes the vast range of cognitive and action-oriented choices you make.* When you plan ahead, ask or answer most questions, handle your everyday tasks, or re-do what you do not consider satisfactorily done, you are making thinking/working choices. On most days you make more thinking/working choices than any of the other choices, and you may make more than all of the other four choices combined.

As with the other choices, you may make your thinking/working choices verbally or non-verbally, for yourself or others, and in sex-, age-, or role-stereotyped ways. You developed your patterns of thinking/working choices by listening to those around you, and most of your thinking/working choices are OK with others—if you have considered them carefully. If there is a problem with these choices it is likely to occur if you stay in a thinking/working mode when others want or need a different kind of choice from you. You may be able to improve some of your key relationships either through making more effective thinking/working choices, or through limiting such choices in response to the needs or wants of others.

The five CREST choices we have explored here are developed further in the chapters that follow. Consider this an introduction. At this point the most important ideas are: we make a variety of choices, we can make them in OK or OD ways, and when we want to improve a relationship or make an effective in-the-moment choice, we can bring to mind the five CREST choices to help us in the process of choosing.

To What Extent are You Like These People?

Roy F.

If the range of choices available in any given moment can be assigned a value of +10 to -10, Roy F., a new assistant assigned to youth ministry, operated almost totally within the +1 to -1 range. He showed little feeling, seldom smiled or varied his voice tone or volume, and was always in control. The young people liked him well enough, especially since for many in his inner city church he was the only young, male role model, but most of them felt cheated somehow—they wanted more from him.

A representative from the nearby district office, Dr. Warren, saw Roy's potential and spent some time exploring with him the attitudes of the young people in the church as well as her own reactions. She took Roy on as a "project" after he convinced her that he sincerely wanted to impact the young people in his church in more positive ways.

"All right," she said at one point, after she had explored with him the idea of accounts in relationships, "your behavior teaches several lessons about traditional adult male behavior: use few words, be serious, and keep your feelings controlled. These choices tend to stay in the +1 to -1 range. It may not be easy for you, but you can make the changes you want if you allow yourself to loosen up." Roy had always been "a quick study" and gradually and persistently he modified his interactions. As he added to the balance in his accounts with others his satisfaction with his position rose significantly.

How much are you like Roy F. *was*? What changes might you want to make?

Frank B.

Frank was a high school English teacher who impressed students and others with his knowledge, but he kept rigidly to the curriculum, and he used a variety of OD choices—putdowns and harsh statements—to maintain control in the classroom. In his first year of teaching he adopted the motto, "Never smile before Christmas," and in his dozen years of teaching he never changed. When he died in a fiery car crash, a number of his past and present students attended services in his memory. The most poignant thing said at the time was a comment passed quietly in the back row. "Too bad he never learned to live before he died."

How much are you like Frank B. was? To what extent do your OK choices outweigh your OD choices? What changes do you need to make?

Louise T.

One of the joys of being around Louise T., a high school counselor, is that she is such a multifaceted person. She is so secure in herself that she is able to respond freely to adolescents and to others who come into her world—and wherever she *is* seems to be her world. She sees and hears her own needs and the needs of others and responds to them; she yields leadership to others who need it or want it, but she is always ready with a suggestion that fills a void; she knows how to enjoy herself and is generous in her appreciation of others; she states what is troubling to her without sulking and making others guess what is wrong, and she never lets her frustrations build to the boiling point. Finally, she uses her mind actively and carries out her tasks effectively—in school, in the community, and with her family and friends.

How much are you like Louise T.? What changes would you have to make in your patterns of choices to be more like her in some way that would be appropriate for you?

Ideas You Can Use

** *Make major OK choices.* Along the way you have probably had many experiences that gave you warm, positive feelings—for example when someone put trust in you or treated you in some special way. Reflect on what you and the other person said or did that helped to create those feelings. Those words or actions are clues for how you can make major OK choices in your life. Think about the implications of those words or actions for your work. What clues do you gain for making major OK choices with young people and others? Find a way to make at least one major OK choice every day, for at least a few moments, with an individual or with a group.

** *Model more ideal behavior.* Think about the best teachers, counselors, or other people you have known who work with adolescents. What sets them apart? Enthusiasm? Interest? Involvement? The depth of their understanding of others? Their facility with their responsibilities, with subject matter?

Select one model. Begin to emphasize the trait you admire most in that person. If you admire a person's enthusiasm—be enthusiastic. If you already have that trait in abundance, select another trait to emphasize. Be an actor or actress if necessary, but take on a trait of the person you admire and let it be useful to you. Start slowly, and gradually increase your expression of that trait. Don't give up in advance or make a brief try and opt out because you cannot be *just* like that person. You *can't* be. But you can *choose* to have more of whatever trait you admire. Let your choice to emphasize that trait help you contribute positively to your accounts with adolescents and others.

** *Focus on one relationship and one CREST choice.* Think about a specific youngster or other person in your life with whom you would like a better relationship. We have explored the five CREST choices very briefly, but even at this point you can ask yourself: Which choice might I use more often in OK ways, or which one might I use less often in OD ways, if I want to move toward my positive goal for this relationship? Try to make a few small changes, then as the balance increases in your relationship account, turn your attention to improving other relationships, one at a time.

Critical Incident

Fourth period class, revisited. Let us return to the hypothetical fourth period assignment we introduced in Chapter 3—a class of young people you find difficult to challenge in an assignment that is unrelated to your credential. Let us say on this particular day that things go quite well, and there is a ten minute block of time left that you might use in a creative way with the group. What might you say right now—as that idea occurs to you? What kind of activity could you use that might be rewarding for those involved? What words might you use to introduce that activity?

Respond to one or more of the Critical Incidents in Chapter 2. Decide what kind of choice seems to be called for in response to the adolescent or the group.

Sharing Choices and Communication Skills with Adolescents

Section B of Chapter 16 presents three sharing suggestions under the following titles: *We can learn to differentiate major and minor OK and OD choices. We can conceptualize relationships as accounts. We can learn to make use of the five CREST choices.*

Journal Entry

Date your entry and label it *Ch. 4, OK/OD CREST Choices and Accounts.* You may begin your entry by reflecting on the ideas presented in the chapter, *you, your major and minor OK and OD choices, your accounts,* and *your CREST choices*—in your work with young people and beyond. You may also use the end-of-chapter activities or the key words on page 31 to further cue you in writing your entry.

5
Caring Choices

** Caring choices are responses to needs, and every person has needs for care.

** Appropriateness and the relationship are keys to OK caring choices with others. Moderation and positive self-talk are keys to OK self-caring choices.

** The right kind of touch can be a caring choice; each person must decide when to use touch to show caring for adolescents and others.

** Listening is a caring choice; it is also an underdeveloped skill for most people. Listening deeply involves pausing, repeating internally what was said, and searching out the feelings in the message.

** Listening can be enhanced by the environment created and the use of relevant nonverbal means of communication.

** Both silence and minimum verbal responses can effectively supplement listening; both may be taken as evidence of caring and concern.

Exploring Caring Choices

Dave has been sick with a cold so severe it bordered on pneumonia. Today is his first day back in your group. The choices that follow are illustrations of various points along the continuum of major and minor OK caring choices and minor and major OD caring choices you might make. The OKness or ODness of each choice depends on the relationship you two have, and the tone of voice you use, among other factors.

"I'm glad to see you're feeling better and are back today, Dave. I hope you'll take it easy for a while."

"Feeling better, Dave?"

"From what I understand you really had quite an ordeal, near pneumonia and all."

"Oh, Dave, you poor thing, you look so pale. Should you be here at all? Is there anything I can do?"

The first step in making a caring choice is observing a need. After ten minutes in a group of yours, Mark, who is usually alert, puts his head down on the table before him. You see a pained expression on the face of your colleague, Patrice. You feel a headache coming on. If you say or do anything that responds directly to any of these needs, you are probably making a caring choice.

Our society sends the message that being quick to admit needs is a sign of weakness. As a result, if you touch Mark gently and say, "I think you'd better go lie down," it is possible that he may shrug his shoulders and reassure you that he is all right. Patrice, who looked pained, may wave away your offer of assistance. You may not acknowledge your own need to change your activity or take an aspirin.

One reason few of us respond well to caring choices is that we are accustomed to people using social forms such as, "Hello, how are you?"—then they don't even stay and listen to the response. Or they say, "I'm all right,"—when we know they are having a problem. **** Social forms serve their purpose by putting us in touch with others, but if we really want to show concern we must go beyond rituals.** People who work with adolescents model suitable behavior if they give themselves permission to respond to direct calls for assistance as well as to the more subtle clues adolescents may offer.

One of the key factors in making any of the CREST choices in a way that is OK is that they need to be appropriate in the relationship and in the situation. In making OK caring choices, then, for your choice to be OK, it must respond to the need of the other person in a way that is appropriate within the relationship.

Self-Caring

We seem to be a nation of extremists when it comes to self-caring. Symbolically, some people pour any fuel in the old tank and expect the engine to keep on perking; they stuff themselves with junk food, alcohol, and sweets and turn down green and yellow vegetables and foods loaded with fiber. That is a bit like expecting fine engine performance on ten-year-old gasoline with a molasses additive. Others are constantly on diets. A long-term fad says: be thin, so they try to be—regardless of what their "natural weight" might be. Some never do anything more than bend an elbow for exercise. Others jog doggedly past a sensible stopping point.

** *For effective self-caring our theme should be: MODERATION IN ALL THINGS!*

It is essential for you to care for yourself physically, but equally important is what you think about and what you say about yourself internally. If you think positive thoughts about yourself, you are taking care of *you* in an important way. If you are highly self-critical or concentrate on what you *cannot* do or be, you are not caring for yourself well. Your attitudes about yourself are important because what you project influences adolescents' and others' views of you, and, indirectly, of themselves.

Adlerians suggest that people will meet their essential needs in some way or other. Those who lack effective skills in self-caring resort to the mistaken goals of attention-seeking, power, revenge, and inadequacy as substitutes for the more genuine goals of love and respect (Dreikurs, 1968; Dreikurs, *et al.*, 1982). These behaviors become surrogate self-caring choices designed to meet the individual's need for affection and recognition. Helping young people learn more effective ways of meeting their needs through self-caring or through asking for the care they want can make a significant contribution to their well-being.

Touching as Caring

In this chapter we have used the language "in touch" figuratively, and we mentioned touching Mark on the shoulder and suggesting that he go lie down. We are aware that some adults who work with adolescents have been discouraged from ever touching young people, while others have been encouraged to use physical restraints in

extreme situations to control behaviors. We will return to the issue of restraining touches, and we will subsequently explore alternative avenues for demonstrating care, but first let us consider some of the positive aspects of touch.

** *When someone is in need, often the most appropriate action you can take involves touch.* Many young children thrive on hugs, and they can be appropriate with adolescents in particular circumstances as well. Perhaps hugging goes beyond what would be comfortable for you—and that is your right to decide. However, with people of any age who are in distress, the reality is that a gentle touch may convey your caring more effectively and more appropriately than any number of words you might say.

Some years ago, Jessie Potter, in *The Touch Film* (1983), made several valuable points. She noted that there are great benefits to be gained from touching, and that negative consequences and even death may result from lack of touch in infancy. Though the form of expression that is acceptable changes as infants become children, adolescents, and then adults, the need is always present. Nonetheless, it is frequently the case that those who actually need touching the most receive the least. Potter noted that boys, whose need for touch is as great as that felt by girls, are weaned from touch prior to adolescence; yet, somehow, they are expected to know how to touch in positive ways by the time they become men. She pointed out that in many secondary school settings the only positive touch boys receive relates to athletic performance; a coach may use a pat on the rear to send a player into a game, and a high five or a hug may greet a fine play or a team win. A rhetorical question may be raised: must positive touch for young people be limited to those who play on athletic teams?

If you work with adolescents in any capacity, you should certainly be cautious in this area, and with persons of any age you need to make sure of the appropriateness of any touch you use. Still, it is not necessary for you to join those who have overreacted to the issue of touching.

Redl and Wattenberg (1959) offered useful guidelines for employing physical restraints. Restraint should be applied only when young people are clearly a danger to themselves or others. If restraint is to be used, care should be taken not to hurt the person. The restraining action should neither be punitive nor rough. The goal should be restraining until control is regained. Finally, as Charles (1992) suggested, physical restraint may risk legal action, so it should be used only when absolutely necessary.

In a camp for delinquents in which one of the writers was employed, that individual tried to turn disciplinary situations in which she took actions that could have been perceived as negative (OD) choices into positive (OK) choices. She made every effort to communicate to the youth how she felt about needing to implement a disciplinary policy, she conveyed her concern for the person, and she stated her willingness to help the individual learn self-control.

Ultimately *you* decide what touching you use, and a variety of matters such as the need of the other person and the setting, will, and ought to, affect your choice. But it is important to note that, often more clearly than anything else, *touch says I care.*

Listening as Caring

In our society, all our lives, people have sent us the message: be strong; don't admit your need for care. That message has been sent to males more strongly than to females, but it affects both sexes. As a consequence, few among us are genuinely comfortable either in receiving or giving care. We may be willing to make caring choices with young children or with older people when they have needs, because we stereotype those choices as appropriate for *them*; but if they have been raised in the same culture, they have received the same message and are likely to deny their needs. We do not have to keep our needs to ourselves or withhold care from others.

*** One expression of caring that we can make to people of any age who are in need is that of listening.**

Most of us are used to two kinds of listening. Some people listen impatiently, waiting for the opportunity to inject their story into the dialogue: "You think you've got troubles. What happened to me last week was much worse. It was early and I was on my way to work. . .." Other people listen superficially, ready to seize the first clue that might help us solve our problems. They are often so busy probing for information and getting ready to tell us what we *should* do, that they may not really have heard us.

You, the adolescents you encounter, and others, can benefit from deep, committed listening—rather than impatient or superficial listening. The deep listener puts aside all urgency to solve the problem for the time being in favor of affording the release of pent-up feelings, and understanding the concern.

In his discussion of Glasser's approach to discipline, Charles (1992) mentioned a listening approach a teacher has used that would seem to have applicability in many adult roles with adolescents. Maureen Lewnes called for a consultation corner, a special kind of time-out location in which the young person is invited to share feelings, interests, and problems while the adult listens; the adult may also talk with the young person about a concern or a misbehavior in order to get insight into what might be troubling him or her. Byron Fox, an Indiana educator, makes a similar suggestion, he offers youngsters what he calls *safe time* during which they may state a concern or complaint without any fear of criticism or reprisal. In these and other appropriate ways, adapted to the situation, adults may structure opportunities for adolescents to be genuinely and deeply heard.

As you work with young people, if you listen deeply to them, you are enabling them to engage in creative problem-solving. Likewise, your listening may help adolescents who are in some kind of difficulty to come to their own conclusions about what they need to do. Even when you talk to young people about disciplinary matters, the need for deep listening is present; perhaps it is even greater then since they often feel misunderstood at such times. Your listening is not a promise that no punitive action will be taken. It is what it is intended to be—a message that you care.

Listening: An Underdeveloped Skill

Listening is arguably the one of most important of the communication skills you have available to you as you work with adolescents and others, and it may well be one of the least developed of your skills for three main reasons. First, listening has been a part of your life since even before you were born; as a result you may not have taken time to consider what the word really means. It is like the word *choice* in that sense—it is a concept that has been with you all your life, but you may never have examined it closely. Second, unless you are a counselor, in all likelihood your professional preparation has not taught you the value or the skills of listening. Third, more likely than not you had inadequate models for listening as you were growing up.

Think about your childhood and youth. If you were among the fortunate, you were listened to deeply and well. On the other hand, you may have been among those who were surrounded by people who cared, but who did not regularly send the message to you that they were hearing you at the deepest level. You may have been brought up on the message, "Children should be seen and not heard." You may have been dismissed as a chatterbox. Or you may have been reinforced for being "the strong, silent type." Whether you were listened to well or poorly, or at some point along that continuum, chances are you were brought up by adults who believed that what they were doing was best for you—based on how *they* were raised.

If you were listened to well, count your blessings, and make an effort to improve on the model you were given. If you were not listened to well, do not blame those who raised you for being thoughtless or inconsiderate; instead, accept the reality that you are not likely to have developed the skills of listening deeply to those around you. If that is the case, take it as a challenge to build the skills of effective listening—both within and beyond your work with adolescents.

Deep Listening:
A Three-Step Process

Listening deeply can be seen as a three-step process (Nelson, 1977).

1. *Pause.* When a young person or a colleague has said something serious within a group, or individually, at least some of the time decide that you will make an attentive, internal pause. Let what she or he has said really register.

2. *Repeat the message internally.* Repeat the message inside your brain. Hear the person's voice and intonation exactly as he or she delivered it, instead of getting your own message or a hastily-conceived solution ready to send. You will look more closely and listen more attentively if you obligate yourself to repeat the message internally, and the other person will be aware of the level of your listening.

3. *Search out feelings.* Identify the feelings behind the other person's message. If you sense sadness, frustration, or excitement, you will be more likely to respond sensitively and appropriately, instead of responding without considering his or her feelings and needs. Note that in subsequent chapters we will suggest additional skills for you to use at such times.

** *Deep listening is a valuable skill; when you are really listening, you are not likely to cut the person off, offer superficial solutions, ignore his or her words, or become defensive.*

It is also important for you to listen deeply to yourself. From time to time, when you are speaking, pause, internally repeat what you have said, and search out your own feelings. The gain is likely to create positive ripples: hear yourself, and you are more likely to be able to take care of your needs; take care of your needs, and you put yourself in a position to be able to hear others more effectively.

Listening:
Non-Verbal Components

** *You let others know that you are listening to them through your non-verbal behaviors and the environment you create.* If you are successful in letting others know that you care, you do such things as maintain *good eye contact*, as opposed to either an unremitting stare or a distracted appearance. You *nod your head* from time to time to demonstrate that you are listening and that you understand. You use *harmonious facial expressions* and *gestures*— that is, smiles or frowns and occasional hand movements that are in harmony with the needs of others—to help them see that you are in tune with them. As you speak, you use a *soft, but firm tone of voice* that conveys your confidence in yourself and your interest in and concern for the other person.

If you are talking one-to-one, you arrange chairs so that you and the other person are at a *comfortable proximity*, perhaps three to four feet apart, at an angle but almost face to face, with no physical barriers between you. You avoid having the other person sit in front of your desk while you sit behind it. You select chairs of about the same height so that your eye contact is close to that person's level. To generalize the point, you create a comfortable physical environment so that the two of you can talk easily.

Silence

** *Silence is a component of listening, and frequently silence is golden.* Here we use the term silence to mean a conscious decision not to speak—as opposed to an interval in which you are waiting for an opening or cannot find anything to say. A well-placed three to ten second pause will often do three significant, positive things. (1) It will encourage the other person to keep talking, unless you are sending a non-verbal message that says, "Wait for me!" (2) You will learn more and will not need to ask as many questions as a result. (3) You will have more time to formulate your idea before you speak.

Many people who work with adolescents have not learned to be comfortable with silence; as a result, when they are in dialogue with them they constantly fill the silence with questions and suggestions. We recommend that you develop a sense of comfort with silence. To do that, you may find it useful to say to yourself, frequently, "Wait. Don't be in a hurry. See if she or he has something more to say."

The point should be made that silence *can* be punitive—so it should not be used indiscriminately. Think about the message that might be received by an adolescent who says to you, "I think I'll end it all," if you merely nod. He or she might decide you do not care a rap about him or her, and that may provide the final, needed nudge in the negative direction. Silence is non-punitive, and therefore most effective, when it is clear that the other person feels a press to talk or when it seems appropriate for him or her to take a moment to think further about what she or he has said.

As the old saying goes, we have been given two ears and one mouth for a good reason. Take that as a signal favoring silence—but make sure your use of silence is motivated by caring and concern.

Silence is useful in the classroom, only teachers call it by a different name: *wait time*. Research on wait time shows that teachers tend more frequently to wait four or five seconds when they call on good students, and they wait less when they call on students who really need more time to respond. Poorer students soon learn that if they hesitate, the teacher will move on to someone else. Let silence be an asset to you in your work with groups, *and* when you are communicating individually with anyone, of any age.

Minimum Verbal Responses

Minimum verbal responses, or MVRs, are supplements to silence that encourage others to continue in the same vein or allow them to direct the discussion elsewhere. Examples of MVRs are: "I see." "Yes." "Mm hmm." "Go on." When it is clear that someone has more to say, an MVR may be a highly suitable response. Note that minimum verbal responses should not be strung together in a series: "Hmm. Yes, I see. Go on." One at a time is likely to be enough. Well-placed MVRs can be very useful in group work and in teaching, as supplements to wait time. They encourage deeper thinking and expanded responses.

Responsible *FOR*, or Responsible *TO*, Young People?

The key in developing effective communication with others is feeling responsible *to* them, rather than *for* them; this is particularly true concerning adolescents. Whether you teach, counsel, or meet young people on other grounds, if you feel responsible *for* them, you try to fix, protect, and rescue them; you control them and listen inadequately. You are likely to feel tired, anxious, fearful, and liable. You are concerned with asking questions to get details, with finding answers and solutions, with being right, with your performance.

If you feel responsible *to* young people, you are sensitive to their needs and you listen, show empathy, encourage, and confront. You are likely to feel relaxed, free, aware, and good about yourself. You are concerned with them, with their feelings, and with relating to them. You are a helper. You expect them to be responsible for themselves and their actions. You can trust and you can let go. You need to establish positive relationships with young people and act in ways that respond effectively to their needs—and listening well is almost always an appropriate way to begin.

In the following chapters, we explore additional communication skills through which you can demonstrate your caring and concern for adolescents. Suffice it to say at this point that you are likely to be seen as caring and concerned if you listen deeply to them, if you create a comfortable environment for them, if you stay in touch with them in effective non-verbal ways, if you allow for intervals of silence at suitable times, and if you use minimum verbal responses to encourage them to share their concerns.

To What Extent are You Like These People?

Marie J.

Marie is a middle school teacher who has learned the value of caring. When her mother entered a nursing home because of mobility problems, Marie joined a support group through which she learned to respond to her mother's upset feelings, through such skills as listening and touching.

Recently, Marie met Jack, one of her students, as they were both leaving the nursing home. She offered him a ride home, he accepted, and she learned that Jack's father was suffering from a terminal illness. Marie listened to Jack share his anguish, and when they parted she gave him a hug. In that moment it occurred to her that all of her students, not just Jack, needed from her the skills she had learned to use with her mother. Marie has organized her teaching so she has more opportunities to move among students as they work; she pats students on their shoulders and listens to them. Never has she felt more worthwhile as a teacher. Never have her students responded to her so positively.

How much are you like Marie J.? How much caring do you give/could you give the adolescents with whom you work?

Fred T.

Fred T., a high school administrator, had the best of intentions, but he had never really learned to listen well to others. On the basis of one or two bits of information the young people in his school could depend on him to lecture them. Debbie, a strong student, had suddenly stopped performing well. After he talked with her about a program that brought them together, he asked a couple of questions, then began his lecture—"Your recent performance is jeopardizing your grades... The colleges you want to go to are highly selective... Consistent effort is needed..." And on and on. Three days later Debbie attempted suicide; she was sure she was pregnant and her life was over. Fred T. went to see Debbie in the hospital and before he left he said to her, "I wish you'd told me how desperate you felt when we talked on Tuesday." Her response caught him up short. "I wanted to. I even tried to," she said.

How different are you from Fred T.? How do you demonstrate that you really listen?

Betty N.

Betty N. is a highly skilled communicator. She listens with genuine intensity, she maintains good eye contact, she senses when to remain silent, and she often uses just a word or two to encourage the person with whom she is speaking to continue. As a university administrator, Betty

N. works with college-age students, faculty, and staff members; still, she communicates so well in the face of high demands on her time that we see her as a model of caring for anyone.

How much are you like Betty N.? In the light of the concepts presented in this chapter, what changes would help you be a more effective communicator?

Ideas You Can Use with Individuals or Groups

** *Choose the form of caring that suits the moment.* Think about the adolescents or the other people in your life whose needs are obvious—who wear them "on their sleeve." In subsequent chapters we will explore other relevant choices, but for now, consider how you might express your concern. What form of caring choice do you—or could you—use to show your caring feelings for them?

** *Employ the three-step listening process.* Find opportunities with adolescents and others to listen deeply. When you hear something that has been said emotionally, stop yourself; don't formulate a response or wait for an opening to inject your idea. *Pause, repeat internally* what you have heard, and *search out feelings.* Then, so you will not break the spell and stop listening, do something that is basically non-verbal: nod, touch the person lightly on the arm, or say, "Uh huh."

** *Use silence, MVRs.* Opportunities abound for all of us to listen. Be alert to the opportunities you have to use the components of listening. Nod your head, maintain silence, use minimum verbal responses. These skills will help you demonstrate your caring for others.

Critical Incident

Debbie. Suppose for a moment that teacher Fred T's Debbie is someone with whom *you* have contact (see above, second segment—*To What Extent Are You Like These People?*), and she has stopped performing well in your group. You have yielded to temptation and have given her a brief lecture and she has agreed to try harder. You are about to end the contact, but her actions seem hesitant. "Is there something else?" you say. "No, I guess not. I'm just thinking about something that doesn't have anything to do with school," she replies. What might you say—if you spoke immediately? How might you respond without words, or what might you do or say if you were to use the three-step listening process? If Debbie shared her concern, how would you try to help her?

Respond to one or more of the Critical Incidents in Chapter 2. Try out deep listening skills in response to the adolescent or the group.

Sharing Choices and Communication Skills with Adolescents

Section C of Chapter 16 presents three suggestions for sharing these ideas with adolescents under the following titles: *Caring choices are responses to needs. Using the three-step listening process. Supplements to listening.*

Journal Entry

Date your entry and label it *Ch. 5, Caring choices and listening.* You may begin your entry by reflecting on the ideas presented in the chapter, *you, your caring choices, your skills in listening,* and *your use of the various components of listening*—in your work with young people and beyond. You may also use the end-of-chapter activities or the key words on page 31 to further cue you in writing your entry.

6
Paraphrasing and Reflecting as Caring Choices

** Paraphrasing is defined as giving back to the other person what he or she has said. Paraphrasing allows the individual who has a concern to choose the direction of the discussion. Paraphrasing can also be used to break a pattern of communication that is not working. In each of these ways, paraphrasing functions as a caring choice.

** Reflection of content is a brief paraphrase that feeds back to people the sense of their ideas.

** Reflection of feeling adds a vital dimension to reflection of content, that of addressing the feelings of the person speaking.

** Three steps in reflecting feelings are: pause, figure out a feeling word that describes the person's emotional state, and make a statement that incorporates the feeling word.

** Reflections of feeling are caring choices.

Paraphrasing

** *Paraphrasing is feeding back to others the major elements of what they have said.* A paraphrase should be long enough to capture the basic ideas expressed. Paraphrase and summarization are closely related, but a paraphrase often contains more detail than a summary. A good paraphrase is an extension of deep listening.

If you paraphrase what someone else has said to you, the other person has three basic options: affirm that you have captured the essence of the statement, tell you how your paraphrase might be modified, or go on with whatever is on his or her mind at the moment; any of these outcomes may be positive.

Let us suppose that you believe paraphrasing might be useful in talking with Jeff, a young man with whom you have a good relationship. When he stops by to talk with you, you tell him that you would like to try out a new skill, and he agrees. "OK," you say, "tell me something about what's going on in your life and I'll try to paraphrase it; then you let me know if I've really captured the spirit of what you've said."

Jeff says to you, "OK, you want to know what's going on in my life? I'll give it to you straight. My life is a mess right now. My parents have been fighting with one another and trying to get me to take sides, I just broke up with my steady, I haven't been able to concentrate in school so my grades are dropping, and I can't figure out what I've done to deserve all this. There, that ought to give you something to paraphrase."

Hearing the anguished tone in Jeff's comment, you ask if he really wants you to paraphrase. "Sure, why not?" he says. "I can't see how it could make matters worse."

If you paraphrase, you might say something like this: "Things are a mess for you, Jeff. Your parents are fighting and want to pull you into it. You've broken up with your steady. School is hard for you right now because you can't concentrate. And you wonder what you've done to bring all this on yourself."

Of what earthly value is a response of this order?

Note that Jeff has raised concerns in four separate areas: parent conflict, relationship breakup, a school concentration problem, and personal responsibility. Which of these does Jeff need most to talk about further?

The best answer is that you have no way of knowing—until you have heard further from Jeff. Any one of these issues might be uppermost in his mind.

The value of a paraphrase like the one above is that it treats the issues equally, thereby allowing Jeff to underscore the one that is most relevant at present from his point of view. A statement or question on your part focused on one of the issues could well pull him away from the matter of greatest concern. For example, a request, "Tell me about your grades and your school problems," if Jeff is most deeply concerned about his parents' arguing, might seem far too limiting or even inappropriate.

Injecting a paraphrase in a conversation with an adolescent, a friend, or a relative may seem awkward since it is not likely to be something you have become comfortable doing. If you decide to try it, you would do well to introduce your paraphrase with an explanatory statement. For example: "Let me see if I've got this straight...." Or: "What I think I've heard you say is...." Or: "I'd like to try giving back to you what you've said, so you know I've heard you...."

Paraphrasing is ideal for sharpening listening skills. It can help you attend better to what the other person is saying, and it can enable you to determine what is most important to him or her. However, the most valuable uses of paraphrasing may well be in working out your own concerns with another person and in helping people clarify their concerns with one another. In both instances it is well to get an agreement in advance that those involved are willing to try paraphrasing.

If you have a concern with your spouse, a friend, or an adolescent with whom you work, your request for an agreement might go something like this: "We're in a stalemate over this issue. I'd like to suggest that we try paraphrasing as a way of coming to understand one another, and maybe it can help us resolve the issue. It works this way. Let's say you start; you'd do that by telling me in a few sentences about how the matter looks from your point of view. I give back what you've said in a paraphrase. You can clarify your point of view a time or two until you're satisfied that I've paraphrased your ideas satisfactorily. Then I talk about the issue from my perspective and you paraphrase what I've said. We keep going back and forth for as long as it seems useful to both of us, or until we resolve the issue."

If two young people are in conflict over an issue, and you believe paraphrasing would help, you may introduce the idea similarly, seek agreement that the two are willing to deal with the issue through paraphrasing, and begin the process. Paraphrasing has great potential for helping problem relationships. It has been used in teaching, in resolving adolescent-to-adolescent and adolescent-to-parent conflicts, with marriage partners, and so forth.

Paraphrasing is content-oriented, but its underlying purpose is that of creating awareness and understanding. We see paraphrasing as a caring choice that responds to the needs of people in interpersonal relationships.

Reflection of Content

** *Reflection of content is a* brief *paraphrase that feeds back to people the sense of their ideas.* At times it can be very useful for people to hear back what they are saying, and a reflection of content provides that opportunity. Although reflection of content may seem "canned" to the sender who has not become comfortable in using it, people are seldom bothered by what might be called "the echo effect," when reflection of content is used skillfully, or if the intention behind it is explained.

Suppose Ginny has told you that other kids sometimes mock her, then she says: "They do everything right, then they call me dumb when I make mistakes—which I do all the time."

An example of a reflection of content could be: "The other kids seem to do everything right, but you make a lot of mistakes." Two advantages of such a reflection of content are: it helps the person reconsider what she is saying, and it allows her to set the direction for continuing the dialogue.

At first blush it may seem kinder for you to say, "Oh, now, you know you're not dumb," or, "I think you're pretty bright," but the results may well be the opposite of what you intend. Ginny may catalog a dozen things she has done recently that are dumb—thereby reinforcing the label; or she may turn you off as "just another adult who doesn't listen when I try to say how I really feel inside."

Reflection of Feeling

** *The essence of reflection of feeling is reflecting back to the person what he or she is feeling.* Paraphrasing or reflection of content can be useful, but it is often even more helpful for people to hear their *feelings* reflected back to them along with some of the content they have offered.

Reflection of feeling says you understand and care about the person.

There are three parts to a reflection of feeling:

** *Pause.* After you have heard the other person speak, pause briefly.

** *Figure out a feeling word that describes the person's state of mind.* Say it to yourself. For example, when Ginny complains to you that others call her dumb, tell yourself that she feels *troubled*.

** *Make a statement*—not a question—*that includes a form of the feeling word you chose.* Using the same example, your reflection of feeling might be: "It *troubles* you that you can't seem to do things right and that some kids call you dumb."

An attempted reflection of feeling is far less effective in question form—and especially in *yes-no* question form—e. g., "Are you feeling troubled about that?" Such a question is likely to be seen as insensitive since in all likelihood Ginny would expect you to know the answer in advance; furthermore, it invites a yes or no response, which "puts the ball back in your court," and sets you up to ask another question. Reflection of feeling is also less effective if a narrow range of leads is used; for example, if most or all of the reflections are begun in the same way: "You feel. . .."

What might you do if your reflection of feeling is met by a long sigh of relief and the single word, "Yes"? At that point it seems most appropriate to wait a few moments and allow the person to enjoy the feeling of relief which often comes when he or she finally feels understood. That brief period of silence plus a simple nod of the head will generally serve as all the encouragement the person needs to continue, elaborating on the matter at hand or illuminating some new concern. Furthermore, your patient response may convey more effectively than anything else you could do that your interest is in hearing what the person wants to talk about with you, rather than in directing the dialogue where you want it to go.

Reflection of Feeling as Effective Caring

You have probably heard the old joke about the psychiatrist who always reflected the feelings of the patient. Patient: "My life is a terrible mess." Psychiatrist: "You're really upset with your life." Patient: "I think I'll jump out the window." Psychiatrist: "You feel so bad you want to end it all." Patient: "Yes, I'm going to climb on the ledge right now and jump." Psychiatrist: "You're so frustrated that you're going to climb on the ledge and jump right now." Patient: "Goodbye, cruel world." As the patient hurtles through the air, the psychiatrist calls out: "You're angry at the world and you're not going to change your mind."

Reflection of feeling can be inappropriate, inadequate, or both, as in our psychiatrist and patient story; or it can be appropriate and sufficient. Oftentimes, reflecting people's upset, frustrated, and angry feelings gives them the kind of relief they need, and allows them to go on—because someone, at last, understands. When a boy you know is in trouble for disciplinary reasons, you can respond with a reflection of feeling. If he appears to be anxious, for example, you might say, "You're concerned about what's going to happen now."

Most adults do not reflect feelings with young people or others because they have not learned to do so, since they did not grow up hearing others respond to them in that way. However, those who develop this skill see it as very useful.

Consider how comforting it would be if a teenaged girl said something innocently that others heard as suggestive, and you said (italics added for emphasis): "I can tell you're *embarrassed* now. It's *frustrating* when something you say turns out a different way than you meant it." Reflection of feeling facilitates problem-solving by the individual who must ultimately solve the problem—in this case, the girl—and it models an effective caring response that may encourage her to develop the same skill.

Reflection of feeling requires practice before it becomes comfortable and easy to use; once the skill is developed, it is often seen by others as a helpful, caring choice.

To What Extent are You Like These People?

Laura R.

Laura R. was introduced to reflection of feelings in her training as a counselor. Whenever possible, which was most of the time, her family had avoided expressing feelings other than anger, so she found it difficult to incorporate this new skill, even when obvious opportunities presented themselves. Through sheer effort she has become more and more comfortable in using reflection of feeling.

How much has your life been like Laura R's? To what extent do you believe you would be able to reflect others' feelings when that would be helpful? How might you go about developing that skill so that you are comfortable in using it?

Rolf W.

Rolf W. used paraphrasing to great advantage in his teaching. Frequently in class when a student gave an involved, convoluted response, Rolf paraphrased it: "So your idea about this is...," he often began; then he captured the essence of the student's comments as accurately as he could. His students often shaped their responses further after the paraphrase, and as a result they learned to put their thoughts into words more effectively. Rolf also paraphrased student's statements when they stopped by to chat after school. Some students needed little more than that to encourage them to work out their own difficulties.

How much are you like Rolf W.? How might you use paraphrasing to your advantage?

Ideas You Can Use with Individuals or Groups

** *Paraphrase.* Look for opportunities in your work with adolescents, and your contact with others, to paraphrase what you hear. Note that in many instances it will be to your advantage to set up the paraphrase with an introductory comment: "So there are two main issues that are troubling you right now. . . ." Be sure to secure the cooperation of those involved if you should decide to employ paraphrasing to any great extent in your everyday communication or with young people or others who are in conflict.

** *Try reflecting feelings.* Look for opportunities in your life to reflect feelings. Notice the excited, happy, upset, and frustrated feelings others around you evidence, and respond. You may wish to tell others you are trying to listen better to them and if it is OK you will reflect their feelings with them from time to time—then do it. You may occasionally encounter a mild negative reaction when you try this skill at first, but when you clarify your intentions—"to help me understand you better"—and when you become more skilled in reflecting, most people will respond very well.

Critical Incident

Dale. You are walking by a recreational field where a practice soccer game is in progress. The sun is hot, so you stop in the shadows of the bleachers to watch for a few minutes. You see Dale walking toward the stash of players' gym bags. Dale, whom you have known for some time, has a reputation for stealing, and has been in juvenile court over the issue in the past. You see Dale unzip one gym bag, then another. Your view is partially blocked, but it appears to you that Dale has transferred something from the first bag to the second, then zipped them both closed.

You step out of the shadow and call, "Dale."

Dale jumps up, looks around, then smiles at you and says, "This ain't what you think it is."

What would you be most likely to say or do right now? How might you use paraphrasing or reflection of feeling in the moment? Think about any extenuating circumstances that might be operating. How might using approaches from this chapter help you avoid turning the situation into a bigger problem than it needs to be?

Sharing Choices and Communication Skills with Adolescents

Section D of Chapter 16 presents two sharing suggestions under the following titles: *Paraphrasing. Reflection of Feeling.*

Journal Entry

Date your entry and label it *Ch. 6, Paraphrasing and reflecting.* You may begin your entry by reflecting on the ideas presented in the chapter, *you, your choices, paraphrasing,* and *reflecting feelings*—in your work with young people and beyond. You may also use the end-of-chapter activities or the key words on page 31 to further cue you in writing your entry.

7
Ruling Choices

** Ruling choices involve leadership—for others and for self. OK ruling choices are often welcome since leadership is needed in a great variety of situations.

* Assertiveness means making ruling choices in ways that are honest and direct. The alternatives to assertiveness are unassertiveness and aggressiveness—both are undesirable.

** Assertiveness involves self-ruling choices, other-ruling choices, and appropriate expressions of empathy.

Exploring Ruling Choices

*** When you show leadership through offering suggestions, giving directions, or issuing orders, you are making ruling choices.*

Suppose Shelley has been late frequently and is late again today—as a result of a conversation with Mr. Jackson, a colleague of yours. The choices that follow are illustrations of the continuum of major and minor OK, and minor and major OD ruling choices you might make in the situation. The OKness or ODness of each choice depends to some degree on the relationship between the two of you, its history, your tone of voice, and a variety of other factors.

"You're doing fine, come join us, Shelley. I'm aware that Mr. Jackson was talking with you," you say, and smile.

"I saw you and Mr. Jackson talking, Shelley; I knew you'd be late today," you say, and you wave Shelley to a seat.

"Come up here, Shelley. I'd like to talk to you after I get everybody started."

"You know I've been on your case about being late, Shelley, and talking to Mr. Jackson is no excuse. You should have told him you had to be on time."

All choices that show leadership are ruling choices. You make ruling choices when you say such things as: "All right, let's begin." "Let's try a fun activity next." "Why don't we stand up and stretch." "It's time to start on that task." "Let's take a break." "Please be quiet." "Keep it down to a dull roar." "Shut Up!" "Stop all that nonsense."

Here we use the term *ruling*, though the term *leading* would serve just as well. The word ruling may offer a warning that it is comparatively easy to go overboard with ruling choices. This is especially so when professional responsibilities demand leadership—as they frequently do in work with adolescents.

The likelihood is that most of the ruling choices you make with most young people and others are seen by them as OK. It is when you go beyond what others can readily accept from you in leadership that your choices are seen as OD. OD choices involve domination—something most individuals tend to resist.

If you are working with adolescents in a group, most of your ruling choices are not just marginally OK; they are welcome—because most of them want the discussion or the activity to move along. A related point can be made concerning the ruling choices you make with friends and relatives. If you are like most people, some of your relationships suffer from a power vacuum. A power vacuum is present whenever two people engage in a dialogue in which they say such things as: "What do you want to do tonight?" "Oh, I don't care, what would you like to do?" In your personal interactions, as well as within your profession, your leadership may be more than OK, it may be very welcome.

When a power vacuum exists, both people are acting as responders—rather than initiators—at least in those moments. If that is typical of you, you may find it difficult to make the heavy load of ruling choices that may be required of you in your work with young people. As a consequence, you may vacillate between being too soft and too demanding; or, like some people who lead youth, you may seize the opportunities your work allows you and issue commands that are too harsh or too frequent.

When you make suggestions or give orders or issue directions to adolescents, you are modeling leadership. The model you present should exemplify fairness, firmness, and suitable expectations. Your choices should tell the young people in your care two important things: that you are in charge, and that you care about them.

Who's In Charge?
How Can We Tell?

Leadership involves more than words. At least six factors either support or undermine your leadership with adolescents:

Poise. Do you meet young people with a pleasant expression, radiating self-assurance, and encouraging their respect?

Appearance. Is your leadership enhanced by your clothing, your cleanliness, your hairstyle, or other appearance factors within your control?

Eye contact. Do you project confidence by making steady, comfortable eye contact?

Voice control. Do you use your voice firmly as a resource, avoiding unnecessary loudness or monotony?

Deliberateness. In stressful situations are your responses deliberate and reasonable, rather than hasty and negative?

Proximity. Do you show that you are comfortable in moving appropriately close to young people without violating their space?

If you are in charge of groups of young people meeting together, there is likely to be no way in which you can function effectively without making numerous ruling choices; you must exercise leadership. Even if you organize subgroups with leaders, or cooperative learning teams, or committees to handle specific tasks, it is likely to be *your* leadership, and the rules and expectations *you* have set, that sustain the group. At the same time, sharing center stage with adolescents allows them to develop their leadership skills. It is an expression of confidence in yourself and faith in young people when you let them participate as leaders. Two criteria by which your work can be judged as successful or unsuccessful with young people are: the extent to which you are seen as genuinely and positively in charge when you need to be, and the extent to which you enable adolescents to exercise leadership on their own.

The literature on various discipline models suggests that with any group of young people it is important to have a clear set of rules and to follow through so that rules are consistently applied (Dreikurs, et al., 1982; Canter, 1976). Some of the models, for example Glasser's (1985), have also suggested that young people should have input in developing the rules of the group and the consequences—both positive and negative—of cooperation or non-compliance. The leader with youth needs to develop rules and consequences and go beyond that to help them to build a creative, positive environment in which everyone has a good chance of feeling successful. Those actions tend to minimize the necessity for OD choices on the part of the adult leader.

Achieving self-discipline, or, in Choice Awareness terms, enabling young people to make suitable self-ruling choices, should be seen as a primary objective of any discipline model. As Jones (1987) suggested, adults should help adolescents to gain in self-control (make OK self-ruling choices); and Redl and Wattenberg (1959) encouraged adult leaders to provide situational assistance—organizing and reorganizing schedules and routines and removing distracting objects—so that young people can more readily control their own behaviors.

*** Making OK ruling choices is central to your success, regardless of your role with adolescents.** Encouraging and enabling young people to make OK ruling choices allows them to feel successful as well.

Assertiveness

In recent years people have been encouraged to develop the skills of assertiveness as antidotes to the sense of powerlessness they often feel. When people respond assertively to the situations they encounter they do so with both self- and other-ruling choices. By contrast, when people do not give themselves permission to respond assertively they end up feeling upset with themselves because they have let someone "walk all over" them. They may then lash out in inappropriate ways once they have endured all they believe they can endure.

Unassertiveness—
Assertiveness—Aggressiveness

*** Most people act in ways that are at times unassertive, assertive, and aggressive.** The two ends of the continuum are especially problematic for those who work with youth. The youth leader who is basically unassertive may bend over backwards to avoid conflict and may be taken advantage of by adolescents and others. The youth leader who is aggressive may take advantage of adolescents and others in ways that meet his or her needs at their expense. By contrast, the assertive leader is honest and direct, communicates both needs and wants clearly, and models behaviors that are useful for young people to learn in a democratic society.

Most likely you were polite and cooperative as an adolescent yourself, and you moved through the educational process without developing a great deal of skill in being assertive. If so, you may unconsciously expect the young people you work with to behave as cooperatively as you did. That expectation could lead you to act in unassertive ways. Unassertive leaders plead, cajole, whine, and threaten—but young people know that their threats are bluffs: "C'mon folks, can't we get *on* with it?" "*Please*, I can't hear what Ralph is saying." "You kids are driving me crazy." "I can't stand all this noise any longer." "Settle down—or I'll have to do something drastic."

Some colleagues in your field may be continuously aggressive (we will assume you are not); they may have consciously or unconsciously selected their work as an outlet for aggressiveness; they expect the worst of young people and they often bring out the worst in them. Probably more of the aggressive acts by leaders with youth, however, are perpetrated by unassertive individuals who endure problems for a time without taking action, and then overreact and become aggressive out of a sense of frustration. "You kids are just stupid." "This is the worst group I've ever had." "Get out of here right now—I don't want to see your face ever again."

Most teachers, counselors, and others who work with adolescents need either to *learn* to respond to them more suitably and assertively, or they need to *enhance* their skills in doing so. Once they have mastered those skills, they are seldom overwhelmed by young people or others, and they do not feel the need to react aggressively.

Assertiveness in Group Work with Youth

** *Being assertive in youth group work situations means stating expectations clearly and repeatedly, if necessary, without anger.* "Jack, I expect you to be in your seat and doing your work." This statement describes the action you want to reinforce. It is far superior to: "Jack, what are you doing out of your seat when you're supposed to be working?" which invites an explanation or an argument; or "Sit down and shut up," which invites further aggression in response.

Being assertive in group situations also means being generous with reinforcement when expectations are met: "This is a great group; it's a pleasure to work with you." "Good, more than half of you are ready for the next direction." Giving attention to positive actions through such statements as these, along with such earned rewards as a brief time block for informal visiting or for a game, and so forth, is far superior to focusing attention continuously on negative behaviors.

According to Lee Canter's assertive discipline approach (1976), leadership in the classroom (and beyond, we would suggest) requires the development of a specific discipline plan that includes a limited number of rules, an agreed-on pattern of rewards for cooperation, and a system of penalties when infractions occur. We commend assertive discipline as an aid to managing youth groups, but it should be noted that some of the behaviors that are most frustrating to those who work with adolescents are not always clear violations of rules.

For example, during a discussion Rhonda raises her hand. You recognize her. She smiles and suggests sweetly, "You said we've been having a good day. May I play one of my music tapes during the last five minutes today?" You could respond unassertively, saying, "We'll see," or you might give a disapproving look and ignore the question. If you respond aggressively you might shout, "Don't interrupt with irrelevant questions!" OR you might slam your notes or your book on the floor in disgust.

Assertive behavior in such a situation can take several directions. You may think for a moment and conclude that Rhonda's question: (1) is a signal that the activity or discussion has been long and the group members are losing interest, (2) is well-meant but ill-timed, or (3) is a pattern in her behavior that you do not want to reinforce. Your response should fit your interpretation.

1. "Rhonda, you've done us a favor by pointing out that we have been working very hard for quite a while. The answer is yes. And in just a moment we'll switch activities."

2. "In about five minutes we should have completed this activity and you may ask about that then." This preserves Rhonda's ego, states your intention to go on with the work at hand, and encourages Rhonda to time her questions better.

3. "I'm not going to answer that now." This response, stated without anger or further explanation, takes less time and causes you less internal stress than scolding would.

The Caring Implications of Assertiveness

From a Choice Awareness point of view, both leadership and assertiveness involve ruling choices. Even so, the underlying motive in assertiveness is often that of caring.

Effective leaders care about themselves too much to allow young people to take undue advantage, and they realize that adolescents ultimately pay a price when they are allowed to run roughshod over adults. Furthermore, effective leaders care about adolescents too much to permit them to behave in ways that are damaging to others their age or to themselves (Charles, 1992).

Adolescents need limits, and those who are in charge of them need both to assert themselves and to make sure the limits they set are reasonable (Canter, 1978).

The Assertiveness Sequence

Regardless of your work role, you are likely to meet situations in which you may need to make a series of assertive responses. For example, a group of young people want you to take them to a statewide contest because their sponsor is ill. You are unable to go, but they keep pushing.

A first step in an assertiveness sequence is making a self-ruling choice:

"Sorry, I can't take you. I have other plans at that time."

A second step may incorporate a moderately-stated other-ruling choice:

"Don't plead now, I've already told you I can't go."

A third step may include an expression of empathy and a reiteration of self-ruling:

"I understand your difficulty, but I can't help you out this time."

In a fourth step you continue to be assertive, but avoid being aggressive:

"Discussion's over." You remain pleasant as you usher the group out the door.

The fact that you begin by listening does not mean that you will yield. The use of the assertiveness sequence takes care of the situation through effective ruling choices.

To What Extent are You Like These People?

Debbie D.

Early in her experience with youngsters in the halfway house in which she works, Debbie D. decided that she would try to counter the sense of powerlessness that characterized the group by empowering the residents as much as possible. She organized the house on a cooperative basis to encourage the development of leadership and to increase interaction among the residents. Most of the time the young people involved lived up to or exceeded her expectations.

How much are you like Debbie D.? To what extent do you involve—could you involve—adolescents in leadership with others?

Greg H.

Greg H. is a high school English teacher who exudes quiet confidence. He has a pleasant smile, a friendly and firm manner, and is well-organized. But what sets him apart most from most of his colleagues is his patience. When it is time for class to start, Greg stands and waits for the students. Before long the noise subsides.

He often begins class with a brief reading, and students like listening to his quiet, dramatic voice.

Yesterday, just after the bell rang, the self-appointed class clown in a ninth grade section was acting up. Greg

raised his voice only slightly above his normal level of speech: "Stan, I'm ready to begin," he said firmly. Stan grinned sheepishly and sat down.

How much are you like Greg H.? What gentle, reasonable means do you use to let young people know you're in charge?

Ideas You Can Use with Individuals or Groups

Two simple strategies for making OK ruling choices are: ** *Take time to think.* And, ** *Make your choices in as pleasant a way as you can.* In the heat of the moment, when a young person has done something that is irritating or otherwise troublesome, tell yourself to think for a second or two about what you want to do or say and then do it or say it as pleasantly or reasonably as you can. That suggestion may seem like little more than common sense, but if you analyze your own behavior you may find that there is little that is common for you in either of those choices. What appears to be "just common sense" may actually be viewed as "uncommonly good sense."

Three strategies for being assertive, for making effective ruling choices, are:

** *Make assertiveness a way of life.* Be gently but firmly assertive with young people and with others in your life. That is, clearly state your needs, wants, and expectations.

** *Use the assertiveness sequence.* When several assertions may be called for, follow the sequence outlined above: (a) a self-ruling choice, (b) a gentle other-ruling choice, (c) a self-ruling choice along with an expression of empathy, (d) a firm other-ruling choice.

** *Invite assertiveness from others.* Invite those around you, including adolescents, to be assertive with you. Encourage them to tell you of their needs, wants, and goals. Create opportunities for them to demonstrate leadership.

Critical Incident

Administrator. When teachers are surveyed about things that trouble them in their profession, many list among their concerns a lack of administrative support. Doubtless the same problem occurs to some extent in other work involving adolescents.

Assume it is a year from now, you are working in a new assignment involving adolescents, and you encounter a boy who causes many problems by his disruptive behaviors. Without success, you have tried a number of approaches to reach him. Today you sent him to the office because of *another* disruption. You did this hesitantly, because other staff members have not felt supported by the administration in disciplinary matters.

You prepared and sent a carefully-worded memo to the administrator describing today's disruption—one that disturbed the group and hurt another person. You also detailed approaches you have used in dealing with the boy's previous infractions.

The administrator arrives at your door, waves the boy to his seat, and speaks to you in a sarcastic voice that all can hear. "I've had an opportunity to meet with this young man. I'm sure you two can work this out." He continues, "Furthermore, I have more important things to do than to settle conflicts between the people in your group. . ., or even between you and this boy." The administrator turns toward the door.

What do you do or say now? Later? If you were to try the assertiveness sequence, what words would you use?

Sharing Choices and Communication Skills with Adolescents

Section E of Chapter 16 presents two sharing suggestions under the following titles: *Introducing ruling choices. Assertiveness.*

Journal Entry

Date your entry and label it *Ch. 7, Ruling choices.* You may begin your entry by reflecting on the ideas presented in the chapter, *you, your ruling choices,* and *assertiveness*—in your work with young people and beyond. You may also use the end-of-chapter activities or the key words on page 31 to further cue you in writing your entry.

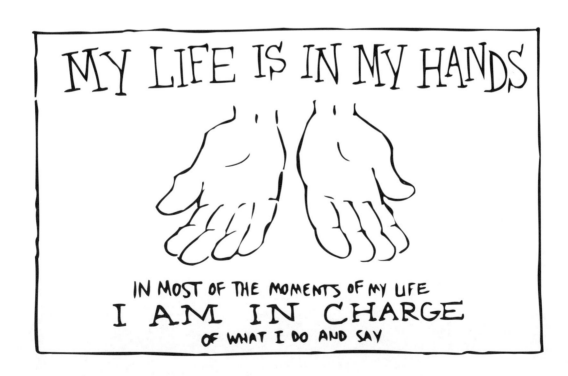

8
Enjoying Choices

** Enjoying choices involve expressions of positive feelings.

** Adults tend to think of enjoying choices as events and believe that most enjoying choices belong to children.

** OK enjoying choices are keys to building effective relationships and developing positive self-feelings; they also act as models of effective choices for young people.

** Enjoying choices can take many different forms. Adults who reinforce adolescents and show a sense of humor in their interactions make valuable and valued enjoying choices with them.

** A variety of relaxation and activity processes contribute to a positive outlook; these processes may include deep breathing, meditation, fantasy, exercise, positive addiction, and laughter.

Exploring Enjoying Choices

Whenever you act directly on your positive feelings you make enjoying choices.

Leading a round of applause for Terry's positive efforts.

Writing a note that says, "Keep up the good work, Gene!"

Giving someone a pat on the back.

Hugging, not as support (which is a caring choice), but because of a small victory.

Chuckling at an amusing incident.

"I really enjoy this group."

"You have such a nice attitude, Chris."

"Thank you for your help, Dale."

"Let's see how many creative ways we can think of to solve this problem."

These are enjoying choices you might make with young people. Through your enjoying choices you let others know of your good feelings toward them and toward yourself. And through enjoying choices you express your own positive self-concept.

Why Do We Hold Back on Enjoying Choices?

Enjoying choices sound great. Why do most adults hold back on them?

** *We think of enjoying choices as events.* We see enjoying choices as evenings out, vacations, and sporting events, and we overlook the value of positive comments and actions—things we can say or do in just a moment. Although sharing a ski weekend or attending a concert or a tennis match may stand out as a memorable event in a relationship, ultimately we weave the fabric of effective relationships with great numbers of small day-to-day choices. Realistically, we know we cannot take time for a major event whenever the idea occurs to us, but we *can* "reach out and touch someone" in some way, or make a positive self-choice, in almost any given moment.

** *We think we must be serious as adults.* We believe we have to "put away *childish* things"—silliness and un-thinking behaviors—and it is appropriate to do so! But then we may also "put away *childlike* things"—open and joyful ways of being, and positive words and actions. As a result we may model dull behaviors, and the young people we encounter may eventually come to imitate the behaviors we exhibit.

** *We have not practiced effective adult enjoying choices enough to be comfortable with them.* Some of the more risky enjoying choices we made as children may seem too daring for us now, and we may be uncertain about what good, grown-up enjoying choices really are. As a result, we may let inhibitions carried over from adolescence keep us from making an enthusiastic statement, tossing off a "high five," or singing out a line of a song—when such a move would help those around us see that we love life and know how to make enjoying choices.

OK and OD Enjoying Choices

** *OK enjoying choices are those that are acceptable to the people affected by them, now and later; OD enjoying choices are unacceptable to those involved.* OK enjoying choices may be made for ourselves or with or for another person; OD enjoying choices may be made at one's own expense or at the expense of another.

Sometimes the line between an OK and an OD enjoying choice is fuzzy. With a few adolescents, a teasing choice may be OK; with others, even though they may appear to be amused by what was said, the teasing may create an invisible hurt. The likelihood is great that marginal enjoying choices like sarcasm or teasing will be OD, thus it is well to steer clear of such choices. Name-calling "in fun" and teasing are examples of the OD enjoying choices young people are likely to make unless the adults around them model more open, truly-positive, enjoying choices.

Modeling Enjoying Choices

** *Our society sends strong messages that suggest that enjoying choices belong to children and adolescents.* "These are the best years of your life—enjoy them." "Have fun while you can." "Go on out and play." As a consequence, many adults offer young people poor models for making OK enjoying choices—exemplifying instead, bland, unenjoyable adult lives. Young people need adults around them who permit themselves the luxuries of smiling, of entering enthusiastically into the joys of living, and of taking time to help others find constructive ways to enjoy themselves.

A teacher friend once commented to a group, "The funniest thing happened in school today and I almost burst out laughing." She described a really amusing event that was neither vulgar nor hurtful; it was genuinely funny. When she finished, she was asked why she didn't laugh aloud with her students. "I'm a teacher," she said.

Many adults believe they must take a very serious approach to the adolescents with whom they live and work. They hold back their enjoyment and enthusiasm because they fear that problems in maintaining control will occur if they give expression to those feelings. Unfortunately, the outcome is that young people find too little to enjoy in the adults they know, in their teachers, and in learning itself. We do not want to suggest that adults get carried away with enthusiasm and leave adolescents behind in the dust, for example, like the mathematician who spends a full hour filling a chalkboard with ecstasies of equations, the derivations of formulas the young people in their charge do not need to know. But more often than not adults err in the opposite direction: they show adolescents too little enthusiasm and humor.

** *Really effective grownups are enthusiastic about what they do and they permit themselves to see both joy and humor in life.* Secure adults share life's little joys with young people and tell anecdotes now and then. They allow those around them to see them as human beings.

You can change—if you have relinquished enjoying choices to young people, or if you relegate such choices to occasional major events, or if you have fallen into a pattern of using sarcasm and teasing instead of genuine enjoying choices. You can, instead, exemplify suitable enjoying choices for the young people you encounter.

It is important to realize that in most instances enjoying choices are the best choices available for building positive relationships. Emphasize creative activities, compliment young people, pat them on the back, thank them for their assistance, write reinforcing notes to them—in other words, make numerous OK enjoying choices—and you enrich adolescents' lives, and you enrich your own life at the same time.

The best basis for making OK enjoying choices with young people is building the habit of making enjoying choices for yourself. Think positive thoughts about yourself and take time to do things for yourself that are renewing and positive. Life cannot be all fun and games, but life with few enjoying choices is barren and dull—and a poor model for young people.

Reinforcing Adolescents

** *Negative behavior may be extinguished by ignoring it, and positive behavior may be encouraged by reinforcing it.* That axiom is well known, but if you listen as you walk through the corridors of most schools, or as you pass many other places where adults are engaged in working with groups of young people, you may wonder whether or not that message is taken at all seriously. Voices raised in annoyance often outnumber voices raised in praise.

When you were an adolescent yourself, you may not have received much reinforcement; nevertheless you matured and learned. So, why should you be generous in praising the young people in *your* charge? As a partial answer, think about the answers you would give to these two questions: Would it have been easier for you to be enthusiastic if the adults around you·*had* given you more reinforcement? Might you have been a more involved group member if the grownups around you *had* acknowledged you more? You may not have needed a great deal of reinforcement to thrive as an adolescent, but reinforcement may make all the difference to the young people with whom you work.

J. Grossman, in an article in *American Education* some years ago (1978), told of major improvements in behavior by boys considered totally incorrigible. The treatment? The staff in the alternative school to which they had been sent used such simple, consistent actions as meeting them in the halls, greeting them with handshakes and verbal statements of welcome, and having positive expectations for their behaviors and their work. You can meet the most difficult adolescents you know with joy, warmth, positive expectations, and reinforcing comments: "Hey, Sandy, you're right on time." "Great! We're off to a good start today." "Glad to see you!"

The behaviors and traits of difficult young people may tend to run counter to the values you hold; as a consequence they may receive little reinforcement from you. However, if you are a courageous adult who genuinely cares about young people and wants to contribute to their development as much as possible, you can find ways to reinforce even difficult adolescents.

** *Often the flip side of a negative trait offers a helpful clue to qualities you might reinforce.* Three examples should make the point: You might tell an argumentative girl, "You know what you believe in and I respect that." You might say to a disruptive boy, "You make sure you get the attention you need." You might even observe to a vengeful adolescent, "You have a strong sense of justice and you're going to make sure things are made right from your point of view. That's a valuable trait." Think creatively about the young people you know; turn the behaviors that bother you upside down, and you may find ways of reaching those you thought were unreachable.

Your immediate reaction may be to question whether or not reinforcement along the lines suggested might encourage an undesirable behavior. We agree there is a risk of that. However, in many instances once young people realize that they are not *totally* disapproved, that there is *something* about them that *someone* in their world can appreciate, they moderate their unacceptable behavior.

When you are working with challenging adolescents, you may become impatient with the mixture of gradual change and backsliding that occurs, and say: "I've tried reinforcing Pat for three whole days, and nothing has changed." In this era of instant cures in print advertising, and twenty-second sound-bite political statements, it may be natural to look for quick cures, but it takes time and patience to use reinforcement well. Patterns that have taken years to build are not likely to change overnight. Nonetheless, the rewards for you and the young people with whom you work can be great.

Developing a resource of verbal and nonverbal reinforcers and using them generously increases the odds of success with young people. Few adolescents are likely to turn away from positive reinforcement that is genuinely and sincerely given: "Wow!" "Nice going." "Right!" "Thank you." "I like that." Stickers. Positive checks. Complimentary notes. Happy faces. A chance to work on a special project. A popcorn party. Felt pens. Posters. Stationery. Awards. Applause.

** *The most capable young people you know should experience your enthusiasm for their abilities and achievements. The average young people you know should experience your appreciation of their efforts. The most difficult young people you know, at the very least, should experience your interest and concern. But, if you are to achieve the highest level of effectiveness of which you are capable, all of the young people with whom you work will receive from you your enthusiasm, your appreciation, and your interest and concern.*

Humor with Adolescents

** *Humor provides an outlet for the expression of feelings, it reduces stress, and it helps to build relationships.* Humor serves a variety of functions with adolescents and others; it creates an easy sense of familiarity, it relieves tension, and it provides an outlet for the expression of feelings. The laughter that results from humor has a positive effect on blood pressure, and it facilitates oxygen exchange and the release of endorphins, the body's natural pain relievers.

A sense of humor is the trait that adolescents say they value most in teachers (Charles, 1992), and we speculate that is true of other adults with whom they come in close contact. The importance of humor cannot be overestimated, but it must be well-timed and well-used. We have suggested that enjoying choices can be overdone, and we would particularly caution against the use of sarcastic humor by adults with adolescents. Often young people feel powerless to react against sarcasm in the ways they would prefer; they may "go along to get along" instead, but the effects of sarcasm may be troublesome, nonetheless.

Goodman (1983) built a checklist for distinguishing between humor that involves *laughing with* someone, an OK enjoying choice, and *laughing at* someone, which is clearly OD. Laughing *with* someone involves caring and sympathy, it builds confidence, it involves people, it invites them to laugh, it is supportive, and it brings people together. By contrast, laughing *at* someone is based on contempt and insensitivity, it destroys confidence, it excludes some people, it offends some, and it divides people.

The potential value of humor with young people is great. It should not be destroyed or diluted with sarcasm or other OD enjoying choices.

Reinforcing Yourself: Relaxation Processes

If you are like most people, you make most of your interpersonal choices in ways that depart minimally from the midpoint on an OK/OD continuum, when you could make more genuinely positive (or negative) choices. Similarly, when it comes to the question of physical activity, due to the rush of daily life, you may spend little time in achieving a high level of activity or in truly relaxing. The systems in your body were designed to handle both highs and lows—to gear up to encounter physical danger or to pursue game for food, and then to relax. If you spend most of your time in the mid-range of tension, you are not using your capacities in the ways nature intended.

It is important to develop strategies for relaxing, and those strategies that can be used in a variety of circumstances are especially valuable.

** *Deep breathing is a most important strategy for countering stress.* When you have responded to a problem, either well or poorly, you may be able to move on more effectively to the next step or situation you must face if you take a few deep breaths and deeply exhale. Even in the face of an argument or another form of perceived difficulty, you may benefit by taking a deep breath and letting it out slowly to allow yourself an additional moment before responding.

** *Meditation is a valuable strategy for stress reduction.* Meditation involves clearing the mind by focusing on a single thought and sweeping away the interferences of life for a time. Far Eastern gurus suggest repeating a mantra—think of it, non-mystically, as a nonsense syllable or sound—that helps to clear the mind of competing thoughts. A word, a saying, a positive self-statement, or a brief prayer serves the same purpose. Try it. Clear away other thoughts and say: "Peace." "There is nothing to fear but fear itself." "I can handle this." "Oh, Lord, give me strength."

** *The simple act of closing your eyes is an important relaxation strategy.* Alpha waves signaling relaxation begin almost immediately when you shut your eyes. If a day is not going well for you, close your eyes if only for an instant, take a deep breath, clear your mind, and you may be better prepared to respond to what is before you, to meet the next group of adolescents, or to face the next challenge.

** *Fantasy can be a valuable relaxation strategy.* Fantasy involves bringing to mind an image, e. g., a coastline, mountain, or lakeside scene, with the purpose of clearing away present difficulties and gaining an inner sense of peace. A closely-related strategy, guided imagery, involves a step-by-step imaging process, for example, of getting on a magic carpet, flying away from the present, rolling all cares in a ball and tossing them over the side, arriving at a peaceful scene, engaging in renewing activities, and, eventually, returning, ready to encounter the world afresh.

** *Relaxation training is a strategy that involves alternately tensing and relaxing muscle groups in a combination of activity and relaxation.* To use relaxation training, start with the extremities, and move toward the body and head, tensing and then relaxing each muscle group two or three times. A common sequence involves the hands, arms, feet, calves, thighs, buttocks, back, neck, and facial muscles.

Relaxation is a choice all of us need to make; actually it is a matter of hundreds or thousands of choices spread over our lives. To maintain effectiveness as a person, you need to find ways to relax that fit your situation, your needs, and your personality.

Reinforcing Yourself: Activity Processes

** *If relaxation is important, its opposite, activity, is at least equally important.* The literature on physical activity suggests that all except those who are infirm need to engage in vigorous exercise that stimulates the entire cardiovascular system for twenty minutes or so per day, from three to five times a week. But for those less inclined to spend that amount of time, recent findings support what logic tells us—that *some* exercise is better than *none.*

Our bodies were designed to meet genuine dangers and challenges, then return to a state of equilibrium, once we have expended the energy necessary to encounter the emergency. In our contemporary world, stresses tend to be psychological rather than physical, but the body prepares to encounter both kinds of stress in the same way. We need to dissipate the secretions and products our systems generate to enable us to react, and we can do this best through physical exercise.

If you often feel weary and your life tends to be sedentary, it may not seem logical that exercise would help you feel more energized and powerful, but it *is* likely to do that. Note: it is important that you consult a physician before engaging in vigorous exercise, and that you build up gradually to the twenty-minute exercise goal.

Positive addiction (Glasser, 1976) offers another activity process that may be useful. Though the term addiction rightfully engenders concern, Glasser has suggested that people need to give themselves over to some kind of positive activity that absorbs a portion of their energy and time so wholeheartedly that they experience some form of withdrawal on those occasions when they cannot engage in it. He has argued that feelings of inadequacy, depression, and other problems may be overcome as a result of thorough engagement in such (alphabetically-listed) positive addictions as: bird-watching, chanting, composing, diary-keeping, gardening, knitting, needlepoint, religious faith, sewing, singing, weight-lifting, and yoga.

According to Glasser the positive addiction should be noncompetitive and freely chosen; it should engage the person for about an hour each day; it should demand a minimum of mental effort; it should not require the involvement of others; it should be engaged in without self-criticism; and the individual should experience it as contributing to his or her personal improvement.

Over time, for many individuals, work with adolescents may become a wearing experience, in part because it can absorb every waking thought. It seems appropriate, then, that you find some activity that is dissimilar to your work to give some time and energy to—whether at the level of an addiction or not. Engaging in an activity that is unlike your work should absorb some of your energy and time, give you a lift, and reduce the likelihood of burnout.

Let us explore one other dimension before we leave the topic of activity processes and enjoying choices: laughter. Proverbs (17:22) says, "A merry heart does good like a medicine; but a broken spirit dries the bones," and contemporary research validates that point of view. Nature's healing chemicals, endorphins, are released in the body through laughter and other positive actions, while negative emotions result in stress responses that have negative side effects. Norman Cousins (1979) argued the case for laughter as an antidote for many illnesses, but we do not have to wait for illness to befall us to benefit from laughter. Cousins used videotapes of Candid Camera episodes and Marx Brothers films to generate laughter as a curative for his illness; to those suggestions we would add such items

as the "Make 'em laugh" sequence in the movie, *Singin' in the Rain*. But a very different format might work for you. The key is to find *something* that works for you to lighten the load you bear and help you laugh.

You can bring joy into your life and into the lives of young people by making enjoying choices and by sharing with adolescents what brings joy to you. What works for you may work for them—and vice versa.

In What Ways are You Like These People?

Both of the examples that follow involve teachers, but the implications reach well beyond the field of education.

Kitty J.

In her personal life Kitty J. was a fun-loving person, but in her teaching she kept her enjoying choices under wraps. Shortly after her husband, Paul, walked in the door one evening she told him, "A funny thing happened at school today, and I had all I could do to keep myself from laughing." A couple of hours later she read about enjoying choices and she felt her cheeks turn red. "I'm just like that teacher I read about," she said to herself. "I could have laughed today. It wouldn't have hurt anything." Kitty discussed her discovery with Paul. "I hold back on enjoying choices with the kids because I've always thought I should, as a teacher. But I know I can get control any time I want, so I'm going to change my ways!" Kitty's students responded well when she infused more enjoyable assignments in the schedule and let her fun-loving nature come through more frequently.

How much are you like Kitty J. *is* or *was*? What changes might you wish to make in your pattern of enjoying choices in your work with adolescents or in your life?

Greg H.

We introduced Greg H. in chapter seven, a teacher known for his confidence and his friendly-firm manner—but mostly for his patience. Greg did something of a turnaround after he explored the topic of enjoying choices. "I think I'm too straightlaced and stiff," he told a colleague. "I'm going to loosen up." When he finished the extended dramatic reading in which he was engaged, he shifted to the use of humor in literature and began class daily by reading brief, humorous selections. As a result he "turned on" several of his students to reading the classics. "Gosh, I never knew good literature could be *funny*," said one of his strongest students.

How much are you like Greg H.? How might you introduce laughter and other enjoying choices in your work with young people?

Ideas You Can Use with Individuals or Groups

** *Plan for enjoying choices.* Find ways to incorporate enjoying choices in your work with young people, either as you meet with them, or infused in your plans, or as rewards. Your work with them might well include activities that are fun. A mathematics teacher has an extensive card file of puzzles and problems and uses them as warmup activities for each class session. With some advanced planning, nearly any effort with young people can be made enjoyable.

** *Take time for yourself.* Spend some time each day doing something you enjoy: recreational reading, exercise, woodworking, needlepoint, and so forth. William Glasser has suggested that each of us should develop a Positive Addiction—something we do regularly in which we can feel involved and absorbed. Take the view that you are a person of worth and you deserve some time for renewal for yourself.

** *Reinforce young people.* Use positive reinforcement generously with adolescents.

** *Reinforce yourself.* Focus on all the little things you can do that you appreciate. Build a list of such items, starting with the simplest of all actions: breathe. Contemplate and savor the many simple, but wonderful things you are able to do—instead of focusing on what is out of your reach, what you cannot achieve.

Critical Incident

Crash! A short time ago you overheard a boy in your group refer to some adult or other as behaving like "an old grouch today." You are suspicious that the reference was to you—so you resolve to turn things around. Several minutes ago you warned Steve about tilting back his chair as he worked. "CRASH!" You see Steve flat on his back, looking up at you and laughing, so you know he is not hurt.

What would you be likely to say right now? What is an alternative *OK* enjoying choice you *could* make?

Sharing Choices and Communication Skills with Adolescents

Section F of Chapter 16 presents two sharing suggestions under the following titles: *Introducing enjoying choices. Promoting relaxation in adolescents.*

Journal Entry

Date your entry and label it *Ch. 8, Enjoying choices.* You may begin your entry by reflecting on the ideas presented in the chapter, *you, your enjoying choices, reinforcement, relaxation, and activity processes.* You may also use the end-of-chapter activities or the key words on page 31 to further cue you in writing your entry.

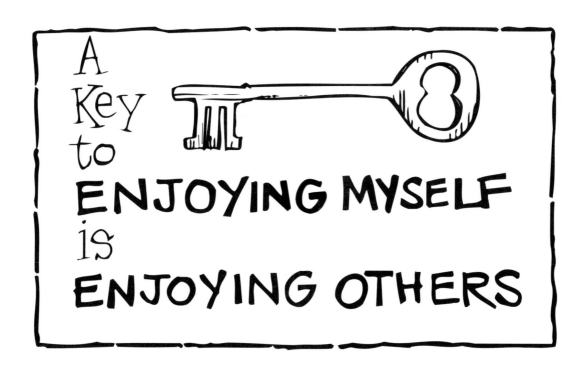

A Key to ENJOYING MYSELF is ENJOYING OTHERS

9
Sorrowing Choices

** Sorrowing choices involve a wide range of expressions of negative feelings, with the most-OK expressions of sorrowing choices involving straightforward statements of feelings.

** Since people in our society are not socialized to accept the need for sorrowing choices, others may not see our sorrowing choices as OK; as a consequence, it is important that we make our sorrowing choices in ways that are at least OK for ourselves.

** In work with adolescents, negative feelings, and therefore sorrowing choices, are inevitable. Effective ways of coping with negative feelings include owning frustrations, sharing concerns, leading discussions concerning problems, sharing observations, stating what is known, and using structured sorrowing choices.

** I-messages and you-messages are interrelated choices. I-messages are best sent when the individual owns the problem; you-messages are best sent when the other person owns the problem. I-messages are sorrowing choices; you-messages generally involve caring.

Exploring Sorrowing Choices

** *Whenever you act directly on your negative feelings you make sorrowing choices.*

Heaving a deep sigh.

Shaking your head and scowling.

"Dad just called. Mom is not doing well."

"I guess today's just not my day."

"That's the dumbest thing I've ever seen you do."

Inevitably, you and the young people you work with encounter frustrating situations, and negative feelings result. The feelings are not necessarily problems in themselves, but what you or they do with negative feelings may be problematic. Adolescents may handle their negative feelings in ways that go beyond the examples cited above, that is: sighing, head-shaking, stating what is wrong, being philosophical, or berating. Their choices may include such behaviors as scapegoating, vandalizing, getting drunk, or even lying, cheating, vandalizing or stealing. As Charles (1992) suggested, young people often (erroneously) feel that hurting others makes up for feeling hurt. All of these sorrowing choices are motivated by underlying negative feelings—most often including negative self-feelings.

Whatever people do with their negative feelings, except order someone to do something (a ruling choice), is likely to involve sorrowing choices. People may want to pretend their negative feelings don't exist, but they *will* act upon them in some way.

Is it possible for your choices to be OK when you are upset, frustrated, or angry?

Yes. At least for yourself.

Although your sorrowing choices come from your internal feelings, they often affect others. In the moment it may feel good to "read the riot act" to an adolescent, but if you look at that choice later, coolly and calmly, will it still be genuinely OK with you? Your answer is likely to depend on whether or not you have helped the relationship.

Most of us make choices we do not like in the moment *or* later—but we have not learned to make more effective sorrowing choices, because we have not seen people around us doing so. Many of the models we see about us for responding to frustrations and concerns are OD models. We see people feeling hurt and troubled—complaining or holding in their complaints—or striking out at young people, their loved ones, strangers, or the world. We see around us many models of miserableness and meanness.

OK Sorrowing Choices

** *OK sorrowing choices are those we use to cope straightforwardly with the sadnesses and frustrations we inevitably face.* If something is troubling you and you sort through your feelings to determine what the source of the frustration is, you are making an OK sorrowing choice. If you write in a letter or a journal, share with a friend, or talk to a counselor about what is troubling you, without rancor or blame, you are making an OK sorrowing choice. If you tell an individual or a group of young people of your upset, briefly and straightforwardly, you are making an OK sorrowing choice.

Two questions are important to ask about any sorrowing choice: (1) Is the choice OK now, and will it feel OK to you later? (2) Is the choice OK now, and will it be OK later, with others around you? Society seems to tell us we are weak unless we work through problems ourselves without "burdening" others. But our looks and our behaviors give us away. An example may make that clear.

Dad, in a traditional household, comes in the door from a bad day at work, slams his briefcase or lunchpail into the corner, throws himself in a chair, and snaps the newspaper up in front of his face. Mom immediately worries that she left something important out of his lunch. Son feels anxious because he didn't put gas in the car after using it. Sis worries that she may have left a rollerskate on the stairs. And even Fido and Tabby spot the steam issuing from dad's nose and ears and slink behind a sofa or chair. Dad's "protecting" others leads each of them to wonder, "*Now*, what did I do?"

It is often far more helpful to share a problem with others than it is to leave them guessing or feeling responsible when they are not. If dad said, "Just give me a chance to cool down. Things were terrible at work today," concern *and* relief would wash over all the members of the household. Similarly, you might say to your friend or to a group of young people, "I'm feeling bad today, and it has nothing to do with you. A relative of mine is sick." That should help your friend or your group to understand your harried look, and they will not assume that they are responsible for your state of mind.

All of us have been socialized to hold in our negative feelings, so there are no guarantees that others will see our sorrowing choices as truly OK—though others are likely to accept our straightforward statement of sadness as being *more* OK than meanness or miserableness. Truly, we need our own acceptance of the sorrowing choices we make more than we need the acceptance of others. Unfortunately, society will not develop acceptance of our sorrowing choices just because we wish it would.

** *It is most important for us to make sorrowing choices that are OK for ourselves.*

Owning Your Frustrations

You can make caring, ruling, enjoying, and thinking/working choices for yourself *and* for others, but you can only make sorrowing choices for yourself. When you respond to another's sadness or frustration you are making caring choices; when you take on the feelings of another person you are making sorrowing choices for yourself.

With sorrowing choices, the important question is: how might you best handle the inevitable frustrations and concerns that come your way?

When you face problems and are frustrated, set time aside to focus on your concerns. Overcoming difficulties requires recognizing them and owning your part in them, distinguishing between what is real and imagined, sorting out what you can change and what is unchangeable, and determining what is temporary and what is permanent. You cannot make others' choices for them, but you can make better choices for yourself—if you focus on your concerns and avoid the temptation to place the blame unnecessarily on others, or wallow in the problem yourself.

Sharing Your Concerns

** *In working through your frustrations, it often helps to talk over your concerns with someone else.* You may want to ask the other person *not* to make suggestions, but rather to just listen and allow you to let off steam, so you may try to figure out for yourself what is really the matter and what you can do about it.

It is often a good idea to mention to young people and others the concerns you have. A brief, straightforward comment is generally best. "I'm a little distracted today because of some news I received in the mail." If you choose, explain a bit more, "A trip I was planning to take this summer has been cancelled." Then stop. A statement that explains your concern reduces the likelihood that others will worry that they are somehow responsible for causing a reaction that has nothing to do with them.

Leading Discussions of Group Problems

Some matters that concern you relate to the groups you encounter. Let us suppose that you sense a lot of conflict in a group of yours. An in-group and a small out-group often bicker. Also, two minority boys and a handicapped girl are not well accepted.

You may want to announce a meeting of the group for a specific time in the near future, sharing briefly what you have in mind: "There are a number of matters I am troubled about concerning this group, so tomorrow I'm setting aside thirty minutes for us to talk. Frankly, I'm concerned about the bickering that goes on, the cliques we seem to have, and the treatment of people who in some way are different. I also want to hear about any issues you believe we have, and what you think about how we work together. My purpose is not to scold or blame anyone for anything. I'm just hoping to see if we can figure out how we might get along better with one another."

Setting a time at a future date encourages prior thought on the part of those involved. Stating the purpose in a concerned way reinforces the point that it is not your intention to be punitive.

You may begin the meeting by asking a member of the group to list the issues of greatest concern on chart paper as they are mentioned, then continue by exploring each item on the list. Two questions you might ask are: What do you think and feel about each of these issues? What do *you* do that creates problems in the group? Later, you may want to ask: What choices could *you* make that would help improve relationships here? Discussing difficulties in this way gives support to group members who choose to change their behaviors, and it minimizes or avoids tale-telling and blaming.

Glasser (1969) suggested that teachers might wish to employ any of three types of class meetings. The example above fits his designation of a *social problem-solving meeting*; his other suggestions include *educational diagnostic meetings*—in which problems involving curriculum and activities are explored, and *open-ended meetings*, in which a wide variety of topics of concern to class members are discussed. The former and the latter are applicable in non-school settings as well.

Sharing Your Observations

** *When what you observe worries you, it is often best to state your worry directly.* A boy who has often taken others' things is reaching into someone else's coat pocket. A girl has what looks like a crib note under a test paper. Instead of scolding or ranting and raving—OD sorrowing choices—we suggest you simply state what you have observed. When you do that you make a thinking/working choice (more on that kind of choice in a subsequent chapter): "I see you have gotten something out of Gerry's pocket." "I see a piece of paper under your test."

Perhaps another boy made a request: "My coat's under yours; when you get your candy bar, would you get mine, too?" The "crib note" may only say: "Do the best you can. That's all you can do." We know adults who have jumped to conclusions about adolescent's behaviors in those precise situations; they accused young people of stealing or cheating, and were themselves reprimanded later.

If you state your observations, then stop and listen, you leave yourself maximum freedom. Once you understand the situation better you can follow-up with whatever action seems necessary. On the other hand, if you immediately scold or put negative labels on the behaviors of young people, you harm your relationships with them and create unnecessary problems for both them and yourself.

Stating What You Know

Confession is good for the soul, but little is accomplished by forced confessions.

** *If the evidence is overwhelming, instead of demanding a confession, it is better to state what you know in as few words as possible*: "I saw you reach into Gene's bookbag a while ago and take something out; now Gene's calculator is missing." Wait briefly for a response, and if necessary, add: "I'd like you to tell me where it is now." If the matter is less clear, state what you know for certain, or indicate what you have heard from other sources: "Several basketballs are missing and a boy said he saw you unlocking the equipment room yesterday afternoon around four o'clock." Wait for a response, then, if appropriate, add: "I would like you to tell me what you know about the basketballs."

Using Structured Sorrowing Choices

You and the young people in your charge will find *some* way to express frustrations and sadnesses, either through an OK outlet, or through meanness or miserableness.

** *One way you can express your negative feelings is through structured sorrowing choices*—a suggestion offered by Betty McComb, a Florida counselor.

1. State the person's name.
2. Say, "When you. . ." and specify what the person has said or done that troubles you.
3. Say, "I feel. . ." or "I felt. . ." and specify your feelings.
4. "As a result I want (wanted) to. . ." and complete the statement.

Pat,

when you yell (yelled) at me for
forgetting that letter,
I feel (felt) really lousy.
(Then, if you choose, add —)
As a result I want (wanted) to
go bury my head in the sand.

Be sure to follow *I feel* with a *feeling word* in step three: *upset, annoyed,* and so forth. Not: I feel *like,* or I feel *that...,* since *I feel like* is likely to be followed by a threatening statement, and *I feel that* is often followed by a statement of blame.

Note that this structured approach can be used to share positive feelings as well, e.g., "Pat, when you smile at me like that, I feel really happy." "Gerry, when you lent me a pen without my even asking, I felt really good."

Using I-Messages

In his books on parent and teacher effectiveness training (1970, 1974), Thomas Gordon has suggested that adults should determine who "owns" the problem that exists in a given moment. If "I"—as the adult in the situation—own the problem, I may beneficially use an "I-message," beginning with: *I feel... I think... I am... I want... I know... I wonder...,* but avoiding: *I feel like..., I feel that...* or, *I feel that you...* (Note that in this section, to avoid confusion about "I-messages" and "you-messages," we have shifted our language to first person.)

If, for example, I walk into a group one minute late and find the room in total disorder with young people running around the room and yelling, when I have recently briefed them on what they should be doing at such a time, I own the problem. I may want to send a sorrowing choice in the form of an I-message. My I-messages might include: "*I feel* annoyed that I can't be a minute late and have you settle down without me." "*I think* I've made it clear in the past how you can begin if I'm ever delayed; please get to it now." "*I want* to be able to trust you to get underway without me if I am detained." "*I know* we've discussed how you should proceed if I am late."

Gordon has suggested that adults in roles of responsibility with young people should take the view: I have a right to my feelings, my needs, and my thoughts. Implicit also is the view that given the ages of the young people I work with, I have a right to expect reasonably mature behavior if I approach the matter appropriately and fairly.

Using You-Messages

When the adolescent (colleague, supervisor, friend, spouse) "owns" the problem, I may appropriately use a "you-message," beginning with: *You feel... You think... You want.. You wonder...,* but avoiding: *You **should**...* OR: *You **are**...* since I may be tempted to follow those beginnings by giving orders or stating a negative label.

Many you-messages are reflections of feeling and content, which we have discussed as caring choices, so here we place the emphasis on I-messages, which are most often sorrowing choices.

Reversing Habit

Gordon has suggested that adults in responsible roles often tend to use I-messages and you-messages in reverse with young people. That is, when "I" have a problem with an individual or a group I may be tempted to blame, attack, or issue orders: "Now you folks stop..." "You are the worst group..." "Don't you ever do that again."

By contrast, when the adolescent has a concern, I may, from force of habit, tend to suggest, judge, or probe: "I think..." "I want you to..." "I'm sure your parents will understand if you..." "I'd like to know..."

From time to time, it may be a good idea to play a modified version of the old button-button, who's-got-the-button game. The modification is: problem-problem, who's-got-the-problem. If "I" have the problem, I should send an I-message. If "you" have the problem, I should send a you-message, instead of the reverse.

In a related point, Ginott (1971) suggested using what he called sane rather than insane messages with young people. A sane message might be, "This is quiet time. It needs to be silent so people can get their work done." An insane message might be, "You are so rude. You have no consideration for those who are trying to work." In sane messages the situation is addressed through OK choices; in insane messages the character of the person involved is attacked, and OD choices abound.

In your work with young people you will inevitably encounter many situations that produce negative feelings in you. You can respond to such situations in a great variety of ways, some of which may be characterized as OK sorrowing choices. Options include owning frustrations, sharing concerns, leading discussions of class problems, sharing observations, stating what you know, and using structured sorrowing choices and I- or you-messages—all sane ways of approaching problems.

In What Ways are You Like These People?

Tony J.

For many years, Tony J. did what he believed was expected of him by "protecting" his wife, Jan, his children, and the young people he was assigned as a social worker, from any difficulty he faced. When Jan gave Tony an ultimatum, "You come with me to see a counselor or I get a divorce lawyer," it was a shock to Tony. The message came through to him loud and clear from Jan and the counselor: "You try to hold in what's bothering you, but everyone knows something is wrong. Your anger and frustration show despite your efforts to hide them. You leave others wondering what you're upset about, and whether or not they're to blame."

It took Tony time to learn to share his feelings and be more open with his family, but he gradually changed in those two ways. Eventually he realized that he could also use some of the same openness he was achieving at home with the adolescents in his groups. From time to time young people hear him share his feelings; for example, "Take it easy, please. Things aren't going well with my dad just now, and since I have that on my mind, I can't handle much clowning around."

How much are you like Tony J. *is* or *was*? What changes might you want to make in your sorrowing choices?

Ann R.

In her work in juvenile justice, Ann R. often tried to get young people to own up to their infractions. "Why do you think I wanted to talk to you today?" she often asked—because that was a question she had heard others employ. She thought the suggestion, "state what you know," was an interesting contrast to the manipulative approach she used, since such questions often seemed to arouse defensiveness in adolescents. An opportunity came her way to try out that idea and she said, "Rex, I notice that the signature on the community service sheet that says you've finished your hours doesn't look like Mr. Wallace's other signatures." Rex opened up, admitted that he'd faked some of the hours, and talked about how far behind he was at school and the pressure he was under at home. When Ann reflected on that event, she realized that she preferred being honest with Rex rather than playing a guessing game.

How much are you like Ann R. *is* or *was*? What changes might you want to make in your patterns of sorrowing choices with young people?

Fred W.

As he began his teaching career, Fred W. had the opportunity to attend a workshop conducted by Thomas Gordon. Fred found I-messages and you-messages intriguing, but he continued to follow his habitual patterns of asking questions and giving orders. In his third year of teaching, he had a junior high school class that troubled him badly. He dug out his workshop notes, reread several chapters in Gordon's *Teacher effectiveness training* (1974), and resolved to give I-messages and you-messages a try. He felt unsure of himself and vulnerable as he told his class one day, when he couldn't get them started, "I feel frustrated when it takes so long for you to get into the work each day and we get so little done. I'm concerned that you're not developing a good base for future studies and that it'll just get harder for you in the years ahead." Miracles didn't occur—they rarely do—but others hushed a classmate who made a wisecrack; Fred thanked the group for their cooperation, seized the moment, and began the day's lesson.

How much are you like Fred W.? How could you use I-messages and you- messages to advantage in your work with young people?

Ideas You Can Use with Individuals or Groups

** ***Be open about your negative feelings.*** If change in this direction seems relevant for you, make a resolve that you will share with those closest to you those matters that trouble you—at first, especially, when the issue does not involve them; perhaps later, even when it does. Mention straightforwardly and briefly to family members, close friends, and young people what you are feeling negative about, rather than holding in your concern.

** ***Make OK sorrowing choices in your work with young people.*** Be alert to the opportunities you have to share your concerns, lead discussions of group problems, share your observations, state what you know, and make structured sorrowing (and enjoying) choices with the young people in your charge.

** ***Employ I-messages and you-messages when appropriate.*** As opportunities occur in your communication with adolescents and others, take a moment to decide who has the problem—you or the other person—and carefully formulate a suitable I-message or you-message. Take the risk of vulnerability to gain the advantages of openness and deeper communication.

Critical Incident

Rob. The setting Peters and Waterman explore in their book *In Search of Excellence* (1982) is that of business and industry, but an important message they offer is relevant to other settings as well. Not only do we *like* to think of ourselves as winners, as those writers suggest, but most people *do* think of themselves in this way. Excellent companies (and excellent leaders with youth) reinforce that notion.

Rob Sanderson is a young person about whom you have concern. You are aware that you have tended to overlook him when your group meets because he does whatever he can to blend into the woodwork and not be noticed. You believe that he sees himself as not very capable or lovable and you resolve to do what you can to help him think of himself as a winner. You have been thinking about Rob when he tiptoes in to pick up his jacket. He whispers, "I forgot this," and starts toward the door.

What would you be most likely to say in that moment? What might be a better initial statement? Subsequently, in what ways (and with what words) might you show interest in Rob and help him feel good about himself? At some point you might want to share your concern for Rob openly through an I-message, a sorrowing choice. What might you say if you decide to do that?

Sharing Choices and Communication Skills with Adolescents

Section G of Chapter 16 presents three sharing suggestions under the following titles: *Exploring sorrowing choices. Structured sorrowing choices. I-messages and you-messages.*

Journal Entry

Date your entry and label it *Ch. 9, Sorrowing choices.* You may begin your entry by reflecting on the ideas presented in the chapter, *you, your sorrowing choices, structured sorrowing choices,* and *I- and you-messages.* You may also use the end-of-chapter activities or the key words on page 31 to further cue you in writing your entry.

THAT THE BIRDS OF WORRY AND CARE FLY OVER YOUR HEAD — THIS YOU CANNOT PREVENT

BUT THAT THEY BUILD NESTS IN YOUR HAIR — THIS YOU CAN PREVENT
— a Chinese Proverb

10
Anger and Grief as Sorrowing Choices

** The feeling of anger is inevitable, but the responses we make to angry feelings are learned, and new response patterns can be learned. Constructive anger management involves recognizing anger as anger, interpreting events in ways that do not hook the ego, and selecting responses that avoid verbal or physical aggression.

** Many young people live in environments in which angry responses appear to be necessary. Youth leaders who encounter angry adolescents need to understand their wants, and have available a variety of possible responses they are ready to use.

** Loss is an inevitable aspect of living, and grief is a normal response to loss. The losses young people experience may be viewed by others as minor or catastrophic, but even what are viewed as minor losses may overwhelm insecure adolescents. The grieving process may include anger, denial, depression, and eventually, re-engagement. The grieving young person needs permission to grieve and encouragement to talk.

Anger

Leaders with youth inevitably feel anger, and they encounter angry adolescents. We will look at adolescent anger subsequently; we concentrate first on the anger youth leaders may feel on occasion—but we encourage you to think of the points we make in both sections as applying to all angry people.

** *Anger as an emotion is neither good nor bad; how you act on your anger is determined in part by how you were socialized—what you learned about how to react when you felt angry.* As you were growing up you may have learned that anger and its verbal expression were tolerated, even encouraged, but physical aggression, except in ritualized settings (sports events or martial arts classes), was looked down upon; if so, you were expected to settle your differences without resorting to physical aggression. If you grew up in another environment you might have learned that physical aggression was necessary for survival.

You need to be aware of your own responses to anger and what you learned about the place of anger in human interactions. Take a moment and think about a situation in which your parents might have approved of your expressing your anger. That may tell you something about where, when, how, why, and to whom it was all right for you to express anger. Now think about the young people with whom you work and what they have been taught. Their learnings may have differed sharply from yours.

The Functions of Anger

Novaco (1975) conceived of anger as serving six functions, alone or in combination—here we look at those functions and how they may affect you.

Anger as energizing. Anger gets you ready to fight or flee when you face danger.

Anger as disrupting. Anger interferes with information processing and attention. You find yourself unable to concentrate and cannot simply go about business as usual; you feel a strong need to respond in some way before you can come back to psychological equilibrium.

Anger as motivating the expression of negative feelings. Anger drives you to express your irritation with the one who has done something you perceive as negative.

Anger as defense against vulnerability. Anger substitutes for anxiety in this function. Rather than allow whatever is threatening to command your attention and lead you to feel vulnerable, you focus the feeling externally so that you do not have to deal with the ego threat involved. If that happens you are likely to get angry rather than let the real issue come to the surface.

Anger as a learned behavior. In your culture you may have learned to respond to any kind of threat with an antagonistic attitude and physical aggression. In that event, any feeling you can construe as anger triggers a single hostile response; no matter what happens, you lash out. This pattern may not be typical of you or of those who work with youth, but you need to understand it when it appears in others.

Anger as an indication that the event involved is a provocation. You see the event as a provocation; this serves as a cue to act in the ways in which you cope with stress. This function of anger can be used effectively to help you to maintain objectivity; it can also alert you to approach the event or concern as a matter for problem-solving.

What Triggers Your Anger?

Many of your friends and relatives may know what to say or do to bring forth an angry response from you. You trust them not to do this maliciously, just as you refrain from pushing their buttons. Similarly, soon after you begin to work with a group of young people, they know what pushes your buttons, too. They may not be so kind as to refrain from doing those things. Take a minute to think about what the important people in your life do that really sets off your anger. Now think about how you respond to each of those provocations. What would happen if you responded similarly to young people? What other responses could you substitute for the ones you believe you need to change—with people of any age?

Constructive Anger Management

*** There are three keys to constructive anger management: (1) recognize your anger as anger when it occurs, (2) interpret provoking events in a way that is non-ego-threatening, and (3) take charge of the situation and select a strategy that avoids either verbal or physical aggression.***

Let us assume that you are about to call a group of young people to order when Greg, one of the more aggressive males in the group, walks into the room, grabs another boy's things, and throws them to the floor with a crash that startles everyone present. You feel your neck muscles getting tense, a sure sign of anger for you.

Recognizing your anger (#1 above) you immediately begin monitoring your own behavior. In order to deal with the situation you must interpret it (#2 above). In an instant you consider several possible interpretations, each of which leads you to different choices: (A) "This is a carryover from something that happened earlier between Greg and Sam." This interpretation may lead you to a calm investigation of what is and has been going on. (B) "Greg is a real jerk, I resent having him in my group, I shouldn't have to put up with this." This interpretation might lead you to exclude

Greg from the room, knowing that he will be back tomorrow with the same load of anger and that you will have the same load of resentment. (C) "Greg surely has problems, I wonder what I can do to help him." This might lead you to request that Greg step outside the room to talk with you or see you at a later time. (D) "Greg doesn't know who's boss in here, I better straighten him out." Your possible responses might include a raised voice, verbal abuse, and the threat of physical punishment or exclusion from the group. (E) "Greg is incredibly angry, I wonder why. Well, whatever the reason, I need to help him regain control of himself. After he settles down maybe we can sort out what is going on here." A non-punitive time-out of some sort might be a possible response; you might ask Greg to take his place in a far corner of the room, make a quiet comment, or encourage Greg to get himself together. (F) "Greg acts like he's drunk or on drugs." A possible response would be to isolate him from the others for their protection and get close enough to him to make a more thorough assessment before deciding how to get him out of the room. A more personal interpretation might be: (G) "Everyone in the group is looking at me to control Greg. If I'd been a better leader, Greg wouldn't be acting this way." This kind of ego-involved interpretation is likely to lead you to act in an aggressive or defensive way.

These are several possible interpretations of what is going on. Notice that each interpretation leads logically to one or more responses. *** To a large extent, the quality of your response is determined by the interpretation you put on the behavior.*** Positive interpretations tend to lead to effective choices, and the converse is true.

Consider the interpretations you might have made. Which would have shown that your ego was hooked and that you felt threatened, anxious, or vulnerable? Which of the interpretations would have shown you and the group that you had matters under control? How would a supervisor or administrator be likely to evaluate each possible response? Which responses would be best for your long term goals with both Greg and the group? Constructive anger management means that you make an interpretation that does not put your ego at risk, and that you select a response in which you take charge of the situation without using verbal or physical aggression (#3 above).

It is not easy to maintain composure under provocation. An American soldier who had been tortured in a POW camp, returned, went to college, and became a teacher. He commented that it was easier to undergo torture for refusal to give information than to remain calm the first time a student decided to make his life miserable. Nonetheless, making an interpretation that allows you to remain calm with young people has several advantages. (1) You *feel* much more in control of what is going on. (2) You *are* much more in control and others feel more comfortable knowing you are in control. (3) You are more likely to make choices that work both now and later. (4) You are less vulnerable to the manipulations of adolescents if you *choose* how to respond to your anger. (5) The feeling that you are in control in the face of anger-provoking stimuli is self-reinforcing; the more often you experience it, the easier it is to maintain control.

If you are not skilled at interpreting behaviors so that they do not hook your ego, or in maintaining control, how do you learn to do those things? Through becoming aware of your choices, through anticipation (you know some behaviors will be repeated, you just do not know when they will reappear), and through practice—in a safe environment where the consequences of your actions are minimized.

The Realities of Adolescent Anger

The key point regarding anger is this: ** *Anger as an emotion is neither good nor bad, and how people act on their anger depends in large measure on how they were socialized.* Many leaders with youth grew up in a culture where they learned that verbal expressions of anger are appropriate, and physical expressions of anger are looked down upon. By contrast, a large and increasing proportion of young people are being reared in circumstances where they have learned that anger and physical aggression are necessary to their survival.

** *When the adult holds one view of anger and adolescents hold another, misunderstanding is almost inevitable.* An idealistic middle class teacher in a ghetto school some years ago nearly lost her job when she tried to teach her students that fighting was wrong. Parents knew their neighborhood and wanted their children to be able to take care of themselves; they saw the teacher's attempts to change attitudes toward physical aggression as a threat to their offsprings' survival.

It is vital that any exploration of anger involving adolescents should emphasize the value of developing a variety of responses for living in a complex world, where one set of rules may apply on the street and another at school or in the workplace. Most young people learn readily that street language is not acceptable in other settings, and that they must exercise greater self-control with one parent or adult leader than with others. They can also learn that expression of anger is powerful in some circumstances, and that selecting a feeling other than anger to express is powerful in other circumstances.

One obvious characteristic of adolescents is that they lack experience in the world. This lack of experience is accepted in some arenas, e.g., subject matter; it is a goal of education to give young people experiences they have not had. Adolescents also lack experience in managing emotional responses; their choices of possible responses to

anger are affected by their limited experiences, and they may well be unaware that a wide range of choices is available to them when they feel angry.

When people talk about the favorite teachers they had as children, they rarely mention the subject matter those teachers explored with them; instead, they talk about teachers who helped them expand their horizons so that they could function more effectively in their world. The reality is the same concerning adults in other contexts who work with adolescents. *You* can help young people develop a broader range of responses for coping with the anger they inevitably feel from time to time. Do that and you help them expand their awareness of choices in other aspects of their lives as well.

Helping Adolescents Control their Responses to Anger

How can you help angry adolescents to gain control over their responses to anger? Think about the six functions of anger we introduced at the beginning of this chapter. Consider adolescents' perceptions. Do they see the situation as one involving physical threat (1)? Must they disrupt ongoing behaviors (their own or others') in order to cope (2)? Do they perceive it as necessary to express negative feelings to others in order to take care of themselves (3)? Do they feel ego-threatened (4)? Are they behaving antagonistically because that is the only response they have learned to use when provocation occurs (5)? Or have they coolly determined that this situation is one that demands coping strategies (6)?

When you work with angry young people (parents, supervisors, or colleagues), it is easy to feel threatened, angry, or overwhelmed. When you understand how the others' anger is functioning you are in a better position to generate responses that will reduce the threat they feel and defuse the anger so the problem can be worked out. Furthermore, if you have an understanding of what others want at such times, you can respond more effectively than if you get overly ego-involved.

We recommend that you develop a deep sense of awareness of the possible wants of angry people so that you can figure out how best to respond. According to Myers and Nance (1986),

1. *Angry people want to be heard.* They often believe that nobody sees their point of view or even cares. ** *Listen!* Use all of the caring communication skills you have learned, but especially—listen.

2. *Angry people want someone to notice their feelings.* Don't try to talk them out of feeling angry; people who are angry can't *not* feel angry until something else changes—at least until someone listens. ** *Acknowledge that they are angry,* and that they may feel hurt, mistreated, or used.

3. *Angry people want someone to see their point of view.* Find a way to agree with them. ** *Agree that the situation they are in is rotten or that the rules often do create inequities.* This helps the angry person understand that you are on his or her side in trying to find a solution to the problem, it reduces your own feeling of threat, and it puts you in a problem-solving frame of mind.

4. *Angry people want help in figuring out what caused the anger,* ultimately, if not immediately. ** *Use your communication skills to facilitate a clear definition of the problem from the angry person's perspective and from yours.* Negotiate if necessary to come to a common definition of the problem.

5. *Angry people want respect.* Evaluate each strategy from the perspective of each person involved, select a strategy that everyone can agree to try, and make a commitment to implement it. ** *Discuss each person's satisfaction or dissatisfaction with the process.* If there is dissatisfaction, deal with it. If things seem to be workable, make a specific appointment to explore whether or not the tactic is working. If not, cycle back through suggestions 1 through 4 above.

6. *Angry people do not process information well.* They may need structure, or they may need more information than they have to work on the problem. ** *After the strongest feelings have subsided, you may want to collect and share information*—to define the problem more clearly and to list strategies for solving the problem.

7. *Angry people need to know that they are still accepted.* This is probably more critical with adolescents than with adults. ** *End the discussion on a positive note; thank those involved for being cooperative about solving the problem;* encourage them to return to discuss with you whether or not things are working out; offer to find someone else to help with the problem if it has not been worked out. In essence, demonstrate your respect for, and acceptance of, those involved—one more time.

8. *Angry people need to know that your effort was sincere.* Keep the followup appointment. Don't assume that no news is good news. ** *If adolescents do not keep the followup appointment, call, visit, or write a note to demonstrate your commitment to the process, and your sincere concern for them.* Many young people will not initiate a second contact if they believe the first one did not work well. If you initiate another contact, you may be able to demonstrate to them that perseverance has merit. If things *have* worked out well, you have the opportunity to reinforce the efforts they have made to solve the problem. You *might* even receive a thank-you.

** *Young people must function in a complex world in which simplistic, knee-jerk, angry responses may work for* them part of the time, but will increase their difficulties in the long run. For the time being, they may be forgiven their adolescent angry responses, but down the road they need to have in hand more effective skills in order to function as workers, spouses, friends, and parents. You do young people a great favor if you help them explore what it is they want, and if you assist them to extend the range of the responses they might use when they are angry.

Grief

** *Grief is a normal response to loss.* What might seem to be a serious loss to one person might be a minor loss to others, and vice versa. The death or illness of a family member, the divorce of parents, and leaving a community are among the triggers for a potentially serious sense of loss in most adolescents. Some young people experience grief reactions to losses that adults may not consider very important: loss of a pet, failure to be accepted by a group or make the honor roll, or the breakup of a teen romance. When young people are grieving, their performance in all arenas often deteriorates. The adult who understands adolescent grief may be able to recognize when additional help is needed, ease the pressures on the grieving person, and minimize negative effects on performance and on the developmental process.

** *Adolescents have been identified as the age group most at risk for serious grief reactions* (Rando, 1984; Wolfelt, 1986). This is due in large measure to developmental characteristics that tend to interfere with grief recovery.

(1) Most adolescents are striving to become less dependent on their parents physically, psychologically, and emotionally; when they experience a severe loss, they may feel helpless and childish, but they may not allow themselves to seek support from a parent or other adult for fear of losing some of their hard-won independence.

(2) Adolescents tend to be sensitive or oversensitive to social acceptability. They want to appear grown up, but they may lack mature models of grieving behaviors. Their self-consciousness may inhibit their expression of grief and their need to seek support. In a grieving family, they may find others' dependence on them frightening, since they themselves feel so needy. As a consequence they may suppress their need for grieving and prolong the recovery process.

(3) Adolescents may be prone to self-pity, believing they are the only ones who have ever suffered such a loss. They may also be secretive about their feelings. Thus they may withdraw into themselves and prolong or put off the grieving process until it cannot be put off any longer.

(4) Adolescents who have experienced a period of normal rebelliousness just prior to the loss of a significant adult may feel guilty about the relationship, or blame themselves for the loss. Their intellectual self may tell them that blaming themselves does not make sense, and as a result, they may fail to deal with their feeling self, which will not let go of the guilt—and that only prolongs the period of deepest grief.

(5) Adolescents who have lost parents or siblings to death often report two or more periods of mourning—the first immediately after the loss and the second three months to a year or more later. At their particular developmental stage, adolescents may be able to tolerate just so much grief, so they "shut down" emotionally for a while to protect themselves. They may believe that they are finished with the grief, and may be shocked some time later to discover that their grief engulfs them again.

A book that many adolescents find useful is *Teenagers face to face with bereavement* by Gravelle and Haskins (1989). It was written by teens in a grief group. Each tells his or her story of grief resolution, offering hope to others that they, too, can heal.

Those who work with adolescents are in a unique position to observe how young people who have experienced loss are handling the grieving process. For many adolescents, a youth leader or favorite teacher may be the only adult to whom they believe they can turn for understanding and help. Those who encounter adolescents daily need to be aware of the variety of feelings and delayed reactions that are possible, and remain alert to signs of unexpressed grief and withdrawal. Feelings and reactions need to be acknowledged as normal for adolescents, because so many of them fear not being "normal." Note that persons other than counselors or psychologists may need to make referrals with young people if their grief seems severe or extends over a long period of time.

Grief Recovery

Elisabeth Kubler-Ross's (1969) report of her work with people who knew they were dying is still the best known model for understanding grief and loss. She proposed five stages of response to an impending death: *denial*, *anger*, *bargaining*, *depression*, and *acceptance*. These stages have been applied to the adjustment to various other losses as well, but many experts in grief resolution see the process somewhat differently for those who survive a loss.

When Kubler-Ross (1969) described the "stages" of grief, it was not her intention to impose an external structure on the grief process. Alan Wolfelt (1986) suggested that *themes* might be a more appropriate word than *stages* because each person's grief unfolds in its own unique way, and all of the themes of grief are present all of the time. The more appropriate analogy might be that of a stew. Sometimes a slice of carrot bubbles to the surface, next a chunk of potato, then a bit of onion. When the pot of grief is bubbling, sometimes anger surfaces, sometimes fear, sometimes happy memories, and more often than not some combination of all of the possibilities bubbles to the top.

Whether the view is taken that stages or themes characterizes grief, there are three tasks that must be accomplished in the recovery process (Parkes and Weiss, 1983): *intellectual recognition and explanation of the loss*—this involves moving past denial and developing an explanation of how the loss happened; *emotional acceptance of the loss*—this is accomplished through repeated review of the loss until it is no longer too painful to face the remembrances; and *assumption of a new identity*—this involves confronting and accepting the difference between the world with, and the world without, whatever or whomever was lost. Assumption of a new identity is often slow and difficult. A "thought mistake," accidentally including in plans whomever or whatever was lost, can be emotionally taxing and embarrassing to a self-conscious adolescent.

In the case of a relatively minor loss—death of a goldfish, failure to be elected class treasurer, having a date cancelled—grief may be resolved in a few hours to a week. The more serious the loss, the longer the recovery is likely to take. The *process* tends to be the same; it is the *duration* that tends to differ. When adolescents are experiencing serious grief for the first time, the interference with the activities of daily living may be out of proportion to an external perception of the seriousness of the event. The grief is nonetheless real. When grief remains unacknowledged at home, adolescents may turn to peers or other adults for support. Knowing the process of grief resolution may enable youth leaders to reassure adolescents of the normalcy of their feelings and to make a referral if necessary.

Anger and Grief

Here we have discussed the topics of anger and grief separately. One aspect of grieving involves anger, and frequently what causes anger involves loss—loss of prestige or the loss of a sense of power. Thus the two issues are often related. Note that numerous suggestions are offered for responding to anger and to grief in the following *Ideas You Can Use.*

Ideas You Can Use: Managing Anger

** *Manage your anger constructively.* Look for opportunities to manage your anger in constructive ways—by recognizing and owning the feeling of anger when it occurs, by putting an interpretation on the situation that does not hook your ego, and by selecting an assertive response—one that avoids either "poor me" feelings or aggressive actions.

When you encounter an angry adolescent or other person you need to have available an array of responses, and you need to fit them to the circumstances. Possibilities suggested by Myers and Nance (1986) include:

** *Internalize the list of wants of angry people and some of the responses that are possible.* Make the list of ideas discussed before (pp. 75-76) a part of you so that your responses become almost automatic. At the very least, review these ideas when you are about to face an angry adolescent, parent, supervisor, or other person.

** *Maintain your own composure.* It is essential that you not lose control. One out-of-control person in a room is enough. Let your composure demonstrate that you are not threatened by anger, that you will not be manipulated by the angry person, and that you may be able to help the angry person to regain control. If you *do* choose to shout a response to the angry person, use a voice tone that communicates self-control.

** *Don't argue.* An out-of-control person is unlikely to be capable of listening and evaluating rational content. The argumentative approach exacerbates a me-against-you relationship, which is likely to prolong the rage. Don't respond to accusations. Paint an image of yourself as stable and firm, but open to criticism and discussion.

** *Choose your initial approach tentatively.* Some angry people will respond with greater self-control when they see that you are not ruffled by their behavior; others will interpret your apparent control as lack of caring. Use your judgment to select one of the two approaches that follow, and be prepared to switch if necessary.

   a. ** *Avoid direct confrontation.* Confrontive behavior on your part is likely to be misinterpreted by an angry person. If you must call for assistance—do it. Do not threaten to do it if something else does or does not happen. But do not call for help unless you see no other reasonable way to protect yourself or anyone else involved. Intervene at the lowest level of authority possible, using a calm, quiet voice. This tends to minimize escalation.

   b. ** *Use the "match and move" technique.* If the calm, quiet approach does not work, "match and move." While maintaining personal control and a calm voice, match the pitch and volume of the angry person's voice, use his or her name, and give a non-confrontative command, such as "Kim come with me" or "Lou, let's talk in the hall." Then move the volume and pitch of your next communication down a notch closer to normal. As the angry person uses a lower pitch and volume, keep decreasing your own pitch and volume until you get back to a normal tone of voice. By then the person will usually be close to a normal tone of voice, though perhaps more agitated than usual.

** *Use the "out and down" technique.* Remove the angry person from the presence of others (without touching) and get him or her to sit down if possible. Moving out of sight of others deprives the angry person of an audience and releases you from your need to "save face" in front of the group. Your options increase when the interaction becomes one-to-one. Further, when people are seated they appear less threatening, and sitting down generally represents de-escalation of a confrontation.

** *Use the "more of the same" technique.* When other attempts to calm the person fail, tell him or her to continue the present behavior. "Go ahead and yell as long as you want, but please do it outside this room." Then escort the person out of the room and say, "When you are ready to *talk*, let me know." If possible, continue your work from a position that allows you to see the person outside the room and your group at the same time.

** *Use the "make me a list" technique.* Ask the person for a list of grievances. While the list is being produced—with you or the other individual writing—make statements like: "So that's the first thing you're upset about." "And that's another thing that troubles you"; or ask questions like: "Is there anything else?" "Are you sure that's all?" This turns the amorphous blob of indignation into concrete issues that can be discussed when the person calms down. And the very task of making the list may calm the person, even though the first few items may come across as angry accusations.

Note that in our suggestions of moving, removing, and escorting the person from the room we have discouraged touch. In a situation involving anger, touch is often interpreted as aggression on the part of the initiator. If you make the first touch in such a situation, you may be held responsible for provoking any aggression that ensues.

Ideas You Can Use: Coping with Grief

Adolescents are easily overwhelmed by the emotions that accompany the developmental processes they encounter, even when nothing unusual is happening in their lives. The adolescent who has experienced a loss is even more likely to be overwhelmed.

** *Reach out.* Bereaved adults do not easily reach out to others, and because of their stage of development, adolescents may be even less likely to do so. Do not avoid the adolescent, do not act as if nothing has happened, do not wait to be asked for help. Express your sorrow about what has happened and, if relevant, suggest how you might adjust work assignments for a while. Then check back often to see how things are going.

** *Turn your thoughts into words and actions.* Many people—leaders with youth included—complain, "I don't know what to say," when they encounter a grieving person. If they turned that thought and others into words, in most instances they would have made an effective response. Examples of thoughts turned into words include: "I wish I knew what to say." "I wish I could do something that would help." "I feel frustrated because I want to do something, but I can't think of anything that would help." "I'm sorry about your loss." And whether tongue-tied or not, a touch that is suitable in the relationship—an arm around the shoulder, a touch on the arm, a pat on the back—is likely to convey concern more effectively than any collection of words. Two useful books on this topic are *How do we tell the children?* by Schaefer and Lyons (1988) and *Death in the school community* by Oates (1993). The first offers constructive advice on talking with young people about death and grief. The second offers specific strategies school personnel can use to help adolescents cope with grief.

** *Give permission to grieve.* Social acceptability discourages adolescents from crying, yet there may be times when tears are needed. You may need to make arrangements with another person, e.g., a counselor or nurse, for the grieving person to go to when he or she feels the need for more privacy. By giving permission to grieve and providing a safe and supportive place, you discourage putting off the grief, and may shorten the period of severe grieving.

** *Involve the person.* The absence of social interaction during grief is a common factor in prolonged, unresolved grief. Adolescents, particularly, need to be reassured that they are still accepted and that others still care about them. You may include the person by inviting his or her opinion on an issue. You may wish to talk with the grieving adolescent yourself, or ask another appropriate person to do so, exploring what others can do to be helpful; or you may encourage his or her friends to explore with the adolescent what he or she needs or wants. Few adults know how to respond to the bereaved; fewer adolescents do.

The following suggestions for responding to others' grief are based on the work of Rando (1984):

The don'ts.

In an attempt to protect ourselves from others' pain, we often get our own needs mixed up with those of others. To avoid doing this:

1. Don't try to minimize or take away the pain.

2. Don't allow your sense of helplessness to keep you from reaching out.

3. Don't expect to be appreciated for your concern.

4. Don't expect recovery to fit your schedule; it must be completed in the griever's own way and on his or her time schedule.

5. Don't try to explain the loss in religious.

6. Don't tell the griever not to feel bad or not to cry; she or he cannot stop feeling bad until the recovery has progressed to the appropriate point.

The do's.

It is important to keep the focus on the responses of the grieving adolescent. This suggests listening without interpreting or lecturing.

1. Do listen nonjudgmentally and with acceptance. This means that whatever the griever expresses is an acceptable feeling or idea, regardless of how illogical it may seem to you. Don't interrupt, don't deny, and don't ignore. Be there and listen. From time to time it may seem vital to confront an idea, e.g., a misunderstanding, or a vengeful or suicidal thought. After listening with acceptance, and before the adolescent leaves, you may wish to return to that idea. By then he or she may well have shifted gears and drawn a different conclusion, without your interference.

2. Do encourage the adolescent to talk repeatedly to someone who cares about what has happened. People often think over and talk over grief-producing events many times until they can do so without strong emotional responses. This is healthy.

3. Do offer hope and confidence. Avoid conveying the idea that things will be "just like before," because they *never* will. Instead, express your confidence that the young person will be able to do the hard work of grieving and get on with life. Adolescents often doubt that they will be able to cope with what has happened. When an adult expresses confidence in them, they may be more able to believe in themselves.

4. Do let young people know that it is all right to seek your help or the help of others in dealing with their grief.

In What Ways are You Like These People?

Ruth P.

Ruth P. grew up in a quiet, middle-class environment in which anger was not an acceptable feeling. As a result when she faced situations with young people that engendered her anger she was so immobilized that she thought at times that she would have to give up her work with youth. "I shouldn't *ever* be provoked to feel anger," she told a counselor friend, who introduced her to the concept of anger management. Ultimately, Ruth realized that she needed to recognize her anger as real, she needed to interpret provoking events so that they did not threaten her ego, and she needed to select response strategies that kept her in charge.

How much are you like Ruth P.? How could you use anger management to your advantage?

Ted W.

Ted W. grew up in the downtown area of a middle-sized city, and he understood the need of many adolescents to express anger in physical ways. When some gang-like behavior began to appear in the community, Ted was influential in persuading the school administration not to overreact, but to find outlets for the hostilities of the young people involved. Ted helped the high school track coach organize gloves-on, supervised fights between two pairs of the would-be gang leaders, threw a pizza and soft drink party immediately following each of the fights, and persuaded several athletes to help initiate a wrestling program at the school—all with parental approval. Ted dealt directly with the two-worlds concept by indicating that he understood that the boys had learned to settle their differences in physical ways, and he urged them to develop alternative strategies for the world ahead as well.

How much are you like Ted W.? How might you respond if angry feelings began to express themselves in gang-like behavior in your community?

Jessica A.

As a high school teacher, Jessica A. was shy about involving herself personally with her students. She was all business in the classroom, and none of her students felt they knew her very well, though they respected her knowledge. When Allen's father died unexpectedly, Jessica did not know what to say or do. She continued her all-business approach and treated Allen's absence as she would have a minor illness. About a week after he returned to school, Jessica was shocked to learn that Allen was withdrawing from her class—especially since, until the death of his father, he had seemed most interested and even gifted in her subject area.

How much are you like Jessica A.? How could you assist a bereaved young person to cope with the tasks you are responsible to assign?

Critical Incidents

Darla. Darla, a member of one of your groups, has learned to push an anger button of yours. Take time right now to decide what that button might be—perhaps using racial or ethnic slurs, picking on a handicapped or disadvantaged peer, making a humorous remark at a serious time. There, she has just done it again, despite your cautions. Your neck is getting red.

What would you be most likely to say at that moment? If you were to use constructive anger management, what interpretation that would not hook your ego, might you put on Darla's behavior? What response would that call for *now*? What might you say or do *later*?

Explore these ideas: What actions push *your* anger button? What physical reactions in you tell you that you are becoming angry? What are some of the alternative choices you have when you are becoming angry?

Sharing Choices and Communication Skills with Adolescents

Section H of Chapter 16 presents three sharing suggestions under the following titles: *Anger buttons. Wants related to anger. Grief.*

Journal Entry

Date your journal entry and label it *Ch. 10, Anger, grief, and your choices.* You may begin your entry by reflecting on the ideas presented in the chapter, *you, anger, grief*, and *how you cope with these strong feelings inside yourself or from others.* You may also use the end-of-chapter activities or the key words on page 31 to further cue you in writing your entry.

11
Thinking/Working Choices

** Thinking/working choices involve cognition and action; these choices overlap to some extent with each of the other CREST choices.

** The OKness of thinking/working choices depends in large measure on whether other choices are wanted or needed. Effective thinking/working choices require depth of thought.

** In communicating individually with young people, *questioning* has many drawbacks. Questions can create dependency or invade privacy, and WHY questions invite rationalization and blaming. Open questions tend to be more useful thinking/working choices than closed questions.

** What we refer to as *solutionizing* also has its drawbacks in communication, e.g., it ignores feelings and it tends to create dependency.

** When the time is right, building lists and considering the advantages and disadvantages of each list item can be effective in exploring options with adolescents and others.

Exploring Thinking/Working Choices

** *When you ask or answer a question, plan your next action, or do what you have planned, you are making thinking/working choices.*

"What do you see as the next thing you need to do, Rex?"

"Your first three steps are correct; your trouble begins at step four."

"OK, group, let's look at Rex's new approach."

"If any of you need help, here's a model you can look at."

Moving among young people and checking their work as they do it.

Puzzling out a way to get two unmotivated young people involved.

Recording a tally mark for on-task behavior.

Designing a special group activity.

The above are thinking/working choices you might make with young people as you conduct daily routines and special activities. While you use words in making many of these choices, you make even more thinking/working choices without words.

** *You make hundreds of thinking/working choices daily as you respond to the different people and situations you encounter.*

Thinking/Working and Other CREST Choices

Any system for looking at behavior has to allow for overlap, and certainly each of the CREST choices overlaps at times with each of the other choices. When words and actions are primarily helpful, we label those choices as caring; when words and actions show leadership, we see those choices as ruling; and when words and actions are primarily responses to positive or negative feelings, we call those choices enjoying or sorrowing. We label choices thinking/working when our words and actions are mainly cognitive or task-oriented, although in a genuine sense thinking/working choices are a part of all choices. We have to *think* at some level in order to make any of our choices, and whatever we do requires some effort or *work* from us.

In every day that passes you make a great many thinking/working choices. The important thing to note is: ** *You can make a great many thinking/working choices daily in your relationships, but you can't build really significant relationships solely out of these choices.*

OK and OD Thinking/Working Choices

You can test the OKness of a thinking/working choice with your friend, a co-worker, or an adolescent. The key issue is whether that person needs or wants another choice from you. If you and your group are working hard at a task, you may each enjoy a bit of humor, but sticking basically to the task may also be OK. If a young person in your charge wants or needs another kind of communication from you in the moment, that individual is likely to see a steady diet of thinking/working choices on your part as OD.

There is no way your choices can be OK all of the time with all of the young people with whom you work, although most of them are likely to understand that you have to attend to other people and to other matters. The important thing, over time, is to remain alert to your own and others' needs, especially for caring and enjoying, and to make attempts to fulfill those needs at least occasionally.
** *You need to develop a reasonable balance among thinking/working and the other CREST choices.*

Shallow Thinking

Much of the time when you are convinced you are thinking, you may just be rerunning old tapes that have been spinning around in your head for a long time. If you grew up with the idea, "children should be seen and not heard," for example, this is likely to have an effect on the ways in which you relate to young people; your expectations of adolescents may be unrealistic, and the young people with whom you work—who may not have been raised to be unheard—may be more verbal or outspoken than you can accept. If you continue to apply that old injunction to *yourself*, you may treat supervisory personnel or co-workers with more deference than is useful, and you may have difficulty asserting yourself even when it would be appropriate.

If you are like most adults, in stressful situations with adolescents you may act hastily. You may well respond to the problem in the heat of the moment with the first thing that comes into your head—and that may be a memorable, too-strong reaction from a grownup you knew when you were younger. As the old saying related to teaching goes, "We teach as we were taught, not as we were taught to teach"—and the same goes for many other people who work with youth. Some old messages are useful, but not all.
** *Shallow thinking/working choices result when we blindly imitate others or when we follow old messages and habits without examining them.*

Deep Thinking/Working Choices

We are all used to either-or, yes-no, now-never, with-against thinking. Once you have come up with two choices you might use in responding to the problem an adolescent presents, you may decide that you can select option A or B. Deeper thinking and planning require time and effort. Considering the problem in the shower or while driving to work may increase your range of options to three or four, but sitting down with a notepad and listing possible ways of approaching the problem—and eventually listing the advantages and disadvantages of each—may lead you to eight or ten alternatives. Our observations suggest that if you list several choices you are more likely to act on responses that occur to you late in your deliberations; thus you may never even consider the two or three best possible options unless you take the time to build a reasonably extensive list. Within limits, the more choices you are able to list, the more options you have available to you to resolve the problem.

Many situations in which you feel stress seem to call for instantaneous thought and action, but a moment's pause—the time span of an eye-blink, or several seconds, or a count of ten—may be your best asset in making effective choices. In some stressful situations, it may be better to delay your response even longer. In the judicial system, sentencing is often delayed for days or weeks after the offender is judged guilty, so the judge, who is used to meting out punishments, can decide on a fair sentence. With young people it may seem cruel to wait any great amount of time to "pronounce" a penalty, but in actuality it may be highly appropriate for you to state, "I want each of us to think this over until tomorrow. Come by then with your suggestions and we'll work out a disciplinary action that fits what happened."

Redl and Wattenberg (1959) have offered a model for dealing with conflict within groups which requires depth of thought. They call the model *diagnostic thinking*, which is analogous to testing an hypothesis. The steps include developing a hunch, fact gathering, taking action, viewing the outcome flexibly, and then approaching the issue from a different angle if the outcome is disappointing. Adults and adolescents alike can make use of this model and other organized approaches to deeper thinking.

** *Thinking/working choices of any depth require time and effort.*

Give Yourself Permission to Think and Act

One of the rationalizations many adults use from time to time as an explanation for inaction is: "My boss/The administration won't let me do that." It is likely that many restrictions by supervisors or administrators are imagined, or are guessed about and used as excuses, because people hesitate to go beyond their usual patterns of choices. Certainly, *some* major alterations in the plan of operation or the curriculum are not likely to be approved by supervisory personnel. But the words leaders use in today's group meeting, and the actions and activities they employ—what they say and do *within* preset guidelines—involve a great many choices on their part.

Effective leaders consider carefully what the expectations are for their work with young people, and permit themselves considerable latitude for creativity in *how* they meet those expectations. If what they plan to do deviates substantially from the standard plan, they prepare and submit a proposal to the administration that tells clearly what the change is and why they believe they should implement it. If the innovation is minor, they act on their own.

A great variety of organizational approaches may be used to enhance efficiency and reduce the likelihood of problems arising when young people are gathered in classes or other groups. For example, adults who are leading young people individually within a group setting need to give maximum assistance without wasting time, so that "down time" and misbehavior opportunities are minimized (Jones, 1987). Furthermore, not all assistance needs to be given by the adult in the situation. Peer helping can be valuable both to the helper and the receiver; at the same time it may maximize the opportunity for the adult to work where she or he is most needed.

** *Effective leaders think through alternatives and give themselves permission to make a wide variety of effective thinking/working choices.*

Difficulties with Questions

Well-placed questions are valuable in communicating with others, but it is easy to become overly dependent on questions. ** *In communicating with adolescents and others, questions have many drawbacks*:

Correct answers. Young people are used to questions that have "correct answers," so they may give answers they believe you, their parents, or others want to give.

Pattern building. When you ask young people two or three questions in a row you may well be setting a pattern for your communication. Many adolescents are quite willing to give away the responsibility for their difficulties, so they will gladly sit back and let you take over their problem. As a result, questions lead almost inevitably to more questions, and the young people involved tend to take less and less responsibility for figuring out solutions or for carrying them out effectively. Young people may be all too willing to give up ownership of the problem and of the ways they might resolve it if others show willingness to take over for them. The trouble is, others cannot do so, effectively.

The expert image. A related point is that asking questions suggests that you are "the expert." Adolescents assume after they have given you all the answers you seek, you will come up with the "perfect solution" that will resolve their problem or concern—so they may be more than happy to answer your questions. But creating an "expert image" is burdensome since it puts the responsibility for solving the problem on your shoulders. It also obligates you to define the problem, when there may actually be several that need attention, and to offer the most relevant assistance. Finally, it teaches adolescents nothing about solving future problems on their own.

The atmosphere problem. Rapid-fire, short-answer questions create a "witness stand" atmosphere—like old Sergeant Friday's "nothing-but-the-facts-ma'am."

Probing/prying. Since young people may not feel free to deflect or reject your probes, they may answer questions that cause them pain or guilt. Or they may lie to protect others. Furthermore, they (and their parents) may see your questions as invasions of privacy and internally resent them or react vigorously against them.

Insensitivity. "How do you feel about that?" "Are you upset?" and similar questions about feelings are often seen as insensitive. Young people say internally, "Why can't he or she tell how I'm feeling?" As we suggested in our discussion of reflection of feeling, your best guesses about feelings may be received more positively than questions about feelings. For one thing, you are not likely to be far off track; but even if you are, adolescents are likely to appreciate the effort you are making to understand them.

WHY questions invite rationalizing and blaming. When you ask a WHY question you may inadvertently be encouraging rationalizing or blaming. "He/She/They...," the reply often begins. From the point of view of many adolescents, *why* almost always involves someone or something else. Often young people do not know the *why* of their behavior. And if they *could* really answer honestly, they might say something like this: "Because I'm no good. Because I don't even like myself and I need to have someone punish me." That would be difficult, if not impossible, for *anyone* to say.

It is often better to be patient, to listen, and to reflect feelings than it is to ask questions. To say it another way, in many instances it is better to offer caring choices than thinking/working choices—especially in the form of questions.

Effective Questions

** *Used sparingly, questions can be very helpful, and open questions tend to be far more useful and effective than closed questions.* Open questions cannot readily be answered by a simple yes or no or in just a few words; they invite elaboration. By contrast, closed questions invite the person to answer in a few words, and "the ball is back in your court," so to speak.

Suppose Josh has complained that he feels a lack of acceptance in the community, even though he moved to his present home almost a year ago. An example of a closed question you might ask would be, "Do the kids just ignore you then?" If he were highly verbal he might answer yes and then elaborate at length. He is not, so he says, simply, "Uh huh." It is your turn again, so you fill the air-space with another closed question, and a question/answer pattern has begun to build.

On the other hand, if you were to take a moment to formulate an open question, you might ask, "What are some of the things others do that show you they don't accept you?" Josh mentions one or two evidences, and perhaps you say, "Uh huh," to encourage him to share with you more deeply. Josh gets the clue that you want him to talk, and—if he is modestly verbal and if you have helped him realize that your task is that of helping him find his *own* way through his concern—he is likely to do so.

In many situations, a frequently-asked question may come to mind: "Have you talked with your mother about this?" Or: "Why don't you talk to your father about that?" If you must ask a question, try one that is more open instead: *"What have you tried so far to solve this problem, Josh?"* (Italics for emphasis.) After Josh responds you might say, *"So two of the things you have tried are. . .,"* and summarize what you have heard to this point. The summary invites Josh to elaborate on either of the items, or to tell you something else he has tried, and it helps you avoid the obvious. Later you might ask: *"What have you thought about, but decided not to try?"* This latter question may be useful because young people often discount good solutions when they cannot figure out how to implement them. At another point, you might ask: *"What do you plan to do about that?"*

Note that in many instances an invitational statement in the form of a reflection of feeling is better than either kind of question. Example: *"It troubles you that after almost a year in this school the other students still don't seem to accept you, Josh."* Josh may respond to such a reflection with a simple, heartfelt, "Yeah!" In that event, a nod, a brief period of silence, and/or a minimum verbal response: "I see," should invite him to talk about the matter from his perspective in any way he wishes.

Questions in Groupwork and Teaching

Before we leave the topic of questions, it seems relevant for us to make a point related to the use of questions in groupwork in general and in teaching in particular. As they stand before groups, many adults depend too much on two basic tools, asking and telling (and some add a third option, yelling). These people are comparable to the carpenter who uses only a hammer and saw. Effective youth leaders use a wide range of verbal and non-verbal responses to adolescents; they can be compared to the carpenter who adds to the hammer and saw such other tools as a drill, compass, screwdriver, plane, square, and tape measure. Effective leaders use such tools as listening, reflecting feelings, and asking open questions that encourage young people to think more deeply, and they create conditions in which adolescents are encouraged to develop their own strategies for solving the problems they face.

Difficulties with Advice and Solutions

The term *solutionizing* is used here to mean offering numerous suggestions, or seizing the opportunity to advise others before they are ready to consider solutions. Clearly, occasional well-placed and well-timed suggestions can make valuable contributions in meeting the needs of young people. However, all too often adults impose their values and contribute their ideas too early and too often, both because they believe they must play the role of expert, and because they are eager to demonstrate their helpfulness.

Even offering good solutions has its drawbacks:

** *Feelings come first.* In many instances, whether you have called in the young person or he or she has asked to see you, he or she may have strong feelings. If so, those feelings need to be aired before the person can deal with the difficulty in a logical way. Think of a time when you were exploding with anger or consumed with frustration. You wanted someone to *just listen* to you. If the person you talked with immediately shifted to "What you should do now is. . .," you may have felt even angrier or more frustrated. "Don't tell me what to do—just listen to how I feel," you may have cried out inside. It is important for you to let the other person's feelings come through before you yield to the temptation to offer advice.

** *Suggestions infer that you know more about the problem than the person involved.* In most instances the adolescent knows a great deal more about the problem than you do. If you give the person time to share with you in some depth, you are less likely to offer a solution that she or he has already dismissed.

It may seem obvious that Gail must explore the problem with mom or dad or her friend; if so, you may be tempted to suggest it. However, if she does not talk about doing that, in all likelihood she has thought about it and eliminated it as a choice. Give her an extended hearing and you may understand why the suggestion might not appeal to her. You may be convinced that she is right, or you may conceptualize a way in which she could approach the problem. If you think it is important for you to know of her reaction to an option—and it probably is not really important in this moment—try stating it as a negative presumption: *"I assume you've thought about talking about this with your parents, Gail, but for some reason that doesn't seem to you to be workable just now."*

A suggestion you offer early in the exploration may appear to Gail or someone else to be insensitive and uncaring. The same suggestion may be offered by the individual later, or it may then seem appropriate and feasible for you to offer it—since you have shown that you care and have listened thoroughly to the other person's point of view.

** *The adolescent owns the problem—you don't.* If we assume that the *problem* belongs to David, rather than to you, ultimately the *solution* to the problem must be his. What seems like logic to you may seem illogical to him; but even if the solution is ideally tailored to his needs, it would be better if he generated it. If David is the one who owns the problem, he is more likely to carry out his own solution successfully than yours. Furthermore, if he is able to come up with an idea that helps to resolve the problem, he has grown in confidence that he can resolve future problems himself.

** *Solutions teach dependency.* Suggestions put you in control and create dependency on the part of those involved. Solutionizing teaches people to put the problem in someone else's hands, so when the next difficulty comes along they are likely to take the same route. By contrast, if you help others to come up with

their own solutions, when the next difficulty arises they may spend some time thinking through the difficulty and assessing the options available. As a result they may eventually learn to resolve some of their problems without seeking assistance.

** *Solutions encourage the* why-don't-you-yes-but *game.* Many young people are highly skilled in playing the *why-don't-you-yes-but* game and they nearly always "win." If you offer solutions early or often in your dialogue with adolescents you may inadvertently be making the first move in that game. Dialogue that encourages open communication and invites young people to pose possible solutions themselves is generally effective in avoiding the game.

Even in those instances in which young people ask, "What do I do?" the early solutions you offer may be of little value. Knowingly or otherwise, they may be setting you up for the *why-don't-you-yes-but* game, or, despite the question, they may have a great need to express feelings before they are able to listen to your ideas for how they might approach the problem. You can contribute more positively to the needs of most adolescents by helping them develop their own strategies for solving problems, rather than by making suggestions.

Listing

After you have listened deeply to the young person for a while, and it seems like the right time for the two of you to explore alternatives, rather than offer numerous suggestions, try *listing*, building a set of alternative behaviors the adolescent might try when the same situation next arises. Take out a piece of paper and a pen (a felt pen has the advantage of filling the page quickly), title the page with a word or two that summarizes the adolescent's concern: *Fighting*, for example, and ask the person to work with you to build a list of a variety of strategies that might help with the problem.

You can enter directly into the process of building the list—brainstorming at first—without evaluating. Try to get the adolescent to offer at least half of the suggestions. Comments such as, "So now we have four possible things you could do," serve two purposes: they reward the effort, and they encourage making further additions to the list. The following figure (Nelson, 1987, p. 26) shows how the page might look.

When I feel like fighting

GR..R..

Choices
1. Fight
2. Walk away
3. Talk to someone
4. Make a joke

The physical presence of a list is likely to be helpful in its own right. The discussion may wander into other avenues, but the page is there before you, encouraging further expansion of the list. Also, since young people are even more likely than adults to think in either-or, with-against, right-wrong, now-never terms, building a list reinforces the idea that there may be many more than two alternatives in any given situation.

The advantages and disadvantages of *using* and *not using* each of the items can be explored when the list is complete. If Perry is involved in one fight after another, he gets some kind of benefit from fighting. You may be tempted to focus only on the disadvantages of fighting, but it is likely to help the discussion if you also explore the benefits of all alternatives, including fighting. "Let's talk about what you gain by fighting, Perry." If Perry shrugs his shoulders, you can suggest: "I think it does two things for you. It tells everybody you're strong, and it keeps people away from you."

It may be equally important from Perry's view that you consider the *dis*advantages of *not* fighting. "What's the problem, Perry, if you don't fight?" Perry may say, "My dad will think I'm a wimp," or, "The kids will think I've gone soft," or *you* may suggest those possibilities. Exploring the advantages and disadvantages of each of the possible choices should help the adolescent consider the likely consequences of each alternative, as well as the consequences that may result if the action is *not* taken.

Listing, used well, can help young people consider a variety of possible alternative choices. The best solutions are those that have the most significant advantages, the least significant disadvantages, and the greatest promise of positive consequences.

Three Observations

Three observations follow concerning suggestions, advice, and solutions:

** ***Some questions are disguised solutions.*** The question, "Have you talked with your mother about this?" is really a hidden suggestion. It implies: if you haven't, you should. As we suggested earlier in this chapter,

open questions, e.g., "What have you tried to do about this so far?" are likely to be more advantageous, and they do not hide suggestions.

** ***Reassurance, as advice-giving, is often inappropriate.*** While it may be tempting to offer reassurance to a young person who faces a difficulty, we suggest that you avoid reassuring him or her unless you are absolutely certain you are on firm grounds. If you were tempted to say, "I'm sure your parents will understand and help you if you tell them about this," could you be *sure*—even if you thought you knew the parents well? Not likely. Reassurance is likely to do more for you than for the adolescent—and that is not what your objective should be.

** ***Plans should be followed-up.*** In many instances, whether the action contemplated by an adolescent results from his or her own suggestion or yours, it should be followed-up by *someone*. Followup can mean referral to a suitable helping person, or it may occur in a planned, future discussion between you and the young person. "I'd like to have you stop in tomorrow and let me know how it went for you. How about four o'clock?" Such a suggestion says, "I care about you. What happens with you is important to me. I don't want to just let this go."

The key in making effective thinking/working choices is timing. Explore solutions when the adolescent is ready to go in that direction—and help him or her develop options from which to choose.

In What Ways are You Like These People?

Bob D.

So that he might communicate more effectively with the young people in the home for juveniles in which he and his wife were house parents, Bob D. elected to take an introductory counseling course. As an optional project, class members who had access to young people were encouraged to check out their listening skills with two different youngsters. Bob made the offer to meet with two of the residents, and talk with them about any of their concerns, and Tina and Warren volunteered. A quick count as he listened to the audiotape from his contact with Tina proved to Bob that he was highly dependent on asking questions, and he resolved to use a broader range of communication skills when he met with Warren. "I made fair progress with Warren, once I learned that I asked questions continually with Tina," he remarked to his counseling class, "but I'm so used to asking factual questions, that it's slow work for me to figure out any other response. I'm getting there, though."

How much are you like Bob D.? To what extent are you dependent on asking questions when you communicate with young people individually or in a group? To what extent do you use other approaches or ask open questions? What other approaches would be most useful for you to practice now and in the future?

Lois K.

Lois K. is a middle school social studies teacher who *thinks* a great deal. She doesn't *act* enough even to suit herself, and she doesn't balance her thinking/working choices with enough caring and enjoying choices to suit her students. She is interested in the subjects she teaches, but her students see her as a kind of walking computer, well-informed, but not programmed to show enthusiasm or excitement.

Last summer Lois attended a workshop on Choice Awareness and she came to the conclusion that she emphasized thinking/working choices. At the time she decided that was all right with her. However, Lois recently overheard one of her favorite students call her class boring. She then decided to make an effort to vary her teaching and use a wider range of choices.

How much are you like Lois K.? To what extent do you balance your thinking/working choices with the other CREST choices in your work with adolescents?

Joy W.

Joy W., a social worker, prided herself on coming up with "innumerable, immediate, and immutable suggestions" when the young people on her case load asked for help. She reacted negatively at first when she read that quickly-formulated solutions might not be sensitive to the needs of others, and that suggestions often create depen-

dency. Her annoyance was still fresh in her mind when she found an I-need-to-talk-to-you phone slip on her desk one morning, and followed it up. "Oh, everything's fine now," Lauren reported, "I worked it out on my own because you weren't here yesterday when I wanted to talk to you." She invited Lauren to share the details and was impressed with the maturity of judgment that fifteen-year-old showed.

"I'd better start listening more and talking less," Joy told a colleague later. "Lauren came up with a great plan for the problem. Maybe others can, too."

How much are you like Joy W.? To what extent have you believed you needed to come up with solutions when adolescents present their problems to you? To what extent do you need to broaden your approach?

Ideas You Can Use with Individuals or Groups

** *Use a broad range of thinking/working choices with adolescents.* Make thinking/working choices that improve your interactions with your groups. Organize interesting activities that heighten the interest of young people. Where appropriate, dramatize, challenge, invite debate, brainstorm, hypothesize, try out, visit, etc.

** *Help young people see that they have some responsibility for their interest.* State the view that nothing in the world is inherently boring, but because adolescents live in an "entertain-me" world they may overlook the fact that they have a stake in creating interest within the setting you share with them. If it is relevant, state that *you* will do more to enhance interest. Also, invite group members to suggest better ways of approaching issues or content and encourage them to ask challenging questions and to share their ideas with others. Place some responsibility on group members for creating interest, invite their involvement, and be open to their suggestions.

** *Think about and work on balancing your CREST choices.* Think about a relationship you want to improve with an adolescent or other person. Do you make too many choices of one kind and too few of another, e.g., too many thinking/working choices and too few caring or enjoying choices? (Many adults do.) Plan ahead and make needed changes in your choices.

** *Limit the numbers of questions you ask.* In your everyday communication with young people, family members, and friends, make a vigorous effort to ask fewer questions. And when you do question, form your inquiries so they are open—so that you show your interest and concern for the other person, rather than just for "the facts."

** *Limit the number of solutions you offer.* In your everyday communication with young people, family members, and friends, avoid taking a know-it-all position when someone presents a problem to you. Make a strong effort to help others find solutions on their own—since their commitment to the solution will be greater.

** *Avoid the* **why-don't-you-yes-but** *game.* When you realize the why-don't-you-yes-but game is on, *stop.* Say something like the following: "I've been suggesting things you could do and of course the ideas fit me, but not you. Let's talk about the possibilities you've thought of, or can think of, and maybe we'll find some approaches that are workable." If that does not change matters, call the game by its name and back out altogether. "You may not mean this to be a game, but I see it as one called *why-don't-you-yes-but;* it's not doing any good, so I'm calling a halt to it now."

Critical Incident

Ralph. Legislation has placed major responsibility on neighbors, educators, and other interested persons for reporting possible instances of child abuse. For some time now you have been concerned about Ralph. Periodically, you see him looking bruised and battered and he tells you he has been in a fight. When you show him concern, he assures you he is all right. Marcie, a next-door neighbor of Ralph's, commented to you one day, "I can tell you're worried about Ralph. I am too. The yelling I hear from his house sounds really bad. His father's always screaming at someone, and he hits all the kids—hard. Especially Ralph." Marcie often exaggerates, so you hesitate to take her word for what is happening. Also, in a conversation about Ralph with your supervisor you were told in so many words, "Don't rock the boat."

You have started your group and Ralph walks in, sweater torn, blood on his upper lip, and a bruise above his right eye. You start the group on an activity and ask Ralph to step outside the room with you.

"Ralph! You look just terrible!" you say.

Ralph replies, "Oh, I'm OK. I just got into a fight with my. . ., uh. . ., some kids—on the way here."

You decide this is the time for you to take action. What are your words, and what do you do, now? Later?

Sharing Choices and Communication Skills with Adolescents

Section I of Chapter 16 presents sharing suggestions under the following titles: *OK CREST choices. Open versus closed questions. Listening versus solutions.*

Journal Entry

Date your entry and label it *Ch. 11, Thinking/working choices.* You may begin your entry by reflecting on the ideas presented in the chapter, *you, your thinking/working choices, questions,* and *solutions.* You may also use the end-of-chapter activities or the key words on page 31 to further cue you in writing your entry.

WITH A LITTLE THOUGHT AND EFFORT I CAN IMPROVE MOST RELATIONSHIPS

12
Components of
Thinking/Working Choices

** Rehearsal and role play can be used to help people prepare to face their difficulties. Role play involves taking someone else's part, while rehearsal involves preparing to act on one's own part. Both procedures afford opportunities for tryout and practice.

** Reframing involves helping someone to see his or her concern from another point of view. Premature reframing often seems insensitive, thus the key in effective reframing is timing. Reframing can help adolescents and adults view life from the perspectives of others.

** A variety of behavioral approaches can be used, directly or indirectly, in an effort to help adolescents modify actions that cause problems for them. Record keeping by adults may involve day-to-day charting, frequency tallies, and timed tallies. Young people may also benefit from participating in self-monitoring procedures.

Rehearsal

What often blocks adolescents from taking responsibility for their own actions is that they have no idea what to say—if they have broken an object of value, or if they need to tell their parents about a pregnancy (their own, a girl friend's) or share with someone any matter of deep personal concern. ** *Rehearsal can be a valuable process for helping adolescents prepare to take action.* Used in a non-threatening way, rehearsal can help young people sort out the words they might wish to use.

As with offering solutions, suggestions, or advice, the question of timing is a key to the effectiveness of rehearsal. The problem needs to be aired, feelings shared, and trust built through listening and caring, before rehearsal is appropriate. When those conditions have been met and the problem is clearly defined, rehearsal may be helpful. Two questions are of value in shaping the rehearsal. "What have you thought about doing?" and "What have you considered doing, but thought you couldn't?"

Suppose Marla comes to you and tells you she is pregnant. You encourage her to talk to her parents and suggest that she see the school nurse or her assigned counselor, but she refuses to talk with anyone but you. "It was hard enough to get up the courage to tell you," she says, sobbing.

Your strategy becomes, first, to let Marla share her feelings and express her concerns; then, eventually, to rehearse with her ways of discussing the concern with her parents in the hope that she will then be willing to talk with them about the pregnancy. You help Marla get her feelings out and listen to her, and when the time seems right you ask her, "What have you thought about doing about this?"

"Oh, I suppose I *have* to tell mom and dad. But I'm *so* scared about doing that—I *know* they'll kill me," she replies.

You reflect her feelings, moderating her statement of the concern somewhat: "You know you have to tell them, but you're really scared to do that."

Marla agrees with a sigh; you decide it's time to offer her the opportunity to rehearse; and she tells you that she would prefer to talk with her mother about it first. "Let's play out what might happen, Marla," you suggest. "I'll take the part of your mom, you say what you think you need to say, and I'll try to respond in the way I'd guess your mother might." Marla nods. "You can tell me if you think I'm off base, and I may make a suggestion or two about what you might say as well."

You rehearse several times until Marla thinks she knows how she might talk about the problem, and believes she has a sense of how her mother might react. She agrees to take her mother aside and tell her after dinner, then come to see you tomorrow afternoon to let you know how it went. You feel confident in her ability to discuss the matter with her mother, but you think through a fall-back position for tomorrow in case she gets "cold feet." Your alternative plan is to offer to have Marla call either or both of her parents and have them meet with the two of you—so that Marla can tell them about her problem in your presence.

Role Play

** *Role play can be a valuable process for helping adolescents gain perspective on a problem.* Role play and rehearsal are closely related; in *role play* a person takes someone else's role, whereas in *rehearsal* a person takes his or her own part and tries out behavior in preparation for its use. In the illustration of rehearsal above, you offered to *role play* the part of the mother, while Marla *rehearsed* what she might say.

With Marla and with many other people, a combination of role play and rehearsal may be beneficial. As a first step, you may encourage her to open the discussion of her problem with you—rehearse in whatever way she can—with you taking the role of her mother. After the two of you have given one another feedback, you might replay the parts with modifications. Next, instead of responding as the parent, you might ask Marla to take the part of her mother and respond as she thinks her mother might. You may then continue with rehearsal and/or role play until Marla is satisfied that she has a way to *initiate* the discussion, at the very least. Two important advantages of having Marla role play her mother are: Marla may begin to see the situation from her mother's perspective, and you can see how Marla believes her mother might react.

Rehearsal and Role Play in Groupwork

** *Within nearly any group setting involving youth there may be numerous opportunities for role play and rehearsal.* People are involved in all curricular matters, and events in history, literature, science, health, and mathematics present rich possibilities for dramatizing, humanizing, and energizing the curriculum. If you meet young people in a non-school setting, you should be able to envision many opportunities for rehearsal and role-play concerning the specific issues and problems they face. Rehearsal and role-play may also be used in such diverse

areas as practicing for employment interviews or coping with on-the-job problems, reentering the family setting after an enforced absence of some kind, and handling concerns involving alcohol and co-dependency. Depending on the basis of your contact, you may find it worthwhile to help young people understand social issues and current events by having them role play the parts of figures in the news, then discuss the events and their implications. Through these avenues you may be able to help adolescents better understand themselves and those around them, and explore the dynamics that affect decisions in the wider world.

Reframing for Adolescents

Suppose an adolescent asks to talk to you, then tells you in a barrage of statements: "My mother has gone to work recently. I have to take care of the little ones all the time. All six of them are four or more years younger than I am... It's really heavy for me—sometimes I feel like a slave... Mom never notices what I *do*— she just scolds me for what I *don't* get done... Sometimes I think she's half-crazy. She yells and cries all the time... Now I understand why Dad left."

If that problem was presented to you, you might be tempted to try to help the adolescent see the problem from the mother's point of view: you want to help the individual *reframe* what is happening. If you put your idea in a statement you might say: "Your mother is probably tired and upset because she has to handle everything by herself. I imagine she has so much need herself that she doesn't think about telling you she appreciates your help." If that is your impulse, it is appropriate, but you may be tempted to offer that view before the individual is ready to hear it. Further, it would be more effective if the adolescent were to verbalize that view. As with many other thinking/working choices, you need first to *listen* and understand the person's strong feelings.

When the time is right, there are five steps you might *gradually* take in reframing:

** *Step one in reframing is: State the reason it is needed*: For example, "When you are in a problem situation it is easy to pay attention to the same things over and over. When you do that you usually see the problem only from one angle. If you can see what is happening from a different angle it may help you feel better." Stop after stating your reason for reframing and allow time for reactions and discussion.

** *Step two in reframing is: Identify what the person attends to.* For example, "What you notice most about your mother lately is that she has put a big burden on you, she doesn't appreciate the helpful things you do, and she cries a lot." OR an open question can be relevant here: "What are some of the things you notice most about your mother these days?" Again, allow time for reactions and discussion.

** *Step three in reframing is: Identify alternative perceptions.* For example, "If you try to understand what your mother thinks, it could be: 'I have all these kids and no husband here to help with them, and I have to leave them with (name the adolescent) and work him or her too hard. I hate that. Life is rotten for me now.'" Or, an open question may help: "What do you believe your mother thinks and feels about her life and how hard it is right now?" Allow time for reactions and discussion.

** *Step four in reframing is: Help the individual tie the new perception to a particular person, place, and time.* For example, "Could you try thinking (new perception) when your mother (person) first comes home after work (place and time), and yells about something: 'She's tired. I know she loves us. I know she loves me. Life is hard for her now'?" Allow time for discussion.

** *Step five in reframing is: Arrange for followup.* Refer the adolescent to an appropriate person or schedule a future appointment with you.

Helping young people to reframe their thoughts is not easy, since reframing is a complex communication skill. You may choose to refer, rather than reframe, when you believe that a young person has a distorted view. However, there may be times when someone will not seek other resources, and skill in reframing may be essential. In any event, it may help just to know that reframing is *possible*.

Reframing for the Leader with Youth

Whether or not you use reframing in discussing problems with adolescents, you can use it to gain a different perspective on the ways in which they behave with you. When you think: "Todd just wants attention." You may be able to reframe the issue and see it differently: "Todd needs attention and I will find a way..." When you think: "Sue's just lazy." Reframe: "Sue is discouraged and needs support." When you think: "This youngster is stubborn." Reframe: "This youngster is independent." And, most important, in your own life, when you think: "I'm bored." Reframe: "I'm letting myself be bored." OR: "I'm boring myself."

If you are like most people you respond to particular behaviors or attitudes on the part of others in habitual ways. Two of the most advantageous actions you can take are: (1) choose to see the behavior or attitude from the

other person's point of view, and (2) put the most positive construction possible on the behavior or attitude.

** *Reframing is an important survival skill in work with youth.*

Record Keeping

** *Behavioral strategies may be useful supplements to other communication patterns; record keeping is a useful behavioral strategy.*

Day-by-day chart. For problem behavior that occurs occasionally, perhaps once each group meeting, a day-by-day chart may be useful. Suppose that Peggy frequently comes to your group late. If you decide that a behavioral strategy would be useful in curbing her habit, for each day that Peggy is on time, you record a plus (+) on a day-by-day chart; otherwise you record a minus (-) for that day. An example of the record for one week might be: M + T - W - T + F -

Frequency tallies. For behavior that occurs more often than once an hour, frequency tallies may be used for each instance. If Darren is often out of his seat, you might wish to tally each instance and discuss his progress with him from time to time.

Example: M """"/"""   T """"/"   W """"/"   T """"/"   F """"
                   (8, 6, 6, 6, 4)

Timed tallies. For high-incidence behavior, timed tallies may be used. If Sandy is seldom on task, you, an assistant, or another adolescent (selected by Sandy), could monitor each five minute period on the minute, and tally plus (+) or minus (-) to reflect on- or off-task behaviors, using a recording sheet prepared in advance.

Example: 9:05 + 9:10 - 9:15 - 9:20 - 9:25 + 9:30 - 9:35 + 9:40 - 9:45 - 9:50 -

The procedures involved in the various record keeping strategies are similar. (1) Select a behavior you want to influence. (2) Collect base rate information for a minimum of two or three time blocks over two or three days. (3) Design and implement a new strategy. (4) Keep an accurate count of the person's behaviors for several days after implementing the strategy. (5) Assess the process and maintain the current direction, or recycle through any necessary steps if the strategy is not working.

Keeping accurate records may mean the difference between perceived success and perceived failure. For example, if you *do* count target behaviors you are likely to notice Darren's gains, you will feel good about your efforts and you may reinforce him for his. If you *don't* count target behaviors, you are not likely to notice the change in his out-of-seat behavior over the first three or four days—since either eight or six instances in an hour is frustrating— and you may discard an effective approach.

It should be noted that target behaviors often increase for a time before they begin to decrease. People of all ages tend to try to preserve the world as they know it until they understand that the change is to their benefit. If patience is not exercised with a new approach, a potentially-effective change may be discarded when it is about to bear fruit.

How you introduce and implement a behavioral strategy is as important as *what* you do. We recommend that, whenever feasible, young people should be included in the planning process so that they can understand why it is being undertaken; doing so may moderate the tendency on the part of some to increase an undesired behavior, thinking, "Maybe he or she just hasn't noticed me yet." Many of the behaviors that frustrate adults involve attention-getting; if you plan a behavioral approach cooperatively with young people, it will tell them that you care and that you are going to give them some of your attention freely, so they do not have to misbehave to get it. Further, it will often help if you take some responsibility for the problem that exists—by saying something like this: "I'm making this change because I think I scold you more often than I need to—and I want to cut down on that."

Record Keeping by Adolescents

** *It is frequently effective to involve adolescents in a self-monitoring process.*

The young person who says, *I cry all the time,* may see the matter differently after counting. Anne, a middle school girl who made that statement, was asked to take notes each time she cried for a week; she was gratified to learn that she cried only five times—she had expected the number of instances to be far higher. Further, she concluded after some discussion that two of those times were thoroughly justified.

Two of the adolescents cited earlier, Peggy and Darren, could have kept their tallies themselves as well. Peggy might have been more readily motivated to be on time if she had been asked to maintain the record. It might also have been useful for Darren to have kept a count of the number of times he was out of his seat. With both young people, teaching them to self-monitor could have clarified for them the dimensions of the problem, and it might also have influenced them to change their behaviors.

The four R's we have discussed here, rehearsal, role play, reframing, and record keeping, offer assistance to the leader in working effectively with adolescents. Each of these thinking/working choices, when used appropriately, can assist young people to understand the choices they have been making and to plan new strategies for encountering the problems they face.

In What Ways are You Like These People?

Randy V.

Randy V. thought long and hard about a career as an actor, but he decided he wanted a more stable lifestyle. Instead, he used his obvious talents in civic theater productions and in his teaching in social studies. "Let's turn this event into a scene tomorrow," he sometimes told his students. "As you read the final page-and-a-half of the chapter I've assigned you, figure out who the characters were, what their motivations were, how they might have reacted to the news they received, and what they might have said. We'll take your suggestions and play them out."

How much are you like Randy V.? To what extent do you/could you use rehearsal and role play in your work with young people? How might these approaches help you assist the adolescents with whom you work?

Jack T.

In a staff development workshop on choice-making, Jack T. was introduced to the idea of reframing. One idea in particular hit home with him. The workshop leader commented, "When you're tempted to make a note on a record, or say to an adolescent or a parent that the youngster would do well if he or she would 'just try harder,' see if you can't reframe that. Is the person discouraged? Are other concerns keeping him or her from focusing on what needs to be done? Do the activities or assignments need to be modified so they have greater appeal?" Jack could hear echoes from similar notes he had frequently written concerning adolescents.

How much are you like Jack T.? To what extent do you attribute problems young people have to "not trying" and the like? How could you benefit from reframing? How could you use reframing with adolescents to help them work through their problems?

Rachel S.

Rachel S., a middle school teacher, uses a variety of self-monitoring approaches and rewards with students—to help them with such problems as tardiness, talking out, and being off-task. She became a believer as a result of her experience with Nellie M., the counselor at her school. Paul was a rebellious seventh-grader who seemed to do everything he could to frustrate Rachel—and she had him in her classroom just short of three hours a day. "I think he hates me" she told Nellie.

Nellie sat down with Paul and developed a behavior modification plan with him that seemed workable; then she turned to the question of rewards. When Nellie reported her findings, Rachel was bowled over with surprise. Paul wanted time with her after school—just to talk, maybe to do some chores in the room—since he thought she was the neatest teacher he had ever had. "All those things he's doing are to get you to pay attention to him," Nellie reported. "He just didn't know any better ways."

How much are you like Rachel S.? To what extent do you know what does or might motivate each of the young people with whom you work? To what extent do you or could you use behavioral strategies to help adolescents work through their problems?

Ideas You Can Use with Individuals or Groups

** *Use rehearsal and role play.* When you have a "sticky" decision to make or need to confront someone about a concern, find a person to role play the part of the other individual, explore the responses you might hear, and rehearse what you want to say. Switch roles, then, and try to see the situation from the other person's point of view. If you have no partner to role play with, write out statements and responses.

** *Reframe.* If you feel bored, irritated, upset, angry, or challenged by an adolescent, a parent, or a supervisor—reframe. Choose to put a more positive construction on the matter; choose to see the problem from another point of view.

** *Use behavioral strategies to improve your communication with others.* For example, attach a piece of tape under your watch band and use it to mark the particular choices (behaviors) you want to increase—such as smiling or giving verbal reinforcement, or decrease—such as scolding or raising your voice, with particular young people.

Critical Incident

Stan. Put yourself in the situation we described when we introduced reframing earlier in this chapter. To avoid stereotyping the problem as belonging exclusively to females, we will call the student Stan.

You invite Stan to meet with you because his work and his motivation have recently deteriorated. You know that Stan's parents have recently been divorced and that he is the oldest of seven children. A bit at a time Stan lets out several pieces of information about his situation—being left with the younger children a lot; feeling like a slave; his mother not noticing what he does, just what he doesn't do; his mother's yelling and crying, etc.—then he stops and looks at you.

What would you be most likely to say at that moment? What do you see as the possible advantages and disadvantages of helping Stan *eventually* to reframe the situation—seeing it from his mother's perspective? If you decide to introduce reframing to Stan, what might you actually say?

Sharing Choices and Communication Skills with Adolescents

Section J of Chapter 16 presents sharing suggestions under the following titles: *Rehearsal/role play. Reframing. Record keeping.*

Journal Entry

Date your entry and label it *Ch. 12, Thinking/working components.* You may begin your entry by reflecting on the ideas presented in the chapter, *rehearsal, role play, reframing,* and *behavior modification, as choices.* You may also use the end-of-chapter activities or the key words on page 31 to further cue you in writing your entry.

13
Consequences, Feelings, and Choices

** What we think of as consequences follow our actions, but not everything that follows what we do or say is a consequence of our actions. The other person makes choices too. We cannot control another person's choices, but when we act positively we increase the odds that more positive consequences will follow. The opposite is also true.

** Although we may have a sense that our feelings come singly, more often than not we choose our feelings in the moment from an array of possibilities. We make choices in our feelings about ourselves and others. The more positive choices we make, the more likely we are to feel good about ourselves.

Consequences

We make choices that are followed by behaviors of others. ** *When we say or do something and someone else responds, we think of the action that follows as a consequence.* Consequences are the results of some of our actions, but other people make choices too, so not everything that follows is a consequence of what *we* have said or done. Our behaviors influence, but they do not control, the behaviors of others.

** *When we make positive choices we increase the chances that others will make positive choices in return.*

CREST Choices and Consequences

If you want positive consequences, make statements and take actions that will increase the likelihood that those consequences will happen. Suppose you work with an adolescent who troubles you, with whom you are often in conflict. Think about the choices *you* make that contribute negatively to your relationship. Would your interaction be enhanced if you were a little less authoritarian, if you used a little less sarcasm, or if you chose less often to feel angry with that individual or less sorry for yourself? Restating that in Choice Awareness terms, if you have a poor relationship with a young person you probably OD on one of the five CREST choices, caring, ruling, enjoying, sorrowing, or thinking/working. Ask yourself: "Which of the CREST choices might I make less frequently in OD ways with the adolescent?"

Now look at the flip side. Would matters improve if you showed more concern for the individual, if you occasionally made a suggestion you believe he or she would like, if you smiled more often, or if you worked on the relationship? In Choice Awareness terms, ask yourself: "Which of the CREST choices might I make more often with the adolescent in OK ways? Should I care more, enjoy more...?"

If you alter your pattern of choices with others, you probably do so in the hope that more positive consequences will follow. But suppose you smile and the person frowns back, or you compliment someone and he or she laughs in reply. Is the person's behavior a consequence of what you said or did? If a consequence is what logically or naturally follows an action you take, the answer is no. The frown or laugh is not a logical or natural consequence of your action. It may be a consequence of something one of you did yesterday, or it may be a consequence of an event or problem that does not relate to you—but it is not a direct consequence of your smile or compliment.

When an unexpected response follows an action of yours it proves that the other person also has choices. There is no guarantee that you will get what you expect. But, as we have suggested, you increase the chances for positive choices from others when you make OK CREST choices with them.

The key to producing more positive consequences in a relationship is persistence. If the account in your relationship with an adolescent is "in the red," two or three positive choices are not likely to turn it around, but, if you are persistent, over time you are likely to be rewarded for your efforts.

Choosing Feelings in the Moment

** *We choose from among our feelings.* From time to time you may think your feelings are in control of you. You may act on your feelings, then say: "I *had* to discipline him." "I was in a bad mood." "She made me mad." You, not your feelings, are in control of what you say and do. *You* choose how you act on your feelings.

** *Strong feelings often mean a mixture of feelings.* A friend of yours calls from out of town and schedules a visit, but the appointed time passes and more than an hour goes by. In the course of waiting, you feel excitement, anticipation, warmth, annoyance, frustration, concern, and fear. When your friend arrives in good condition you could share any of those prior feelings—or your immediate feeling of relief. But how might you spell relief? A-N-G-E-R?

When one of your favorite adolescents shirks a responsibility, you feel a mixture of upset and disappointment; but on the positive side you still have a reservoir of feelings of appreciation, enjoyment, and affection. When one of the more difficult young people you work with gets in trouble, you may allow fewer of your positive feelings through, but behind the obvious feeling of frustration, or even of vindication, you may feel concerned and worried because of your interest in the person.

With each of these people, your friend, the favorite adolescent, and the problem young person, you may have many opportunities to make a response, but what you say *first* is particularly important. You could say to your friend: "I'm relieved to see you're OK. I was worried about you." You could say to your favorite adolescent: "I've come to think highly and expect a lot of you, and I'm disappointed with the way you handled that responsibility." You could say to your problem young person: "I feel bad that you got in trouble. We don't always get along, but I want only the best for you."

You may think that you have only one feeling at a time, and must act on it, but that is rarely true. At times your smorgasbord of feelings may include a large helping of anger, however, there are usually other feelings on which you can choose to act that could contribute to the relationship.

Anger is a strong feeling, and when you are angry you may believe that you should act on that feeling. Albert Ellis (1979) observed that anger almost always comes after another feeling, and he suggested that people ought to act on the feeling that came first. In the case of the friend, the main prior feeling may be frustration—that you were kept waiting in favor of some unknown person or situation. With both the favorite and the difficult adolescent, your prior feeling may be disappointment. Sharing your frustration or disappointment is likely to be a better choice than acting on your anger.

A choice is more often effective if you take time to consider your mixture of feelings, then draw on a positive feeling that serves a positive purpose. ** *You can choose to act on feelings that move you toward your goals.*

Choosing Feelings About Yourself and Others

Some of the most important choices you make in your life involve how you choose to feel about yourself and others. If you are among the fortunate few who received considerable reinforcement in the process of growing up and who continue to feel good about yourself, count yourself blessed. If you were raised on criticism, or if you have become overly self-critical or critical of others, we suggest you give yourself permission to like yourself and others more. Love your neighbor is an important injunction, but don't lose sight of the full text: *Love your neighbor AS YOURSELF*—that suggests that you must feel love for yourself *before* you can love others well.

It is possible to overdo on self praise and even on compliments to others, although our observations suggest that the opposite more often occurs. If you are like most people, though, you can be far more generous with compliments and supportive comments to yourself and to others without having any concern about overdoing them.

We have suggested that you make CREST choices with others that can increase the chances of positive consequences coming back to you. The same idea can work for your choices about yourself. *Make CREST choices that help you feel good about yourself.* And while you are at it, also: *Make CREST choices that help you feel good about others.*

In What Ways are You Like This Person?

Darrell S. After an injury to his younger sister when he was a teen-ager, Darrell S. volunteered to work in the children's ward of the county hospital. Through that experience he developed skills in caring for young people. He is now a sensitive and enthusiastic educator who works very well with young people in general and with special needs learners in particular. Because Darrell learned well the lesson of reinforcing small steps that indicate progress; he looks for small, positive consequences of his efforts. His positive outlook and the reinforcement he gives act together to encourage the adolescents he works with to reach beyond themselves and gain the maximum from their potential.

How much are you like Darrell S.? What specific efforts do you make or could you make to produce positive consequences with young people—especially those you experience as most challenging?

Because of the frequent reinforcement Darrell S. gives special needs learners, when the city paper wanted to do a feature article on a model teacher, the principal of Darrell's school recommended the reporter write about him. He was cited as an example of how the positive self-concept of a teacher, and his or her belief in students, can encourage young people to learn.

How much are you like Darrell S.? To what extent does your view of yourself and of young people contribute to your success in working with them? What specific efforts do you make, or could you make, to act on your positive feelings about young people—especially those you experience as most difficult? What could you do to enhance your own self-concept?

Ideas You Can Use with Individuals or Groups

** *Take time to be positive.* When you are tempted to be negative with young people, pause briefly, think of a more positive or a less negative way to send your message; your effort should increase the likelihood that you will experience positive consequences.

** *Act on your positive feelings.* Whenever you have a mixture of feelings, as may often be the case, make a strong effort to choose to act on your more positive feelings—at least some of the time.

** *Appreciate yourself and others.* It may be easy for you, or it may not be, but you can *decide* to have positive feelings about yourself and others. It is your choice.

** *Make choices you value, and value your choices.* The best insurance for having positive feelings at the end of a strenuous day's effort is being able to look back and feel good about the choices you have made. The positive choices you have made benefit young people; they also benefit you and add to your own sense of well-being.

Critical Incident

Professional satisfaction. In recent surveys, a significant proportion of teachers have stated that they do not envision themselves teaching five years hence, and similar kinds of data appear when others who work with youth are surveyed. This can be taken as one important piece of evidence that satisfaction with youth work is not as great as it could be.

You are waiting for a meeting to start and several of your colleagues are discussing an article that reports similar current survey information about your field.

"I expect I'll find a place in industry before long," says one young colleague.

"We'll probably expand the family business and I may go into it," says another.

"Well, I'm going to be right here on the job with kids, and glad to be," says the person across from you.

After a while others realize that you have not voiced your opinion. The person across from you asks: "What do you think you'll be doing five years from now?"

What do you believe you would most likely say at that moment? What day to day choices can you make that will help you feel good about yourself as a person and as a professional? What special things might you do to avoid burnout?

Sharing Choices and Communication Skills with Adolescents

Section K of Chapter 16 presents two sharing suggestions under the following titles: *Consequences. Choosing feelings.*

Journal Entry

Date your entry and label it *Ch. 13, Consequences, feelings, and choices.* You may begin your entry by reflecting on the ideas presented in the chapter, *you, the consequences of your behaviors, your feelings in the moment and about yourself,* and *the choices you make.* You may also use the end-of-chapter activities or the key words on page 31 to further cue you in writing your entry.

14
Better Choosing and
Better Group Management

** Good group management requires good planning and effective use of each of the CREST options, expressed in OK ways.

** Three basic management models appear in the literature to date—one may be referred to as *youth-centered*, another as *environment-centered*, and the third as *interactive*. The three models are based on different interpretations of child development. A fourth model, the *Choice Awareness* model, is choice centered, it emphasizes the role of *choice* in interactions.

** The interpretations of child development, and the resulting models youth leaders use, affect their actions with individuals and groups in a variety of significant ways.

Group Management and Choosing

Management of groups of young people has been given a great deal of attention in the literature, particularly in the literature in the field of education. Here we have borrowed generously from the writings on classroom management since most of the good ideas for managing classes are relevant in other situations in which adults meet young people in controlled environments.

** *Good group management is the result of good planning, followed by effective moment-to-moment choices of words and actions that lead young people toward appropriate behaviors.* While different leaders of youth may achieve the kind of climate they seek in a variety of ways, there are some leadership behaviors that are found almost universally in environments in which adolescent achievement and satisfaction are high.

Based upon their analysis of research, Greenblatt, Cooper, and Muth (1984) offered the following list of leader behaviors found in situations in which achievement is high. In such environments the youth leader:

1. provides clear, businesslike instructions
2. keeps young people on task
3. offers corrective feedback in a positive way
4. structures activities for maximum learning or use
5. limits disruptions, and
6. paces action appropriately.

Mosley and Smith (1982) asked young people what they liked about the ways their teachers helped them learn; their suggestions apply to other professionals as well. The adolescents' most common responses were the following:

a. makes the process fun, has a sense of humor
b. communicates clearly what is expected
c. maintains a positive, relaxed learning atmosphere.

While some leaders stress achievement over satisfaction, and some stress satisfaction over achievement, the most effective youth leaders strive for high levels of both achievement and satisfaction. This may seem like an admonition to "walk on water," but it should be noted that all the items on the two lists above are behaviors that can be cultivated. These lists emphasize OK thinking/working, enjoying, and ruling choices—the latter gently applied—and it is clear that there needs to be an undergirding of OK caring choices as well. Note that not one of the items on the lists above is a personality characteristic. Indeed, there is no set of personality characteristics that guarantees effective youth leadership (Wlodkowski, 1977). So, where do you begin if you want to be the most effective leader you can be?

As in most other areas of self-improvement, it is a good idea to begin with self-knowledge. If you do not know where you are, it is almost impossible to plan to get where you want to go. To figure out where you are, we invite you to join us in breaking the pattern we have created by making a journal entry right now. Take some time to think about what you know about yourself, then make an entry of several lines on each of the topics listed below. Later, as you explore a number of group management models, refer to these lists and decide how the various ideas relate to your personal strengths and needs in your work with youth.

Journal Entry

Date your journal entry and label it #14.1—*Choices and group management.* Label the subsections of your entry with the italicized headings below.

a. *Personal strengths.* Discuss some of your strengths and why you believe they serve (or will serve) you well as a youth leader.

b. *Personal weaknesses.* Discuss some of your weaknesses and why you believe they serve (or will serve) you poorly as a youth leader.

c. *Preferred atmosphere.* Using elements from both the Greenblatt, Cooper, and Muth (1984) and the Mosley and Smith (1982) lists above, discuss the kinds of choices you use to help you create the kind of work atmosphere you prefer.

d. *Problem atmosphere.* Using elements from the same two lists, discuss the kinds of choices you use that might create problems for you in achieving the kind of work atmosphere you prefer.

e. *Adolescent reactions—task(s).* Discuss how you want the young people with whom you work to think about and feel about the *tasks* or *subjects* for which you are responsible and what kinds of choices on your part are likely to engender those reactions.

f. *Adolescent reactions—personal.* Discuss how you want the young people with whom you work to think about and feel about *you,* and what kinds of choices on your part are likely to engender those reactions.

g. *Adolescent reactions to themselves.* Discuss how you want the young people with whom you work to think about and feel about *themselves,* and what kinds of choices on your part are likely to engender those reactions.

Four Models of Classroom Management

Life might be simpler, though it would not be as interesting, if all psychologists agreed about the nature of human motivation, but they do not. The result is that we have a variety of theories that attempt to explain why people behave as they do. Wolfgang and Glickman (1986) suggested that there are three basic psychological interpretations of child development and that group management models for youth work can be categorized by the interpretation of development upon which they are based. The models they cited, modified here to apply beyond classroom management, include: *youth-centered models, environment-centered models, and interactive models.* To those models we add a fourth: *the Choice Awareness model.*

Youth-centered models.

The assumption in youth-centered models (Ernst, 1973; Gordon, 1974; and Simon, Howe, & Kirschenbaum, 1978) is that to a large extent each growing person possesses within him- or herself all that he or she needs for successful living; the goal of education is to unfold the inner potential that is already there. The focus is the young person and what he or she needs in order to unfold and become all that she or he is able to become, and to make effective choices in his or her life. Group activities focus at least in part on self-expression, and behavior management focuses on supportive/reflective techniques that maximize the opportunity for young people to solve their own behavior problems in their own way. The youth leader may use a silent stare, state what he or she has just seen happen, ask a non-judgmental open question to encourage reflection, or send an "I-message." Ordering, moralizing, warning, solutionizing, lecturing, criticizing, analyzing, or even praising and consoling are outside this approach—because in those behaviors the input for solving the problem comes from the adult rather than the adolescents. The goal is to get young people to generate their own solutions to alleviate their problems; and although the process may not be rapid, it is seen as advantageous for adolescents all along the way to retain ownership of both the problem and the solution.

Environment-centered models.

Underlying the environment-centered models (Axelrod, 1977; Canter, 1976; Hessman, 1977; Jones, 1987; and Kounin, 1971), also often referred to as behavioral, is the assumption that children and adolescents develop according to the conditions of the environment. The focus is that of providing an environment that will assure that proper socialization of young people occurs. Without strict control of the environment, proponents of this view believe, proper learning behavior is not likely to occur. Under this approach, leaders have not only the right, but the responsibility, to take control of the environment in which they work. Typical leader behaviors include positively-focused questions, positively-stated directives, modeling, reinforcement, rewards for appropriate behavior, and punishment for inappropriate behavior. In some of the environment-centered models there is much emphasis not only on what is said, but on how it is said and what body language accompanies it. A variety of non-verbal communications, such as notices, bulletin boards, the appearance of the leader's space, materials available for use, and physical arrangements of the environment, may be considered important as well.

Interactive models.

The interactive models (Dreikurs, 1968, Dreikurs, et al., 1982; Ginott, 1969 & 1971; and Glasser, 1969 & 1985), which are sometimes referred to as developmental, assume a complex interaction of internal and external forces that simultaneously act upon young people to push or pull them forward developmentally. The focus is that of setting broad boundaries of acceptable behavior and allowing freedom within those limits. When boundaries are crossed, leaders encourage negotiation for compromise until mutually acceptable resolutions are achieved. Expected responses to problems may include silent observation and analysis of the situation, reflective and directive statements, questioning, and modeling. Under the interactive models, there is a strong emphasis on helping young people to understand and take responsibility for their behavior and to make the kinds of choices that produce positive results for them.

The Choice Awareness model.

This source has introduced a fourth model of child development based on Choice Awareness theory (Nelson, 1977, 1989, 1980 & 1992). In this theory the view is taken that while both inside and outside forces act on young people to push or pull them forward developmentally,

young people are active participants. They begin very early in life making ever-increasing numbers of small and large choices daily that have impact on the development of their potential. The focus is that of helping young people become aware of the patterns of their choices and the alternatives available to them, while setting broad boundaries and allowing them freedom to make their choices within reasonable limits. At the same time, youth leaders serve both their own needs and the needs of youth more effectively when they choose to function creatively within their own broad boundaries.

In the Choice Awareness model, expected responses to misbehavior include helping young people understand the choices they are making and exploring with them alternative choices and consequences. As with the interactive model, the Choice Awareness model places strong emphasis on helping adolescents to understand and take responsibility for their behavior. This is accomplished through modeling positive, expansive choices and through assisting young people to make the kinds of choices that produce positive results for them.

In Chapter 15 we explore how Choice Awareness concepts and skills might be made part of a classroom management plan. In Chapter 16 we suggest how these concepts and communication skills may be shared with young people.

As a leader, you can interact with adolescents and work with them effectively using any of the above models; likewise you may interact with young people ineffectively regardless of which model you accept. Within the overall model you choose, it is important that you interpret individual instances of adolescent behavior in ways that are both as reasonable and as positive as possible.

In Chapter 10, we noted that it is often the interpretation of events that results in negative attitudes and behaviors; similarly, the overall interpretation of child development may result in negative attitudes and behaviors. If you choose to believe that young people need a rigid environment and that they will not grow positively unless you continually point the way, those beliefs may lead you to work with them in ways that stifle creativity and joy. On the other hand, you may choose to believe that young people need both structure and creative opportunities, and that may lead you to create an atmosphere of freedom within reasonable boundaries. You can encourage the young people you encounter to see life as a sequence of small and large choices, and help them understand that although there are genuine limits on the freedom they have to act, within the limits that exist they have a great deal of freedom to choose.

Ideas You Can Use with Individuals or Groups

Effective leaders know that prevention of misbehavior makes far more sense and is less disruptive and time-consuming than correction of misbehavior. Below is a list of preventive techniques that fit with most of the group management models.

** *Develop adolescent self-esteem.* Behavior problems and low self-esteem tend to go hand in hand. The following are effective choices you can make that are designed to increase the self-esteem of young people:

** *Communicate individually with adolescents.* If at all possible, schedule some kind of opportunity in every group, during each meeting, to walk about so that you might comment to individual young people as they work on their tasks or activities; use names whenever you speak to adolescents; pat shoulders, give "high fives," or shake hands with adolescents when appropriate; give "understanding looks"; and write encouraging notes to adolescents. While it may be argued that these efforts take vital seconds, it is frequently the case that those leaders who do not make such efforts spend far more time handling disciplinary difficulties.

** *Structure time so adolescents feel successful.* Encourage young people to participate by thanking them for their comments. On some assignments, give credit for completing the task rather than for its correctness. Ask questions from time to time about the *process* being explored. To use a teaching example, it is at least as important to know that an adjective tells which one, what kind of, or how many, as it is to be able to find the adjectives in a sentence. Nearly all young people can learn the definition through repeated statement of it, though some may have difficulty applying it.

** *Recognize both progress and success.* Comment as favorably as you honestly can on your pride in the accomplishments of the adolescents with whom you work. Encourage them and help them try to surpass their own personal achievements on the next task. Avoid recognizing only those for whom the work is easy; offer a small award or post the name and picture of the young person who improves most in any relevant way during a particular week or month or other time period. And send notes home commending adolescents for their effort, progress, or success.

** *Vary the presentation strategies you use.* Avoid boring *some* of the young people by using a variety of methods and appealing to various modes of processing. Employ relevant activities, use visuals but do not overdo their use, use auditory modes as often as you reasonably can in conjunction with other modes of presentation, and involve young people in hands-on activities whenever reasonable.

** *Teach students how to fight their own boredom.* As a youth leader you would rarely set out to bore adolescents, but you need to recognize that at any given moment, somebody is likely to choose to be bored—because the task or the topic is not of interest to the individual, the method of presentation does not fit his or her preferred learning style, or he or she is distracted by other things going on in his or her life. Recognize that, while you can work hard to make your groups interesting, you cannot reach all of the young people all of the time. Let the adolescents with whom you work know that they can make some choices concerning their own level of interest. Explore with them these techniques for combatting boredom:

  a. *silently explain the task or the content to yourself in your own words*
  b. *take notes and write reflections continuously*
  c. *ask questions about whatever is being presented*
  d. *think about how the topic relates to other information you know*
  e. *consider in what inventive ways you might be able to apply the ideas.*

** *Encourage a sense of group purpose.* Human beings are social creatures. They like to feel that they are a part of what is going on. Encourage *esprit de corps*, a genuine sense of group feeling, making sure that everyone in your group feels included—especially you. This helps establish to each individual that you and other group members are on their side as they attack their tasks. Where appropriate, encourage cooperative learning by assigning tasks to groups and by structuring situations in which cooperation advances them toward the goal faster and more efficiently than individual work. Encourage young people to acquire important information and skills and to share what they know, then make use of the information in some way that makes a difference; this lets them know that what they and others learn has value, and it encourages them to learn from each other.

In What Ways are You Like This Person?

Rhonda T.

Rhonda T. was a beginning teacher who was scheduled for an eighth grade history class in the inner city school to which she was assigned. She had heard stories about the tough kids at her school, and particularly in that section, but she was confident that she could succeed. Several weeks before school began, she talked with the assistant principal about discipline plans that had been effective for other teachers at the school. She settled on a plan, she had it approved by the administration, and she posted rewards and consequences on the bulletin board.

On the first day of school her students groaned when they saw the bulletin board. When she explained the plan, one student said, "We had a teacher with one of them plans last year, but we never saw no rewards." Rhonda told the student she appreciated his honesty and his concern; then promised to carry out the plan—with rewards and consequences—as they were earned. She wondered if she had chosen the wrong kind of plan and if she could carry it out fairly, but she promised herself she would give it her best effort and revise it if it did not work.

What evidence is there that Rhonda may not be successful with this class? What evidence is there that she might be successful? How much would you be like Rhonda in similar circumstances? What could you do to increase your chances for success if you were assigned a particularly challenging group of young people?

Critical Incident

Sally—a chatterbox. Sally is a fourteen-year-old you meet in one of your groups. She has always been social, but has rarely acted in a disruptive manner. However, the last few days she has been talking constantly when you have needed to give instructions, and when others in the group have the floor. You are suspicious that something is wrong in her life, but in a conference with her she repeatedly asserts that nothing special is going on.

How would you proceed under a youth-centered group management plan? Under an environment-centered plan? Under an interactive plan? Under a plan based on Choice Awareness theory? What differential expectations would you have for the outcomes under these different plans?

Sharing Choices and Communication Skills with Adolescents

Section L of Chapter 16 presents one final sharing suggestion under the title: *Boring.*

Journal Entry

Label these additional sections of your journal entry with the italicized headings below.

14.2. My management model. Based on the brief discussion of models, and drawing on your learnings gained through this source and others, try to determine which of the models—youth-centered, environment-centered, interactive, or Choice Awareness—best fits your own knowledge, beliefs, and feelings about adolescent development. In making your selection, consider how each model might help you or hinder you in establishing the kind of atmosphere and relationship you want with young people, and discuss the apparent fit between your preferred management model and the strengths, characteristics, and goals you enumerated in your *14.1* journal entry.

14.3. You may use the end-of-chapter activities or the key words on page 31 to further cue you in writing your entry.

15
Creating a CREST Plan for Group Management

In Part 2 of this source, we have explored choices and communications skills and suggested how you might share these concepts and skills with adolescents. In essence, we have provided you with the vocabulary, the skills, and the activities necessary to make more effective choices, and to assist young people to do the same. In this brief chapter we offer a guide for building a model Choice Awareness group management plan that incorporates the skills and choices we have explored.

Lee Canter (1976), in presenting the Assertive Discipline model for the classroom, recommended that a specific set of guidelines be established so that members are aware of the *rules*, *rewards*, and *consequences* of their behaviors within the group. We agree that rules, rewards, and consequences for behavior are three key essentials, and that leaders of youth, regardless of the group setting in which they function, need to have a plan and ensure that the plan is carried out. We believe that such a plan may be used to great advantage initially.

However, we believe that more ideal management plans than those suggested by Canter can advantageously be created over time. Once the group has been formed for a while the question can be raised: Are we ready to explore a new plan (if appropriate, an alternative arrangement to Assertive Discipline) that is designed to promote a positive working environment? If the response by the leader and by the group is resoundingly positive, the plan offered here may be explored and adapted for use with the group.

The Choice Awareness, or CREST, model for group management offers a proactive, comprehensive plan centered around three main ideas, stated here as they might be presented to young people: (1) It is important for us to treat one another so that all of us feel valued and respected. (2) We all make choices and our choices affect our relationships with others. (3) We can all make choices that enable us to work together more cooperatively and productively, and enjoy our time together.

These three ideas provide the framework group leaders can use to assist youth in identifying interactive objectives for the group. The use of the pronoun *we* is stressed to emphasize the reality that the group leader is a part of the group, and that he or she acts as a role model for making better choices.

What follows first is a set of questions, focused on the five CREST choices, that leaders can use with groups to help them develop their own plan for promoting individual growth and self-discipline. Based on the responses to these questions, a CREST group management plan can be created. This list of questions should be considered a guide. We encourage you to build your own CREST-focused questions so that they are appropriate to your setting and group.

We have included two examples of possible CREST group management plans, one group-based, the other classroom-based, since one format or the other may be more relevant to you. We encourage you to develop the concepts of Choice Awareness with your groups, then explore with them how you might work together to build a management plan that fits them and you.

CREST-Focused Questions for Building a Group Management Plan

Caring Choices—Making caring choices for ourselves and others in the group

What caring choices are OK within our group?

How may we let one another know that we care?

How might we encourage others to take effective care of themselves?

What kinds of self-caring choices can we make that will help ourselves and the group?

Will asking for caring choices be acceptable in our group?

What caring choices may be considered OD within our group?

How might we respond appropriately to caring choices that feel OD?

Ruling Choices—Making ruling choices for ourselves and others in the group

What leadership, or ruling choices are OK within our group?

What primary and specific rules do we need for our group to function effectively?

What kinds of self-ruling choices can we make that will help ourselves and the group?

What ruling choices may be considered OD within our group?

How might we respond appropriately to ruling choices that feel OD?

Enjoying Choices—Making enjoying choices for ourselves and others in the group

What enjoying choices are OK within our group?

What specific rewards or reward programs should we set up for responding to effective individual and group behavior?

In what ways might we encourage one another to make OK enjoying choices?

What enjoying choices should be considered OD within our group?

How might we respond appropriately to enjoying choices that feel OD?

Sorrowing Choices—Making sorrowing choices for ourselves

What sorrowing choices are OK within our group?

How can we help others and ourselves express negative emotions, including sadness, pain, grief, and anger?

What specific penalties should we set up as responses to problem behavior in the group?

How might we respond effectively to others' sorrowing choices?

What sorrowing choices should be considered OD within our group?

How might we respond appropriately to sorrowing choices that feel OD?

Thinking/Working Choices—Making thinking/working choices for ourselves and others.

What thinking/working choices are OK within our group?

How can we help one another go beyond shallow thinking and old habits to achieve more depth of thought and more appropriate action?

What kind of schedule should we have for reviewing choice patterns within the group?

What thinking/working choices should be considered OD within our group?

How might we respond appropriately to thinking/working choices that feel OD?

A Sample CREST Plan for Group Management

(A Model for Groups)

Our two primary rules for the group are:

We will show respect for ourselves and others and encourage others to do the same.

We will help to make this group a positive place to be.

The details of the plan which follow show the choices we expect to make in implementing these two primary rules.

Caring Choices

We will show that we care by listening—deeply—when someone needs to talk.

We will use additional communication skills that show we care.

We will encourage each other to make OK self-caring choices, and discourage making OD caring choices, such as self-indulgence or babying, and other OD choices such as using alcohol and drugs.

We will work toward making the group a safe place in which people can say what they think and feel and not be "cut down."

Ruling Choices

We will offer suggestions to each other without being "bossy."

We will respect the need for order and not talk when others are talking.

We will clearly state our needs and wants.

We will be polite and respectful when offering corrections to each other; we will use such statements as: "Please be quiet and listen, and when I get through, I'll be happy to listen to you," and we will avoid saying things like "Shut up!"

We will respect the leader's guidelines and rules; and we will ask for discussion time when we see problems with the rules or the task assigned.

Enjoying Choices

We will share our good feelings with one another.

We will recognize each others' accomplishments.

We will expect positive statements and other appropriate recognition for strong individual and group effort.

We will regularly set aside 5-minute or longer time blocks for activities that help us feel good about ourselves.

We will laugh *with* people rather than *at* them.

Sorrowing Choices

We will accept each other's needs to express negative feelings from time to time.

When someone is angry or has other negative feelings we will try to help them talk about their feelings and needs rather than hold them inside.

We will not "take out" our negative feelings on one another or ourselves.

When our negative feelings are particularly strong we will seek help, and we will encourage others to do the same, rather than make OD choices.

We will accept the consequences and the penalties when we violate rules.

Thinking/Working Choices

When others need help we will assist them to come up with their own solutions through such means as brainstorming, listing alternatives, and rehearsing, but we will avoid giving others solutions to their problems.

We will recognize that giving someone the answer to a problem only helps temporarily; it does not assist the person to be independent and responsible for working through future problems.

We will stop and think about our choices and options before we react, and we will encourage others to do the same.

We will balance thinking/working with the other four choices.

Choices and Respect for the Group

We agree to respect each other and the group, and to help each other make positive choices.

On those occasions when we do not show respect for the rules of the group, when we continuously make major or minor OD choices, we will expect to be asked to reconsider the kinds of choices we are making.

We will help other members of the group to understand how their choices are affecting the group and to reconsider the kinds of choices they are making.

Any person who is unwilling or unable to eliminate major OD choices may be asked to leave the group for a brief or extended period of time until she or he is ready to make more OK choices; when the person returns he or she will be welcomed and respected.

A Sample CREST Plan for Classroom Management

(A Model for the Classroom)

Our two primary rules for the classroom are:

We will show respect for ourselves and others and encourage others to do the same.

We will help to make this class a positive place to be.

The details of the plan which follow show the choices we expect to make in implementing these two primary rules.

Caring Choices

We will show that we understand that others have lives within and outside of school by listening—deeply— when someone needs to talk.

We will use additional communication skills that show we care.

We will encourage each other to make OK self-caring choices, and discourage making OD caring choices, such as self-indulgence or babying, and other OD choices such as using alcohol and drugs.

We will understand the need people have for a quiet place to work and we will respect that need.

We will work toward making the class a safe place in which people can say what they think and feel and not be "cut down."

Ruling Choices

We will agree to a set of rules that will help our class run smoothly.

We will help one another follow the rules of the class.

We will offer suggestions to each other without being pushy or bossy.

We will respect the need for order and not talk when others are talking.

We will clearly state our needs and wants.

We will be polite and respectful when offering corrections to each other; we will use such statements as: "Please be quiet and listen, and when I get through, I'll be happy to listen to you," and we will avoid saying things like "Shut up!"

We will respect the teacher's guidelines and rules for homework and assignments; and we will ask for discussion time when we see problems with the work assigned.

Enjoying Choices

We will take some responsibility for our own interest and help make this class fun.

We will share our good feelings with one another.

We will recognize the good work that everyone is doing.

We will expect positive statements and other appropriate recognition for strong individual and group effort.

We will regularly set aside 5-minute or longer time blocks for activities that help us feel good about ourselves, and occasional longer time frames in which we can share our assignments and accomplishments with one another.

We will laugh *with* people rather than *at* them.

Sorrowing Choices

We will accept each other's needs to express negative feelings from time to time.

When someone is angry or has other negative feelings we will try to help them talk about their feelings and needs rather than rather than hold them inside.

We will not "take out" our negative feelings on one another or ourselves.

When our negative feelings are particularly strong we will seek help, and we will encourage others to do the same, rather than make OD choices.

We will accept the consequences and the penalties when we violate rules.

Thinking/Working Choices

When others need help we will assist them to come up with their own solutions through such means as brainstorming, listing alternatives, and rehearsing, but we will avoid giving others solutions to their schoolwork or other problems.

We will recognize that giving someone the answer to a problem only helps temporarily; it does not help the person on tests or assist him or her to be independent and responsible for working through future problems.

We will stop and think about our choices and options before we react, and we will encourage others to do the same.

We will balance thinking/working with the other four choices.

Choices and Respect for the Class and the Teacher

We agree to respect each other and the class, and to help each other make positive choices.

On those occasions when we do not show respect for the rules of the class, when we continuously make major or minor OD choices, we will expect to be asked to reconsider the kinds of choices we are making.

We will help other members of the class to understand how their choices are affecting the others and to reconsider the kinds of choices they are making.

Any person who is unwilling or unable to eliminate major OD choices may be asked to leave the class for a brief or extended period of time until she or he is ready to make more OK choices; when the person returns he or she will be welcomed and respected.

16
Choices and Communication Skills for Adolescents

The activities presented in this chapter are designed to make it easy and fun for you to share the concepts of Choice Awareness with the adolescents in your charge. Note that the sections cited below parallel the previous *Choices and Communication Skills* chapters. Those who elect to present the concepts of Choice Awareness to young people will want to review the chapters in order to lead discussions effectively and to make the best use of the activities.

We encourage you to use these activities with young people in a group setting. If you work outside the world of education, or if you work within education but lack a group with whom you might share these ideas, think creatively and you may be able to arrange a group experience. To offer one example, a group of counselors in Indiana are involved in a field study in which they are presenting the concepts of Choice Awareness to groups of adolescent delinquents. (Note: Preliminary data suggest that the outcomes will be both valuable and statistically significant.) If you work in the world of education you may have a homeroom period, an advisor/advisee program, or a guidance class for which you are responsible; or you may wish to consider spending ten to twenty minutes on the concepts each Monday or Friday in any class—perhaps as a reward for effort.

Regardless of the setting in which you share the concepts, the adolescents you work with will reap significant benefits if you help them make better choices. Let this portion of *Working with Adolescents: Building Effective Communication and Choice-Making Skills* help you lead adolescents toward making more effective choices; it will benefit both them and you.

Feel free to adapt and add to the ideas presented in the following sections in ways that are appropriate to your group. Help group members see that they choose their way through life, and that they can live more effective lives when they see their words and actions as choices. If it seems relevant, stress the point with your group that as the members show that they are growing and maturing, they are likely to be permitted greater freedom of choice in the important matters that involve them, and that with greater freedom comes greater responsibility.

Build journal entries in which you reflect upon the activities and their effects on the young people in your charge

A. The Ways in Which We Make Our Choices (See Chapter 3)

We make many choices. Most young people have a great deal of freedom, but they perceive their world as controlled by others. They complain: "Dad sets the time when I have to be home, Mom tells me what to wear, and teachers say when I've gotta do my work." It is important for you to help adolescents understand the frequency and variety of choices they make.

Try this: Give your group members small pieces of paper and have them write down a number that indicates how many choices they believe they have made "since this time yesterday." Request that they not put their names on the papers. Have someone collect the papers and scramble them, then read the numbers aloud. Avoid evaluating responses as right or wrong. Lead a discussion concerning why some in the group think they make very few choices while others think they make far more.

Each opportunity to choose allows for a wide variety of choices. Try this. Have your group members list 3 or 4 situations that are relevant to them. Situations may be simple (e.g., entering a room where three friends are present) or complex (e.g., having a person you really like tell you she or he intends to go to a major up-coming social activity with someone other than you). Invite the group to brainstorm ten responses that would be possible if the event occurred to them. Encourage inclusion of positive, negative, and neutral responses—based on the different attitudes individuals might *choose* to have. Explore each of the responses in the discussion. Point out that many responses are possible in most situations. Discuss this point: we choose our attitudes and our behaviors follow.

Choices can be based on goals. Try this. Again, have the group list 3 or 4 simple or complex everyday situations they face—if they listed school situations in the previous instance, suggest that they list home situations, or vice versa. (1) Invite them to brainstorm a list of at least five varied responses that would be possible if the situation occurred to them. (2) Ask them to speculate on the long term relationship goals suggested by each response. (3) Have them write a positive, possible goal for each relationship. (4) Invite them again to brainstorm at least five new responses that would be possible if the event occurred to them—and they were determined to act on the positive goal. Be sure these ideas are considered in the discussion: Adolescents and others around them have goals in their relationships, and they show their goals by the ways in which they act. If young people want to achieve their goals they need to make choices that move them in that direction.

B. OK and OD CREST Choices (See Chapter 4)

We can learn to differentiate major and minor OK and OD choices.

Try this. Explore the idea of major and minor OK and OD choices with your group, then present two or more of the following situations and invite them to suggest major and minor OK and OD choices they could make in each situation.

An acquaintance tells you his parents are really angry at him over something.

A friend scored well in a game or received an excellent grade on a paper—and she is very excited.

A close friend says, "I'm really worried—my favorite uncle was in an accident."

Someone near you drops a cafeteria tray and glass shards litter the floor.

After considering two or more of these sample situations, invite group members to suggest others they would like to explore. See if they can propose major and minor OK and OD choices they could make in each situation. Help them explore the likely effects of the major and minor OK and OD choices they make.

We can conceptualize relationships as accounts.

Try this. Discuss accounts in relationships, then, depending on the time available, have group members fold 8 1/2 X 11" (or half sized) sheets of paper so they have either four, six, or eight boxes. Ask them to put a numerical estimate of the present balance for the most positive account they have in the upper left box, and an estimate of the present balance in their most negative account in the lower right box—based on a +10 to -10 range for the choices each makes. Suggest they code those two sections in their own way, e.g., BR for brother, RV for rival. Ask them to select two, four, or six other relationships (with siblings, friends, relatives), estimate those balances, and enter names or codes in those sections.

Brainstorm with the group how they might *maintain* the balance in their positive accounts and *build* the balance in the accounts that are "in the red." Then have them note in the appropriate boxes a choice they plan to use to build or maintain the account. In discussion, make sure the point is made that adding to or subtracting from accounts is done through major and minor OK and OD choices.

We can learn to make use of the five CREST choices.

Introduce the five CREST choices by adapting the discussion in this chapter. Draw ideas from group members. If it is true, and it is likely to be, indicate that you are not sure that you can always discriminate one choice from another but that the really important thing is to differentiate OK and OD choices.

Try this. Form groups of four or five. Give each group a paper cube or die you have prepared in advance with the letters C, R, E, S, T (or T/W), and CREST, on the six sides. Have group members pose different situations; the person who has the cube tosses it and responds to the situation with the kind of choice that appears on top. If the CREST side comes up, the person may make any of the CREST choices, then name the kind of choice he or she made. Others are to help as needed. If the choice made initially is OD, have group members also suggest an OK choice that might be made in the same circumstances. In the discussion, make the point that most of the time we can make any of the CREST choices, and most of the time in OK ways.

C. Caring Choices (See Chapter 5)

Caring choices are responses to needs. Explore caring choices with your group. After some discussion, ask the members to help you build a list of caring choices they might be able to use from time to time. Choose two or three examples and. . .

Try this. Discuss how those choices might best be made, then form groups of 3 or 4 and have each individual in turn be the focus person. For just a minute or two the focus person shares a need, real or invented. The others try out various caring choices and get feedback from the needful one concerning how their responses felt. In the discussion that follows, give reinforcement for all efforts, and strong reinforcement for those that seem to be most caring and helpful. Make the point that new behaviors, like new skills in sports, often seem awkward; suggest that group members give many tries to the ideas they have explored with you.

Using the three-step listening process. When young people in school settings are asked to suggest activities that might be used as rewards for hard work, they often ask for brief free time periods in which they may talk quietly with one another. Suggest to your group that if they like, you will add five or ten extra minutes to bonus time they may already have earned so that you might work with them on their listening skills.

Try this. Form pairs or triads by counting-off or in some other way so that those involved get a chance to talk with others they might not normally work with as partners. Take the group step-by-step through the three-step listening process. Write the three steps on a chart or chalkboard: *pause, repeat internally,* and *search out feelings.* Prepare one or two volunteers and have them share with you three or four sentences on a topic such as: Some things I like about this group. Demonstrate the three steps by saying aloud what you are thinking. "E.g. I'm pausing. I'm repeating internally: X said (as near exact words as possible) in a (what

kind of) tone of voice. The feeling I heard was (use a feeling word—excitement, frustration, etc.)."

Have each person pick a personal, yet everyday, topic they'd be willing to talk about with their partner(s)— something funny that happened to me last summer, one of my favorite relatives, a pet I had. Have them decide who will go first. Give the group enough time so that each person has two or three opportunities to practice listening.

When the time allotted is up, invite volunteers to share how it felt both to listen and to be listened to. Stress two points: that listening is beneficial, and that it is a choice.

Supplements to listening. Explore with your group the components of listening, and such topics as posture, proximity, touching, silence, and minimum verbal responses in communicating with others.

Try this. Have group members form pairs so that they get a chance to talk with another person they don't know very well. For one minute one person presents a topic and the other listens, uses silence and MVRs, etc. Then have them switch roles. In the discussion make sure that the benefits of the various components of listening are brought out. Make the point that the components of listening are choices all people may exercise dozens or even hundreds of times each day.

D. Paraphrasing and Reflecting as Caring Choices (See Chapter 6)

Paraphrasing. Introduce your group to paraphrasing, stressing its values.

Try this. Ask for two volunteers to help you model paraphrasing. Invent your own issue or use the one that follows—you may want to consider writing out the situation on index cards—or you may verbally assign the A and B roles and say: "The problem is that A dislikes Z, a third person, rather intensely, and doesn't want him or her involved. But because B includes Z in activities, you are often a trio. A has been complaining about this to B, one-on-one, so you decide to use paraphrasing to bring the issue into the open. A, the disliker, begins by making several statements. B, the liker, paraphrases A's comments. After A is satisfied with the paraphrase, B makes several statements, which must in turn be paraphrased by A. And so on. I'll help you as needed." In the discussion following, make sure that the costs *and* benefits of paraphrasing are explored.

As a followup, have group members form triads (or pairs, if necessary) involving people they don't know very well. See that each group has someone in it with a watch that can time a half minute accurately. Prepare them, then have them continue on their own. For a half minute one person presents a problem, real or invented, while another listens, then paraphrases. First the original speaker, then the observer, gives brief feedback or makes a suggestion about how the paraphrase might be improved. Pairs then go ahead and rotate roles until all have had a chance to paraphrase.

Reflection of feeling. Use points in the chapter to introduce your group to reflection of feeling. Some may express discomfort at first, preferring to ignore feelings or ask about them.

Encourage them to practice using reflection of feeling *many times,* in *statement* form, and *then* decide their judgment about whether they will use it in the future.

Try this. Form two groups and move between the two so that you can help. Each person in turn is to make a comment that involves some kind of feeling. The person on his or her right is to (1) *pause,* (2) *name the feeling,* and (3) *make a statement* (not a question) *that includes a form of the feeling word.* Others in the group may assist, or suggest other feelings and statements—reflections of feeling. The person on the left of the speaker in each instance may be asked to act as recorder, writing down the words of both persons, the feeling named, and the reflection—for later discussion.

Discuss the approach. Point out that reflection of feeling, like any new skill, is difficult to master and use comfortably; but that, once mastered, reflection of feeling is a caring choice that is often valuable in interactions with friends and family members.

E. Ruling Choices (See Chapter 7)

Introducing ruling choices. Use relevant points in the chapter to explore ruling choices with your group. Since few young people really believe they make ruling choices, help your group members see that they do so quite frequently, particularly with others their own age and younger, and especially in activities and games.

Try this. In small groups or all together, have group members specify a number of game or activity situations in which they make ruling choices. Have them offer examples of the ruling choices they might make: "Let's go." "I'm next." "I got it." "It's your move." Etc. Encourage mostly OK choices. Next: To extend the point that ruling choices can be very welcome, hand out slips of paper, have individuals write their names on the slip along with a code that indicates a person they see frequently, but with whom they seldom exercise positive leadership—make OK ruling choices. Ask them to write down a positive suggestion they

will make to that person—play cards with me, sit and talk with me for a few minutes, go with me to a game or a movie. Tell them that you will put the slips away for a specified time, then you will ask each person who wishes to share how the other individual responded to their leadership—their OK ruling choice. Followup as agreed. Generously reinforce both efforts and successes.

In the followup discussion, make sure two points are made: (1) young people can use OK ruling choices to build their accounts with others; and (2) when young people take the lead they experience a greater sense of positive involvement and power.

Assertiveness. Introduce your group members to the assertiveness sequence.

Try this. Illustrate the assertiveness sequence a few times, then present one or more of the situations below. Organize your group in 3's or 4's. Have them figure out a series of assertive choices they could make in each selected situation.

You have been waiting to buy tickets for a long time and someone cuts in line ahead of you.

You receive change for ten dollars, but you gave the clerk a twenty dollar bill.

At a friend's house you see a video of yours that has been missing for a while.

A friend pleads with you to stay an hour more, but you have to be home right away.

A stranger asks directions, then says, "You're going my way. Hop in, I'll give you a ride."

Ask those present to suggest situations in which they believe they might be reasonably assertive, and explore the assertive choices they might make—and the possible consequences of their choices. In the discussion, be sure that your group members understand that neither unassertiveness nor aggressiveness serves them well in many everyday situations. Point out that assertiveness and a sense of personal power are related, and that both depend on the effective use of ruling choices.

F. Enjoying Choices (See Chapter 8)

Introducing enjoying choices. Share with your group the idea that OK enjoying choices can be very important if they want to add to their accounts with others. Help them see that events that take a lot of time may be valued enjoying choices, but they can also make significant enjoying choices in just a few seconds. You may wish to lead a discussion on the differences between childish and child-like behaviors. *Childish* actions are silly, foolish, and thought-less, and are best "put away." *Childlike* suggests the qualities of innocence, trust and enjoyment, qualities that should be retained. Invite group members to talk about adults they know who have childlike qualities.

Try this. Form a circle. Invite each person in turn to make a positive statement, beginning "I enjoy. . .," about the person on the right *and* on the left. Lead off with statements of your own that mention positive personality traits, such as: "I enjoy your enthusiasm, Gerry. You're often eager to get into new ideas and explore them." Consider using this activity periodically to create a more positive environment.

Young people often feel powerless to affect others. In the discussion, help them see that their choices *do* affect others, and that it is possible for them to make OK enjoying choices that affect others positively.

Promoting relaxation in adolescents. Use relevant points in the chapter to help young people expand their concepts of enjoying choices.

Try this. Discuss the benefits of relaxation and exercise as important enjoying choices. Then, over several days, take your group through various relaxation procedures. Spend a few minutes each on deep breathing, meditation, fantasy, and relaxation training.

One caution. Make sure that the procedures you use do not violate stated community norms or institutional policies. Some fundamentalist Christian groups have taken exception to the simplest relaxation procedures, e.g., "Imagine a quiet, pleasant place," and tensing/relaxing exercises. It would be well to educate parents concerning relaxation before using it with young people. Here the position is taken that it is appropriate and necessary for young people to learn how to relax in our hectic, busy world.

G. Sorrowing Choices (See Chapter 9)

Exploring sorrowing choices. Share with your group the idea that all people encounter times when they will make sorrowing choices, and that the range of possible sorrowing choices can be very great.

Try this. Build a list of five or six situations young people might face that could *lead* them to (not *make* them—they have a choice) feel frustrated or annoyed. Form groups of three or four. Ask each group to select a recorder. Have the groups brainstorm one or two sorrowing responses some-

one is likely to make in each of the situations, and one or two OK sorrowing choices they might use instead—involving straightforward and brief statements, perhaps inside themselves or to a third person. Note that none of the responses should involve issuing orders or strongly worded suggestions—since those are ruling choices.

Example: Someone mispronounces a word and others laugh. The person's likely response might be, "Oh, you're not so smart yourselves!" An OK sorrowing choice to a third person might be, "Wow I felt really rotten today in third period. I blew it when I mispronounced *nuclear* and everybody laughed."

In the discussion, help group members see that when they are frustrated or annoyed they can share their feelings through sorrowing choices that are at least OK for them-selves. Also, point out that the sorrowing choices they make affect others and influence the consequences they receive.

Structured sorrowing choices. Discuss with your group the idea that sharing sadnesses, rather than letting others guess what is wrong, can contribute to their relationships and increase the value of their accounts; it is clearly better than leaving others to blame themselves. Teach them the use of *structured sorrowing choices.*

Try this. Have group members suggest situations that frustrate or annoy them and help them role play *structured sorrowing choices* they might use in such situations. Set up a sequence around a circle, for example. Invite those who wish in turn to mention something that has happened—it may be real or invented—that might have led them to make sorrowing choices. Ask them to tell what choice they made in the situation. Then have them mention a *struc-tured sorrowing choice* or another more positive choice they might have made at the time. To broaden the range of possibilities, have group members suggest one or two alternative *structured sorrowing choices* the individual might have used.

In the discussion, emphasize the point that although young people may feel powerless, they often affect others adversely—through making OD sorrowing choices.

I-messages and you-messages. Share the concepts of *I-messages* and *you-messages* as sorrowing choices. Empha-size *I-messages.* Relate *you-messages* to reflections of feel-ing and paraphrases which have previously been consid-ered.

Try this. Have group members suggest situations that frustrate or annoy them. Assign individuals to groups of three or four and have them plan brief role plays in which they send *I-messages* in response to those situations. In the discussion following, emphasize the points that they can send *I-messages* that convey their sorrowing choices, and that the choices they make affect the responses that are returned.

H. Anger and Grief as Sorrowing Choices (See Chapter 10)

Anger buttons. Explore with your group the idea of "anger buttons." Invite group members to suggest figures in literature, television, or motion pictures who give evidence of having easily-triggered "anger buttons."

Try this. Assign those present to groups of three or four and have each group prepare a brief role play in which they demonstrate a literary, television, or motion picture situation in which someone pushes a character's "anger button." In the discussion following, explore alternative responses (e.g., OK sorrowing choices) that might have been possible in the same situation. Also, discuss the weaknesses and strengths inherent in having "anger buttons" that others know they can push.

Wants related to anger. Considering the maturity and age of your group, introduce them to the first three, four, or five of the wants they have when they feel angry, and help them see that what they want when they are angry suggests a way someone else *could* respond to them (see pp. 75-76).

Try this. On slips of paper, sufficient so that each person may have one, write *one* of the first three (or all five) of the following wants: (1) *Angry people want to be heard.* (2) *Angry people want someone to notice their feelings.* (3) *Angry people want someone to see their point of view.* (4) *Angry people want help in figuring out what caused the anger,* but not necessarily right away. (5) *Angry people want respect.*

Group those present according to the slip they drew. Have each group settle on one situation in which a member once felt angry, then share how it would have felt, and how another person might have responded, if she or he had really understood what the person wanted. Share both the situations and the possible responses in the total group, then invite suggestions from people who had a different assignment.

Now ask the members of the small groups to act as if *another* person within the group—not themselves—felt the same anger. Have them respond to the want in the best way they can.

Discuss the situations and the responses. Help group members see that what they want—and the ways they would like others to respond—can give them the best clues as to what others want and need.

Grief. Grief can be a volatile subject for adolescents. It is easy to unwittingly uncover a case of unresolved grief in the course of a simple discussion. In your discussion of grief, try to keep the group on an intellectual level to guard against this, but be prepared to make a referral, if necessary. Begin with the following activity.

Try this. Ask your group to pretend that their best friend's grandmother has died. Tell them that their friend has been away for three days to attend the funeral and has now returned. Ask them to write briefly what they would probably say or do when they first saw their friend. Collect the papers and anonymously read some of the responses, omitting any that do not contain serious responses to the situation. Help the group select two or three of the most helpful responses from the pool. Then talk briefly about reaching out, about including the grieving person in activities, and about listening. Adolescents who have been through grief often report that, of the people in their lives, their peers were both the most helpful (usually by just being there and by listening) and the most hurtful (usually by acting as if nothing had happened).

I. Thinking/Working Choices (See Chapter 11)

OK CREST choices. Help your group members see that they make a great number of thinking/working choices daily. Encourage them to balance their thinking/working choices with the other CREST choices. Help them see that they can plan ahead to make better choices with people who are important to them.

Try this. Have individuals spend a few moments thinking about someone who is important to them, with whom they would like a better relationship. Encourage them to select one OK CREST choice they want to *increase*, OR one OD CREST choice they want to *decrease*, with the person, and figure out how they might go about making the change. Invite them to share their plan with the group, naming the person or not, as they choose.

Begin the activity by modeling the kinds of statements you want to encourage your group members to make. For example: "With my friend, Dale, I need to make more OK ruling choices. Too often I wait for Dale to make suggestions about things we can do together. I'm going to say more things like, 'Dale, I'd really enjoy meeting you for lunch on Saturday.'"

In the discussion, make the point that we can improve many of our relationships by planning more effective choices and following through on our plans—and by balancing our thinking/working choices with other choices.

Open versus closed questions. Help your group members see the advantages of open questions over closed questions.

Try this. Pose an everyday situation that tends to call for questions, e.g., you meet a friend whose mother has been ill. Hand a slip of paper to three or four volunteers in one part of the room that says: *Group A. When your group is called on, be prepared to ask one or two* factual *questions or questions that can be answered yes or no. Example. What kind* of medication is your mother taking? Is she doing any better now? Hand another slip of paper to three or four group members in another cluster that says: *Group B. When your group is called on, be prepared to ask one or two open questions that do not call for details and cannot be answered yes or no. Example. How are you getting along since your mother has been ill?* While the two groups are planning their questions, explain to the other members of the class that they are to evaluate the two approaches.

You play the part of the friend whose mother is ill. Allow a couple of minutes for the individuals to get ready to ask their questions, move first in front of Group A, then go to Group B. The groups in turn ask their questions, and you answer them hypothetically in ways that make sense.

In the discussion that follows, ask the observers to discuss how well the two groups carried out their assignments, and what they thought of closed versus open questions. Develop the point that one way they can demonstrate their interest and caring to others is to remember what they talked about when they last met someone, and comment on, or ask about, the interests or concerns of that person.

Listening versus solutions. Help your group members see the advantages of listening over offering solutions.

Try this. Pose a situation that tends to call for advice or solutions, e. g., a friend says, "I'm in terrible trouble with one of my teachers. He thinks I cheated on our unit test, but I didn't." Choose a new group of three or four individuals in one part of the room (not those you selected for the activity above), and hand them a slip of paper that says: *Group C. When your group is called on, be prepared to offer one or two solutions. Example. You might want to talk to him. I bet he'll listen.* Hand another slip of paper to three or four other group members that says: *Group D. When your group is called on, be prepared to listen and to encourage the person to talk; if you wish you may ask open questions, but don't offer any suggestions. Example. Gee, I can see you're really strung out about this.* While the two groups are planning their responses, suggest to the other group members that they should be ready to evaluate the two approaches.

You play the part of the adolescent whose teacher thinks you cheated. After a couple of minutes for the individuals to get ready, move first in front of Group C, then go to Group D. The groups respond in turn, and you reply to them hypothetically in ways that make reasonable sense.

In the discussion that follows, ask the observers to discuss how well the two groups carried out their assignments, and what they thought of the two approaches. Develop the point that young people can often demonstrate their interest and caring more effectively by listening than by making suggestions, and that applies to adults as well.

J. Components of Thinking/Working Choices (See Chapter 12)

Rehearsal/role play. Explore with your group members the idea of using rehearsal or role play to encounter their problems.

Try this. Have those present specify five or six situations which lend themselves to rehearsal and/or role play, e. g., *A friend borrows things from you, including tapes and money, and does not return them; you want the person's friendship, but you don't like being taken advantage of.* As each situation is offered, summarize it on chart paper or chalkboard in a few words or a sentence or two.

Form as many groups as you have situations listed, by counting off. Assign each group a different situation and ask them to rehearse and role play as if one of the members actually faces the difficulty. In each instance, the person who has the problem is to tell another member of the group about the problem and the two will then rehearse and/or role play what the person might say. Other members of the group are to observe, give feedback, make suggestions, and report on the situation later.

In the discussion that follows, ask the observers to report on the rehearsal and role play and tell what they thought of these approaches. If time permits, reenact some of the situations. Develop the point that people can often ease their difficulties by rehearsing what they want to say before they say it.

Reframing. Explore with your group members the idea of using reframing to help them deal with their problems.

Try this. Begin by having those present take from three to five minutes to write down conflict situations they have heard about—not their own. As an example, use the situation that was described under the title *Reframing for Adolescents* in Chapter 12. Make the point that the individual could be male or female. Ask them to include in their writing some of the kinds of details in the example.

Then. Share information from Chapter 12 and explore with group members the idea of reframing. Either in the total group, or in groups of four or five, have them share the conflict situations they wrote about and try to figure out how the person who has the problem might reframe it.

In the discussion that follows, help those present see that they are often frustrated because others do not understand them, but in all likelihood they do not take time to understand others, either. They may be able to make matters better for themselves if they consider the viewpoints of others. Suggest that they look for opportunities to reframe. Announce a future time for reporting on reframing experiences, and build that into your schedule.

Record keeping. Explore with your group the idea of using self-monitoring and record keeping to help them encounter their problems.

Share information from the chapter and explore with your group members the idea of self-monitoring as an approach to problem-solving. The general guidelines are as follows: (1) Decide on a behavior you want to increase or decrease. What is it? (2) Collect base rate information for a minimum of two or three days—at first without trying to change. How many times did the behavior occur? (3) Figure out how you might wish to change and try it for a few days. What do you need to do? (4) Keep an accurate count of your behavior for the next several days. How does the count change over time? (5) Evaluate your progress and maintain the current direction, or recycle through any necessary steps if the strategy is not working. Do you want to continue your present approach or make changes?

Try this. Have group members take five minutes to write down a behavior they would like to increase or decrease (Step 1 above), and make some notes about how they might be able to change (Step 3).

In the discussion that follows, ask those who are willing to share the changes they would like to make. Take time after an appropriate interval for group members to discuss their progress. Reward gain *and* effort.

K. Consequences, Feelings, and Choices (See Chapter 13)

Consequences. Use relevant points in this chapter to explore the concept of consequences with your group members.

Try this. Form three groups and move between them so you can assist. In turn, without naming names, each person is to describe a situation in which he or she would be tempted to respond in a very negative way. The person to the focus person's left is to respond in what he or she thinks would be the most likely way—with the most likely consequence. Others in the group are then invited to suggest unlikely, but possible, responses. Then the person to the individual's right is to respond in what she or he thinks would be a less-likely way—with a less-likely consequence. Others in the group are then invited to suggest other possible responses and consequences.

In the discussion that follows, be sure the point is made that expected consequences tell us that the world is somewhat predictable, and unexpected consequences make it clear that other people make independent, and sometimes unrelated, choices.

Choosing feelings. Take time, perhaps over a period of several days, to help your group understand and use two significant ideas: (1) It is likely that you can choose more positively than you do from among your feelings in many of the moments of your life. (2) You can choose to feel good about yourself and others.

Try this. In the total group, have members mention some incidents that have really troubled them in the past. For each of the incidents, build a list of the many feelings that might be possible concerning the people and the situations involved. Make sure the group considers the underlying positive feelings: e.g., admiration, affection, respect, loving, liking, adventure, interest, etc. Compare and contrast the choices they might make, and the consequences that would likely follow, if they acted on their more positive feelings versus those that were more negative.

In the discussion, return with some frequency to the two main ideas summarized in the first paragraph above.

L. Better Choosing and Better Management (See Chapter 14)

Boring. Develop the concept that boredom and interest are choices.

Try this. In big letters, write the word BORING on a chart or chalkboard. Ask the group members for contributions of things they have from time to time found boring. Add items of your own, specifying whether you have personally found them boring or have heard others say they were boring. Keep asking for suggestions until you have a list large enough to contain conflicting items. Put items in specific terms, e.g., going on an archeological dig in Turkey, attending a baseball doubleheader between the White Sox and the Yankees, visiting Switzerland or Cleveland, eating soda crackers. Have each person list on paper the three items from the list they find most boring. Have two group members tally on the chalkboard the number of "votes" each item received. Invite them to discuss the extent of agreement they showed as a class. Open the topic for discussion: What did someone else (others) find boring that you find interesting?

Help group members see that, when different people find different things boring, it is not possible to keep everyone interested in everything all the time, and that they need to take some responsibility for avoiding boredom. Share with them the techniques for avoiding boredom under *Ideas You Can Use,* and help them expand the list. Make the point that being bored and finding or creating interest are *choices.*

Part 3
Supplementary Materials

Part 3 of *Working with Adolescents: Building Effective Communication and Choice-Making Skills,* includes various materials that are intended to supplement the text and provide suggestions for enhancing the involvement of the readers. The program presented here has a particular context which is described briefly below, but it is readily adaptable to a variety of other situations, such as extended staff training, in-service education, intensive workshops, and college or university courses.

The program presented here has been offered most frequently as an intensive course for teachers-in-training scheduled in the six weeks prior to a ten-week student teaching experience.

In addition, alternative experiences based on the same model have been arranged for a number of experienced teachers and others who wish to maintain or meet state certification requirements.

The overall purpose of the first cluster of Supplementary Materials is to provide specific guidelines to participants for preparing Team Presentations and Handouts for use with the group. These presentation experiences put the participants in the role of team leaders who develop and present content related to adolescents to their colleagues. It is often said that the best way to learn a skill or content in great depth is to present it to others. Thus, awareness of the abilities, needs, and concerns of adolescents is greatly enhanced through presentations to colleagues. This cluster of materials includes:

- **Team presentations:** Adolescence. A brief introductory statement.
- **Expectations for the Team Presentation Handout.** Expectations are spelled out in detail. These expectations and all subsequent materials can be adapted to the needs and purposes of the particular group for which they are designed.
- **Sample Handout:** Theories of Adolescence.
- **Expectations for Team Presentations.**
- **Sample Team Presentation Planning Guide.**
- **Team Presentation — Evaluation Form.**
- **Team Presentation — Guide for Small Group Discussion.**
- **Team Presentation — Self-Evaluation.**

The second cluster of Supplementary Materials relates to another set of experiences involving communication skills training and taping experiences which we have found to be very valuable. This cluster of materials includes:

- **Communication Skills.** This list includes an array of communication skills that may be targeted for increase or decrease, depending on the individual's needs.
- **Taping Experiences — Introduction.**
- **Sample Taping Activity — Instructions.**
- **Outline for Tape Critique Paper.**

The final item in the Supplementary Materials is:

- **Instructions for Preparing a Critical Incident.** Participants are asked to design incidents that include the setting and dialogue, then end in a challenge that demands an immediate response, and may require later followup. It is most valuable if critical incidents reflect real life, rather than the extremes of issues. One adaptation that may be especially useful is that of creating mini-case studies for exploration. If this is done, where feasible, we recommend that each case study end with an immediate challenge for dialogue or action of the sort we have offered in Chapter Two.

- **Journaling.** In addition to the assignments and materials specified above, we request that the participants keep a journal on such matters as their reactions to their readings, their responses to the critical incidents and the end-of-chapter activities, and their experiences in applying the communication skills and choices they acquire through the program. Journal entries have afforded the participants excellent opportunities for self-expression and for gaining in self-understanding. They have also provided valuable feedback that has been used to evaluate and re-structure the program so that it meets participants' needs more directly and effectively.

- **Return Date.** We have included in the design of the program what we refer to as a Return Date. In the middle of the Student Teaching experience we ask students to return for an extended session. This session functions as an opportunity for exploration of concerns that have arisen, and for reinforcement of the choices and communication skills. These two- to three-hour discussions have focused on real-life critical incidents experienced and written by those involved, and have proven very meaningful to those concerned. In a few instances, individuals who were about to quit student teaching decided to complete the experience based on the feedback and support they received on the Return Date. While the Return Date design may not fit your circumstances, you may wish to consider whether it might be possible to provide a similar opportunity for followup, and for reinforcement of the skills learned through the program.

Team Presentations: Adolescence

Teams will be formed within the group and each team will draw the assignment of a topic or a cluster of topics on adolescence for presentation. Each team is to prepare a handout on the adolescence topic, and distribute it in the session prior to the presentation date. On that date, teams are expected to present the topic in a creative way, then engage others in a Presentation and Evaluation discussion (see page 129). The three major goals of the presentation are: (1) to provide you with an opportunity to work with a team; (2) to develop your self-evaluation skills; and (3) to allow you to learn more about adolescence through making a presentation on the topic and through affording you the opportunity to experience others' presentations.

Expectations for the Team Presentation Handout

The team presentation handout should provide others with information about the topic that individuals may use for future reference. See Sample Handout. The handout need not be exhaustive, and it need not cover every suggested element of the topic. Team effort is preferred, but the handout may be produced in individual, named segments.

You are asked to include all of the following kinds of information in your Handout:

Cover page with names and section in upper right corner; 5-8 markers on the topic.

> Optional. You may wish to incorporate a skill(s) as one (or more) of your markers. For example:

> "Upon completion of the reading and the activity you will be able to_____."

> The number of markers may be reduced if you include skills.

> If you take this route, be sure your handout and related activity(ies) encourage skill development.

Research findings on your topic.

Close the formal portion of the handout with conclusions about the topic based on the research. Personalization is expected (See Sample Handout). Individual contributions to team effort should be clearly designated, otherwise the assumption of equal contribution will be made.

A list of 6-10 properly-cited references for teams (APA format, see below), so others may follow-up.

You *may* wish to include any or all the following kinds of information:

> Background information to help others understand your topic.

> An outline of your presentation—6-10 lines for a team, depending on its size, is sufficient.

> Tables or graphs or extended quotations may be photocopied. All sources should be fully cited.

> Additional information you do not plan to explore in the presentation.

The handout and the presentation should reflect fresh effort on your part; it should not be a rerun of prior effort.

Your Team Handout should be:

> Typed, with cover page, then 6-8 pages. (Extra material will be considered supplementary, optional.)

> Prepared in sufficient copies for all members of your group, including your leader/instructor.

> (Make an extra copy of your handout to include with your Team Presentation Self-Evaluation.)

> Prepared in current American Psychological Association (APA) style. Three examples follow:

Cruickshank, D.R. (1987). *Reflective teaching: The preparation of students of teaching.* Reston, VA: Association of Teacher Educators.

Horan, J.J., & Williams, J.M. (1982). Longitudinal study of assertion training as a drug abuse prevention strategy. *American Educational Research Journal, 19,* 341-351.

Sprinthall, N. A., & Collins, W. A. (1984). *Adolescent psychology: A developmental view.* Reading, MA: Addison-Wesley.

Sample references in text: (Sprinthall & Collins, 1984), or (Cruickshank, 1987, p. 28) if directly quoted.

Sample Handout:
Theories of Adolescent Development

Markers

- Adolescence is a contemporary phenomenon.

  Prior to the Industrial Revolution and resulting child labor laws, young people were rushed into adulthood or were eased gradually into adult responsibilities; it was not until this century that adolescents were recognized as having special physiological and psychological needs.

- Very early in this century, G. Stanley Hall presented a view of adolescence as basically biological.

  In 1904, Hall, the first major writer on the subject of adolescence, developed a biological view; he conceptualized adolescence as a social and emotional process, as a period of rapid physical growth, characterized by storm and stress.

- Sigmund Freud conceptualized adolescence from a psychoanalytical perspective.

  Freud's psychological theory suggested that individuals use particular ego defenses — repression, sublimation, displacement, and identification among them — because of the urges and conflicts of this stage of their lives.

- Margaret Mead presented an anthropological view of adolescence.

  Mead's anthropological theory suggested that the experience of adolescence is culturally determined. In some primitive cultures the process of growing up is smooth and gradual, in others the process is delineated by rites of passage, while in Western societies expectations are ambiguous, and adolescents experience difficulties in some measure because they are seen as "marginal" people.

- Albert Bandura contended that adolescence is affected primarily by social learning.

  Bandura, in his social learning theory, suggested that the behavior of adolescents is determined by social and environmental factors. Modeling, and the ways in which others respond to the individual, significantly affect adolescents' behaviors.

- The developmental or sociopsychoanalytical view of adolescence was propounded initially by Erik Erikson.

  In the developmental view, adolescence is seen as the time individuals move from identity diffusion to achieving identity. Erikson postulated seven parts of the identity conflict: temporal perspective versus time confusion, self-certainty versus self-consciousness, role experimentation versus role fixation, apprenticeship versus work paralysis, sexual polarization versus bisexual confusion, leadership and followership versus authority confusion, and ideological commitment versus confusion of values.

- Adolescent development may also be viewed from a Choice Awareness perspective.

  Previous theoretical views of adolescence stress that behavior is either due to inner changes, or outer events, or the interaction of the environment and inner changes in the individual. The role of choice — how the individual chooses to respond to events — can also be viewed as central in whether storm and stress, or smoothness, characterizes the adolescent period of life.

Does it Make a Difference What View Youth Leaders Take of Adolescence?

Youth leaders who take the view that adolescents make choices in response to inner changes and/or to outer events — and who accept the idea that those choices can be brought to awareness — are likely to respond differently to adolescent problems than those who believe otherwise.

Theories of Adolescent Development

Adolescence is an invention of modern civilization... [in] urban-industrial countries. While probably no epoch of history has been entirely free of youthful tension—whether it be the normal trials and tribulations arising from the process of converting the young into culturized beings, or some degree of juvenile delinquency—our age witnesses a strikingly new development... A youth subculture has arisen that developed into a veritable counterculture during the 1960s and 1970s. (Sebald, 1991, p. 1)

For long centuries it was thought that as soon as a child reached the age of six or seven, the child was ready to be trained as an adult... Except for a tiny proportion of the rich and the well-born, they worked alongside adults in the fields, they fought adult wars, they worked in the mines, and with the coming of industrialization they worked from dawn to dusk in the factories. (Sprinthall & Collins, 1990, p. 2)

Sprinthall & Collins (1990) went on to make the point that Western societies didn't really recognize childhood as such until the last 150 years; young people were simply rushed into adult responsibilities in their teens or even earlier. To illustrate that point, those authors presented a copy of the 1806 US Navy enlistment papers of William Wellman as a Seaman at age 13, a not uncommon phenomenon. And in this century the father of one of the two authors was bound over as a dry goods clerk in England at the same age—13. In the mid-1800s free public schools began to appear, and laws were passed to protect the health and welfare of children, but it was not until [the 20th] century that adolescents were recognized as having special physiological and psychological needs. In this country the extension of education beyond the eighth grade gave recognition to some adolescent needs, while creating others.

The Biological View. G. Stanley Hall is often referred to as the Christopher Columbus of adolescence: he completed a two-volume work in 1904 which was the first major source on the subject. Hall presented a view of adolescence that was basically biological; he believed that all individuals relive the major stages of evolution in the course of their development. He saw the period before adolescence (7-13 years) as one of barbarism, in which children recapitulate their animal past, an idea he believed was confirmed by their fondness for such actions as climbing trees and camping out. He considered adolescence as a kind of new birth at a higher level, following which such human traits as love and altruism could be developed for the first time. Although Hall's notions of evolution and recapitulation are no longer accepted, his work on the topic is considered seminal. He contended that adolescence is as much a social and emotional process

as it is a period of rapid physical growth, and he characterized adolescence as a period of storm and stress (Atwater, 1991).

The Psychoanalytical View. Sigmund Freud took a psychoanalytical view of adolescence, interpreting adolescence in terms of the id, ego, and superego, and postulating a latency period from ages 6 to 11, followed by a genital stage from ages 12 to 18. His daughter, Anna Freud, held that adolescence is a turbulent time because of sexual conflicts brought on by sexual maturation. Both theorists suggested that particular ego defenses are evoked within the individual because of the urges and conflicts of this age: repression, in which impulses are blocked unconsciously; sublimation, the unconscious redirection of sexual energy toward more socially acceptable goals; displacement, sexual impulses are displaced onto other emotionally safer objects or persons (e.g., a girl's preoccupation with clothes or makeup, a boy's interest in sports cars or motorcycles); identification, giving attention to parental substitutes such as teacher, coach, or peers as a way of coping with sexual impulses in ways that produce less anxiety; intellectualization, using newly-developed powers of abstract thinking to discuss various topics (e.g., sex, the issue of living together versus marriage) in an impersonal, intellectual manner to create some emotional distance between ideas and impulses; and asceticism, an unconscious denial of sexual urges and the avoidance of pleasurable associations with sex (joining a group that rigidly limits premarital sex and other behaviors—dancing, use of alcohol...).

The Anthropological View. The anthropological view of adolescence was initially presented by Margaret Mead, based on her observations of Samoan traditions. She noted that the experience of growing up was quite smooth in that culture; the main events of life, including birth, death, and sex, were handled frankly and openly; the tasks of the culture were learned very young as duties were assigned that were appropriate to the abilities and suitable to the age levels of the young people involved; and there were institutionalized ways of dealing with interpersonal conflicts—including those between adolescents and parents. In other primitive cultures tasks of children and adults were found to be more clearly differentiated than Mead observed in Samoa, and in such cultures rites of passage often marked the stage of readiness for the responsibilities and privileges of adulthood. In contrast to these primitive cultures, Western industrialized societies present far more complex environments and expectations to which young people must adjust; the smooth transition into adulthood Mead observed in Samoa may not be an option for many; and the rites of passage are far less clear for young people. Kurt Lewin described adolescents in Western societies as marginal people who face ambiguous expectations and unclear rights and privileges, and that marginality contributes to the difficulties of adolescents' experiences. The lesson of cultural anthropology is that the degree of storm and stress in adolescence depends not only on the maturation of the individual, but on the demands and expectations of the culture in which the adolescent lives (Sprinthall & Collins, 1990).

The Social-Learning View. The social-learning theory of adolescence was developed by Albert Bandura, who contended that behavior is determined primarily by social and environmental factors. Social learning theorists see human development as a life-long process of socialization in which our biological drives are shaped through modeling and reinforcement of behavior. Children and adolescents observe and imitate the behavior they see modeled by others, most especially their parents. This is how they acquire much of their language, as well as their habits, attitudes, and values (Atwater, 1991). Bandura and Walters (1959) came to the conclusion that the fathers of overly aggressive boys were more rejecting of them, so their sons became less dependent on them and spent less time with them. Parents of aggressive boys tended to use harsh punishment, so their sons were more apt to imitate their harsh actions than to follow their parents' verbal warnings not to do so. By contrast, parents of better adjusted boys showed more accepting attitudes toward their sons, explained their discipline and demands, and were less likely to use physical punishment—these boys developed more inner controls of aggression, such as an adequate conscience and a sense of guilt.

The consequences of behaviors also affect learning. When aggressive behavior is rewarded, is reinforced, rather than punished, young people are more likely to imitate it. Vicarious reinforcement for aggression may come from watching socially-approved aggression: TV crime shows, violent sporting events. (Question: Do we see confirmation of this in the matter of how drivers act after watching the Indianapolis 500, for example?) Spectators who see the advantages of aggression are more likely to engage in aggressive behavior themselves; they discover the payoff value of aggression in their own lives—thus they administer their own reinforcement that is as effective as external reinforcement.

Adolescence is a time when individuals are exposed to different models and environmental influences: rock and sports heroes, different hair and clothing styles, and changing social values. In Bandura's view, adolescence is not necessarily a time of storm and stress; except for the deviant minority who lack positive models, most adolescents tend to develop in positive ways (Atwater, 1991).

The Sociopsychoanalytical or Developmental View. The major contributor to the sociopsychoanalytical or developmental view of adolescence has been Erik Erikson. Erikson (1968) postulated eight stages of human development: (1) infancy, achieving trust vs. mistrust; (2) early childhood, achieving autonomy vs. shame and doubt; (3) play age, achieving initiative vs. guilt; (4) school age, achieving industry vs. inferiority; (5) adolescence, achiev-

ing identity vs. identify diffusion; (6) young adult, achieving intimacy vs. isolation; (7) adulthood, achieving generativity vs. stagnation; and (8) mature age, achieving ego integrity vs. disgust, despair. Erikson viewed identity formation as a lifelong process with its roots in childhood; during adolescence the individual must establish a sense of personal identity and avoid the danger of identity diffusion. Establishing identity, also referred to as ego identity, requires individual effort in evaluating and learning to use personal assets and liabilities to achieve a sense of who one is and who one wants to become. Erikson postulated seven parts of the identity conflict. (The following summary has been adapted from Erikson, 1968 and Rice, 1992).

1. **Temporal Perspective Versus Time Confusion.** During adolescence young people begin to gain a sense of time and of the continuity of life, relating the past to the present and the future. They learn to estimate and allocate their time and they gain a concept of how long it may take to achieve their life plans. Research suggests that a true sense of time does not develop for most young people until relatively late in adolescence—around age fifteen or sixteen.

2. **Self-certainty Versus Self-consciousness.** In adolescence, most young people develop a greater sense of self-confidence based upon their past experiences. They come to believe in themselves and sense that they have a reasonable chance of accomplishing future aims. Adolescents go through a period of increasing self-awareness and self-consciousness; this is especially true concerning their physical self-image and their social relationships. If their development is reasonably normal, they acquire confidence in themselves and anticipate future success; they take an increasingly positive attitude toward growing up.

3. **Role Experimentation Versus Role Fixation.** Adolescents experiment with the different roles they believe they will play in society; they also experiment with different identities, with various personality characteristics, with different ways of talking and acting, with different philosophies and goals, and with a broad range of relationships. The sense of personal identity develops through this experimentation. Young people who are restrained or feel too much guilt, who lack initiative, or who fix on their adult roles prematurely, do not learn who they are or what they could become.

4. **Apprenticeship Versus Work Paralysis.** Adolescents have opportunities to explore and try out a variety of occupational roles before they decide on their career. Once they have entered the world of work, their jobs play a large part in determining their identity. A negative self-image and inferiority feelings can prevent them from generating the energy necessary for success in school or on the job. Erikson criticizes schools for the destroying the spontaneity, the creativity, and the joy of learning in young people. Other

authors place emphasis on the importance of sex-role identity, socioeconomic status, family background, and socialization as influences on the achievement motivation of adolescents.

5. Sexual Polarization Versus Bisexual Confusion. During adolescence the struggle to define what it means to be "male" and "female" continues. Erikson suggests that it is important for adolescents to develop a clear sense of identity with their own sex as a foundation for a firm sense of identity and as a basis for future heterosexual intimacy. He also emphasizes that for communities to function effectively, men and women must be willing to assume "suitable roles"; thus, he sees sexual polarization as necessary. Much of the contemporary analysis (and some criticism) of Erikson's work focuses on his emphasis on the desirability of sexual polarization.

6. Leadership and Followership Versus Authority Confusion. As adolescents expand their horizons through friendships, educational opportunities, work, and new contacts with other people, they have opportunities both to take on leadership responsibilities and to follow others. During adolescence they are likely to experience conflicting claims on their allegiance. Their parents, their friends, their sweethearts, their teachers, their employers, and the state all make demands, and many adolescents experience confusion. They wonder where they should place their allegiance, whom they should follow, to whom they should listen. In sorting out the answers adolescents must examine their values and priorities.

7. Ideological Commitment Versus Confusion of Values. This conflict relates to all the others because the individual's ideology guides other aspects of his or her behavior. Erikson labels this struggle the "search for fidelity." He suggests that people of all ages, but especially adolescents, need something to believe in, a group or organization to join and follow, something to which they might relate and devote themselves.

Individuals who are able to resolve these seven conflicts, develop a firm sense of identity. The adolescent crisis is over when they have found a sense of self-identification.

The Choice Awareness View. The above views of adolescence suggest that the behaviors of young people are either due to inner changes, or outer events, or the interaction of the environment and inner changes on the individual. These views imply that internal and/or external forces act on the individual who then responds, as it were, in some automatic way. By contrast, Choice Awareness theory (Nelson, 1992) assumes that internal and external factors may exert strong influences on adolescents' behaviors, but, in addition, choice plays a very significant part in the behaviors of young people. The individual, in fact, chooses the ways in which he or she will respond to the

persons, places, and situations he or she encounters; this is apparent since habitual patterns of choice may be brought to awareness and modified. The individual's choices, and not just internal presses and outer events, affect the extent to which he or she experiences storm and stress, or smoothness, during the adolescent period of life. (Note: This topic is dealt with in abbrieviated form here, since this source deals with Choice Awareness theory in depth.)

Conclusions

In this paper we have presented in brief form six of the views of adolescent development: the biological, psychoanalytical, anthropological, social-learning, sociopsychoanalytical, and Choice Awareness views. This research brought to our attention two particularly interesting ideas: that adolescence may well be a new phenomenon — a result of cultural changes; and that earlier theorists' views of adolescence tended to stress that adolescent behavior is either due to inner changes, outer events, or the interaction of the environment and the individual. Until recently, choice had not been noted as an influence on adolescents' behaviors. It is our view that when we were adolescents we made a great many choices, often poor ones, often unaware, in how we responded to changes and events. When we chose carefully, and acted with the likely consequences in view, our experiences tended more often to be positive. Further, we think that the youth leader's theory of adolescence is important. The leader who believes that adolescents make choices in response to inner changes and outer events, and that those choices can be brought to awareness, might well respond differently to adolescent problems when compared to the leader who sees adolescent behavior resulting exclusively from inner changes or outer forces, or both.

References

Atwater, E. (1991). Adolescence (3rd ed.). Englewood Cliffs, NJ: Prentice-Hall.

Bandura, A. & Walters, R. H. (1959). Adolescent aggression. New York: Ronald Press.

Erikson, E. (1968). Identity: Youth and crisis. New York: W. W. Norton.

Rice, F. P. (1992). The adolescent: Development, relationships, and culture (7th ed.). Boston: Allyn & Bacon.

Nelson, R. C. (1992). Choice Awareness: A systematic, eclectic counseling theory. Minneapolis: Educational Media.

Santrock, J. W. (1990). Adolescence: An introduction (4th. ed.). Dubuque, IA: Wm. C. Brown.

Sebald, H. (1991). Adolescence: A social psychological analysis (4th ed.). Englewood Cliffs, NJ: Prentice-Hall.

Sprinthall, N. A. & Collins, W. A. (1990). Adolescent psychology: A developmental view (2nd ed.). Reading, MA: Addison-Wesley.

Expectations for Team Presentations

Given the time constraints for your presentation it is recommended that your team emphasize key aspects of the topic important to group members, rather than attempt to "cover" it in full.

Use your time creatively. Involve the group actively; vary the activity when you are in charge.

Have learners take particular roles, draw cartoons, move about in some significant way, recall an adolescent experience, write a paragraph, share an adolescent concern, observe a particular person or behavior. Take a role yourself, use an overhead transparency, have learners respond to a puzzle or a quiz; use a picture, a brief article from the newspaper, a record, etc., as the focus.

Your activity should extend knowledge, attempt to change attitudes, or help others develop a skill.

Direct your presentation to a specific audience and tell why it is relevant to that audience.

You may ask the group to envision themselves as teachers, a high school FTA group, parents, etc.

We will assume the presentation is directed at teacher education students unless otherwise specified. Organize seating and the group in any way that suits your presentation.

Take a position in the front of the group; include at least one change of activities involving the group when you are in charge; and change your own position or location at least once in your portion.

Use group members' names—ask for others to display name cards if you cannot recall all names.

Teams: Complete presentation within the allotted time.

Group members are encouraged to score you lower if you take substantially more or less than your share of time.

After the presentation, all group members are to fill out presentation evaluation forms.

Ask a member of the group to collect and hand your evaluations to the leader/instructor—evaluations will be given to you at the end of the session. Each member of the team should fill out an evaluation form for him/herself and a separate one for the other team member(s). As soon as you have completed your own form, hand it to the leader—who will read it and return it at the end of the session along with his/her evaluation and the evaluations made by other group members.

Your team is expected to intersperse varied activities, presentations, and discussion.

Use the Planning Guide (below) and adapt the suggestions to the time allotted.

Feel free to deviate from this plan, so long as you remain within the time limit and get to your first activity within the first few minutes of your assigned time.

Sample Team Presentation Planning Guide (30 minutes)

Either begin with an activity or limit yourself to 3 minutes in preliminaries before beginning an activity.

In general, each team member should participate in each element of the presentation.

3 min.	I.	Attention-getting initial activity, pretest-quiz, or other preliminaries
3 min.	II.	Overview of markers on cover page, other remarks
		Don't lecture—assume others have read the handout
15 min.	III.	Activity(ies) involving group—interspersed or followed by discussion and/or quiz
		Design for creativity and genuine learning. Specify time limits to group; keep to them
4 min.	IV.	Concrete examples based on information from: interviews with other professionals, experience, case histories, and research findings
3 min.	V.	Implications for your work with adolescents
2 min.	VII.	A brief summary /conclusions statement

Lead group in evaluation. See *Team Presentation—Guide for Small Group Discussion*

Team Presentation—Evaluation Form

Name of Team Member _____   Name of Evaluator (Optional) _____

Nonverbals - posture, movement, appearance   Verbal presentation - voice, grammar, expression

_____   _____

Activity - creativity, involvement   Content - evidence of research, organization

_____   _____

Use of time - respect for time limit

_____   _____

Major strengths of this presenter   Major weaknesses of this presenter

_____   _____

Circle an overall rating for the portion contributed by this presenter.

10	9	8	7	6	5	4	3	2	1
Highly effective			Somewhat effective			Somewhat ineffective			Highly ineffective

Make an overall comment below:

_____

_____

_____

Team Presentation—Guide for Small Group Discussion

Upon completion of your presentation you are to lead a five to ten minute discussion with all members or a portion of the group, in which you reflect on what you did and how effectively you did it.

Begin the discussion of your part by following the * directions in Items #1 and #2 below.

*1. Make a statement about your part of the presentation in which you discuss such matters as: goals, objectives accomplished, and the effects of your planning.

*2. Invite learners to discuss the creativity of the effort and the choices made in the planning. Be sure to get feedback on your part of the presentation and not feedback on the subject.

 3. Share how you felt during your part of the presentation, how you feel about it now, what you liked and did not like about what happened.

NOTE: During your small group discussion, do not reopen the topic or deal with other issues.

If time remains, your leader/instructor may reopen the subject.

Team Presentation—Self-Evaluation

Your Presentation Self-Evaluation is due the second class day after your presentation.

It should be between four and six pages double-spaced in length. It should include the following:

Discussion of your preparation and your involvement in the team process.

A brief topical outline of your part of the presentation, mentioning the nature of your activity—5 to 8 lines.

Do not summarize the presentation in detail. Use the paper instead to analyze what you did, how you did it, and what the reactions of other group members mean for you as an educator/other professional—as follows:

Discussion of the strengths and weaknesses of your part of the presentation—be sure to include both.

You are encouraged to include points made in the Small Group Discussion.

Include a summary of verbal and written feedback you received from others.

Include a list of scores, the total, the average score, and any comments you have on the results for your part of the presentation. Arrange feedback forms in descending order by scores.

Discuss what you learned about your profession and about yourself through your presentation.

Attach to your self-evaluation paper:

(1) all Presentation Evaluation forms (or specify that they are attached to one of your partner's papers. If possible, all should be submitted on the same date);

(2) a copy of your handout, with all portions you personally prepared clearly marked, or specify on the cover that all the work on the handout was cooperative, and

(3) a copy of any materials used in your portion of the presentation.

* NOTE:

Evaluation of your Self-Evaluation paper is independent of the quality of your part of the presentation

Communication Skills for Taping Activities

Throughout *Working with Adolescents: Building Effective Communication and Choice-Making Skills,* consideration is given to a variety of communication skills. Those skills are abstracted here for emphasis and for use in the taping activity and in the Communication Skills Paper. Note that the first seven items below suggest some ways of communicating that are often overused, thus may be targeted for decrease, whereas items 8 - 14 suggest ways of communicating that might be increased. Note that items 3, 4, 6, 7, 13, and 14 have not been specifically developed in the text, but are treated here as self-evident.

1. *Questions.* Count the number of times you spoke. What percent of your comments included questions? Overdependence on questions is not desirable (for discussion, see pp. 83-84).

2. *Non-word utterances.* Count the number of non-word utterances (uh, mm, er), unnecessary words or phrases (well, you know, like), etc. Non-word utterances suggest confusion and personal inadequacy and block smooth communication.

3. *Word ratio.* Estimate the ratio of words, you to adolescent. Developing a listening mode in communication with young people with young people is highly desirable; thus the word ratio in your communication should either be in balance or skewed in favor of the adolescent.

4. *Words per minute.* Roughly count the number of words you used per minute.

    High speed tends to encourage superficiality. By contrast, thoughtful, considered communication is likely to be slow.

5. *Solutions.* Count the number of suggestions/solutions *you* offered. Include repeats and questions that infer solutions. "Have you talked with your mother about this?" Overdependence on early or numerous solutions is not desirable (see pp. 84-85).

6. *Changes of topic.* Count all changes of topic, major or minor, you introduced or reintroduced. Smooth, considered communication with young people does not bounce around, and the adolescent is given many opportunities to direct the discussion.

7. *Multiples.* Count the number of multiple statements, questions, or restarts. Or count the number of times you spoke, then determine what per cent of your comments included multiple statements, multiple questions, or restarts. "Well, John... Well, you know... I'm really concerned... Well, John, I'm concerned about what's happening here." Clean, brief, straightforward statements are preferred over multiples and restarts.

8. *Silences.* Count the number of 3 to 10 second intervals of silence you used effectively following the adolescent's comments. Effective communication often includes brief periods of silence — so each person can think, and so the young person can take the lead (see p. 48).

9. *Minimum verbal responses (MVRs).* Count the number of MVRs you used effectively. I see. Yes. Uh huh. Go on. (It is better if MVRs are not run together, since they are no longer *minimum*, so count MVRs only if you use one at a time). MVRs are often useful in encouraging young people to explore issues from their point of view (see p. 49).

10. *Feeling words.* Count the number of feeling words you used appropriately. "Feeling sad." "Really *annoyed*." "Kind of *lonesome*." The insertion of appropriate feeling words in communication with young people greatly increases the chances that they will sense that they are understood. Adolescents who feel understood often provide much information.

11. *Reflections of content.* Count reflections of content you used appropriately (see p. 52).

12. *Reflections of feeling.* Count reflections of feeling you used appropriately (see pp. 52-53).

13. *Summarizations.* Count the number of times you effectively summarized what the adolescent said. When many details have been offered, or when a topic appears to be complete for the moment, summarize. The adolescent may either return to the previous topic or open another.

14. *Clarifications.* Count the number of times you effectively clarified what the adolescent said.

    "A few minutes ago you said you and your sister never get along, now you've mentioned a situation in which you two teamed up to cope with a neighbor kid. It sounds like you two get along now and then, anyway."

    Note, *stating* a clarification as in this example is generally far more appropriate than forcing a choice. Asking the question, "Which is it? Do you two get along or not?" as an addition to the above statement, would suggest that mixed feelings do not exist. The reality is that we and the young people with whom we work very often have mixed feelings.

Taping Experiences—Introduction

Effective conferencing with adolescents and others in their lives is important to your professional success. You will be asked to audiotape two role-play conferences. For each of these experiences you and your partner will tape on your own according to printed instructions. You will take turns playing an adolescent and an adult in specific situations to help you to assess (a) your communication skills in this activity, and (b) your progress in developing communication skills and choices.

Readings and discussion will focus extensively on improving communication skills and choices, on specific, reasonable goals for achievement, and on determining the extend to which those goals are achieved. After the second taping, you will be asked to write a critique of your efforts and hand in your tape with the critique. You will receive further information about the critique after you make your first tape.

IMPORTANT: You will need your own individual audiotape cassette, preferably standard size, in each taping session. Using one tape for two people is a problem, since you will each need to hand in your tape with your tape critique. Your leader/instructor will need to be able to find the content on which you are heard as the adult while reading your tape critique.

NOTE: There are no specific expectations for your performance during the first taping—except that it should be a full five minutes in length. The idea during the first taping is to develop a base rate on two or more variables for your personal improvement—those variables will be explored later. Go into the experience with the attitude that you will get to hear how you might relate to an adolescent. That is it! We will build expectations for the second tape, but for now we ask only this: Just be yourself.

PLEASE NOTE THAT THE SAMPLE TAPING ACTIVITY ON THE FOLLOWING PAGE IS AN EXAMPLE OF THE KIND OF ACTIVITY THAT YOU WILL ENCOUNTER WHEN YOU ACTUALLY TAPE, AND THAT WILL ULTIMATELY BE USED TO DEVELOP THE TAPE CRITIQUE PAPER.

YOU ARE ENCOURAGED TO USE THESE SAMPLES AS PRACTICES SO THAT YOU MAY GET USED TO THE PROCESS AND THE TIMING WITH YOUR PARTNER.

THE ACTUAL ACTIVITY MAY PROVIDE A LITTLE MORE INFORMATION, AND IT WILL BE ONE YOU HAVE NOT SEEN OR REHEARSED IN ADVANCE.

A SECOND SET OF INSTRUCTIONS FOR PERSON "B" WILL REVERSE THE ORDER OF ASSIGNMENTS.

Sample Taping Activity—Instructions, Person A

Arrange to get together with your partner on your own with a recorder, and follow instructions as given.

Take your own standard audiocassette tape to the session. When you play the part of the adult, specify your assignment (camp counselor, teacher, etc.); adolescent should represent the age group that is relevant for you.

Do not rush these interviews—You do not have to solve the problem. In each, act as if you have 15 or 20 minutes— more later if necessary. In each, check to see that recorder is picking up. Adolescent should keep track of the time and see that 5 full minutes are used. Adult begins the interview with a greeting.

DO NOT READ AHEAD UNTIL YOU ARE READY TO TAPE

xxxxxxxxxxxxxx cover page to here, and slide down cover to the next x's as you get ready to tape xxxxxxxxxxxxx

Roleplay Number 1

In the first roleplay, you are the adolescent. Your partner will play the adult. Your partner should put his/her tape in the recorder and test it to see that it is recording. *You* keep track of the time. Below is your role.

You are from a complicated home with step- and half-brothers and sisters. Your biggest complaint is that you feel you have no privacy, no place. Your relationship with this person is good, so you unload if you feel listened to.

xxxxxxxxxxxxxxxxxxxxxxxxxxxxxxxxxxxxxxxx cover page to here xxxxxxxxxxxxxxxxxxxxxxxxxxxxxxxxxxxxxxxxxx

Roleplay Number 2

In the second roleplay, you are the adult and you begin the dialogue. Your partner will play the adolescent. You should put your tape in the recorder and test it to see that it is recording. Below is your role.

You called in the individual because his/her work has trailed off to nothingness, and you are troubled. The person is capable of at least average work, and you suspect a change at home may be causing problems.

xxxxxxxxxxxxxxxxxxxxxxxxxxxxxxxxxxxxxxxx cover page to here xxxxxxxxxxxxxxxxxxxxxxxxxxxxxxxxxxxxxxxxxx

Roleplay Number 3

In the third roleplay, you are again the adolescent and your partner is the adult. Partner should put his/her tape back in the recorder so that this taping follows the previous one. Again, *you* keep time. Below is your role.

You have been called in because you seldom complete your work. You are exceptionally bright, and proving twenty times over that you can do something you could have done years ago bores you out of your mind. Your parents, too, are concerned that you are so seldom challenged.

xxxxxxxxxxxxxxxxxxxxxxxxxxxxxxxxxxxxxxxx cover page to here xxxxxxxxxxxxxxxxxxxxxxxxxxxxxxxxxxxxxxxxxx

Roleplay Number 4

In the fourth roleplay, you are again the adult; your partner is the adolescent. You begin the dialogue. You should put your tape back in the recorder so that this taping follows the previous one. Below is your role.

The young person has just moved to your community after living in a big city, and, rumor has it, functioning as a gang member. All who have met him/her are worried about his/her moves to start a gang in your area. You share this concern.

Outline for Tape Critique Paper

1. *Title for Paper: Tape Critique* (5 - 7 pp.)

2. *First Taping.* Critique one of the first two tape segments you recorded in general terms: What happened? How did you respond? What do you see as your strengths? What do you see as your weaknesses?

3. Critique the same tape segment in specific terms: What specific responses of yours did you see as effective? Ineffective? Select two of the COMMUNICATION SKILLS—one to increase, one to decrease (see Communication Skills list above). Discuss your tape in relation to these factors. Indicate why change in that communication skill is relevant for you.

4. *Second Taping.* Critique one of the second pair of tape segments in general terms: What happened? How did you respond? What do you see as your strengths? Weaknesses?

5. Critique the same tape segment in specific terms: What specific responses of yours did you see as effective? Ineffective? Discuss your success in modifying the two COMMUNICATION SKILLS you selected—one to increase, one to decrease.

6. Compare specific verbal responses you made in the second taping with those in the first. Be specific about the gains/losses apparent in the second taping as compared to the first. Indicate any ways you see that you have gained beyond the taping—with those around you.

7. State your goal(s) for your future communication with adolescents—what you could still do better.

8. Indicate what the gaps were in your knowledge about the issues raised in the roleplays that would need to be filled in order to enhance your effectiveness.

9. Discuss the relevance of the taping experiences for your future as a professional in your field, and the value of the taping experiences for you personally—be sure to do both.

Your name should show on both the tape and the paper.

Be sure your tape is at the point where listening should begin and the side to be listened to is clearly marked.

Provide clear instructions on how to find the second taping segment (beginning of second side may be easiest).

Wrap your paper around the tape and fasten it with a rubber band or string.

Please don't turn in cases.

References

Achenbach, T. M., & Edelbrock, C. S. (1981). Behavior problems and competencies reported by parents of normal and disturbed children aged four through sixteen. *Monographs of the Society for Research in Child Development, 46* (1, Serial No. 188).

Axelrod, S. (1977). *Behavior modification for the classroom teacher.* New York: McGraw-Hill.

Canter, L. (1976). *Assertive discipline: A take-charge approach for today's educator.* Seal Beach, CA: Canter and Associates.

Canter, L. (1978). Be an assertive teacher. *Instructor, 88,* 60.

Charles, C. M. (1992). *Building classroom discipline.* White Plains, NY: Longman.

Clark, B. (1988). *Growing up gifted* (3rd ed.). New York: Macmillan.

Cobb, N. J. (1992). *Adolescence: Continuity, change, and diversity.* Mountain View, CA: Mayfield.

Cousins, N. (1979). *Anatomy of an illness.* New York: W. W. Norton.

Dobson, J. (1970). *Dare to discipline.* Wheaton, IL: Tyndale House.

Dreikurs, R. (1968). *Psychology in the classroom* (2nd ed.). New York: Harper Row.

Dreikurs, R. & Grey, L. (1968). *Logical consequences.* New York: Meredith Press.

Dreikurs, R., Grunwald, B. & Pepper, F. (1982). *Maintaining sanity in the classroom.* New York: Harper & Row.

Ellis, A. (1979). Rational emotive therapy. In R. Corsini (ed.), *Current psychotherapies.* (2nd ed.). Itasca, IL: Peacock.

Ernst, K. (1973). *Games students play and what to do about them.* Mellbrae, CA: Celestial Arts.

Frankl, V. (1959). *Man's search for meaning.* New York: Washington Square Press.

Ginott, H. (1969). *Between parent and teenager.* New York: Macmillan.

Ginott, H. (1971). *Teacher and child.* New York: Macmillan.

Glasser, W. (1969). *Schools without failure.* New York: Harper & Row.

Glasser, W. (1976). *Positive addiction.* New York: Harper and Row.

Glasser, W. (1985). *Control theory in the classroom.* New York: Perennial Library.

Glasser, W. (1990). *The quality school: Managing students without coercion.* New York: Harper and Row.

Goodman, J. (1983). How to get more smileage out of your life: Making sense of humor, then serving it. In P. E. McGhee, & J. H. Goldstein (Eds.), *Handbook of Humor Research: Vol. 2. Applied Studies.* (pp. 1-21) New York: Springer-Verlag.

Gordon, T. (1970). *Parent effectiveness training.* New York: P. F. Wyden.

Gordon, T. (1974). *Teacher effectiveness training.* New York: David McKay.

Gravelle, K. & Hoskins, C. (1989). *Teenagers face to face with bereavement.* New York: Basic Books.

Greenblatt, R., Cooper, B. & Muth, R. (1984). Managing for effective teaching. *Educational Leadership, 41,* 57-59.

Grollman, E. A. (1993). *Straight talk about death for teenagers.* Boston: Beacon Press.

Grossman, J. (1978). This school means what it says. *American Education, 14* (9), 6-12.

Hessman, T. (1977). *Creating learning environments—the behavioral approach to education.* Boston: Allyn & Bacon.

Jones, F. (1987). *Positive classroom discipline.* New York: McGraw-Hill.

Kounin, J. (1971). *Discipline and group management in classrooms.* New York: Holt, Rinehart & Winston.

Kubler-Ross, E. (1969). *On death and dying.* New York: Macmillan.

Manaster, G. J. (1989). *Adolescent development: A psychological interpretation.* Itasca, IL: F. E. Peacock.

Mosley, M. & Smith, P. (1982). What works in learning? Students provide the answers. *Phi Delta Kappan, 64,* 273.

Myers, P. & Nance, D. (1986). *The upset book.* Notre Dame, IN: Academic Publications.

Nelson, R. C. (1977). *Choosing: A better way to live.* Lake Park, FL: GuideLines Press.

Nelson, R. C. (1980). The CREST program: Helping children with their choices. *Elementary School Guidance and Counseling, 14,* 286-298.

Nelson, R. C. (1987). Graphics in counseling. *Elementary School Guidance and Counseling, 22,* 17-29.

Nelson, R. C. (1989a). Choice Awareness in a residential setting. *Journal for Specialists in Group Work, 14,* 158-169.

Nelson, R. C. (1989b). Of robins' eggs, teachers, and education reform. *Phi Delta Kappan, 70,* 632-638.

Nelson, R. C. (1990). *Choice Awareness: A systematic, eclectic counseling theory.* Minneapolis: Educational Media Corporation.

Nelson, R. C. (1992). *On the CREST: Growing through effective choices.* Minneapolis: Educational Media Corporation.

Nelson, R. C., & Friest, W. P. (1980). Marriage enrichment through Choice Awareness. *Journal of Marital and Family Therapy, 6,* 399-407.

Nelson, R. C., & Link, M. D. (1982). Teen-parent enrichment through Choice Awareness. *School Counselor, 29,* 388-396.

Novaco, R. W. (1975). *Anger control: The development and evaluation of an experimental treatment.* Lexington, MA: D. C. Heath & Co.

Oates, M. (1993). *Death in the school community: A handbook for counselors, teachers, and administrators.* Alexandria, VA: American Counsling Association.

Parkes, C. M. & Weiss, R. S. (1983). *Recovery from bereavement.* New York: Basic Books.

Peters, T. J. & Waterman, R. H. (1982). *In search of excellence.* New York: Warner Books.

Potter, J. (1983). Touch film with Jesse Potter. (Film). Chicago: Sterling Productions.

Rando, T. A. (1984). *Grief, dying and death: Clinical interventions for caregivers.* Champaign, IL: Research Press.

Redl, F. & Wattenberg, W. (1959). *Mental Hygiene in teaching* . New York: Harcourt, Brace and World.

Rice, F. P. (1990). *The Adolescent* (6th ed.). Needham Heights, MA: Allyn and Bacon.

Rogers, D. (1985). *Adolescents and youth* (5th ed.). Englewood Cliffs, NJ: Prentice-Hall.

Rosenthal, R. & Jacobsen, L. (1968). *Pygmalion in the classroom.* New York: Holt, Rinehart & Winston.

Schaefer, D. & Lyons, C. (1988). *How do we tell the children? Helping children understand and cope when someone dies.* New York: Newmarket Press.

Simon, S. B., Howe, L. W. & Kirschenbaum, H. (1978). *Values clarification: A handbook of practical strategies for teachers and students.* (Revised). New York: Hart Publishing.

Sobal, J. (1987). Health concerns of adolescents. *Adolescence, 22,* 739-750.

Solorzano, L. Hogue, J. R., Peterson, S., Lyons, D. C. & Bosc, M. (1984, August 27). Students think schools are making the grade. *U. S. News & World Report,* pp. 46-49.

Wlodkowski, R. (1977). *Motivation.* Washington, D. C.: National Education Association.

Wolfelt, A. D. (1986). Death and grief in the school setting. In T. N. Fairchild (Ed.). *Crisis intervention strategies for school based helpers.* Springfield, IL: Charles C. Thomas.

Wolfgang, C. H. & Glickman, C. D. (1986). *Solving discipline problems: Strategies for classroom teachers.* Boston: Allyn & Bacon.

Index